Keeping the Vow

KEEPING THE VOW

The Untold Story of Married Catholic Priests

——◆——

D. PAUL SULLINS

OXFORD
UNIVERSITY PRESS

OXFORD

UNIVERSITY PRESS

Oxford University Press is a department of the University of
Oxford. It furthers the University's objective of excellence in research,
scholarship, and education by publishing worldwide.

Oxford   New York
Auckland   Cape Town   Dar es Salaam   Hong Kong   Karachi
Kuala Lumpur   Madrid   Melbourne   Mexico City   Nairobi
New Delhi   Shanghai   Taipei   Toronto

With offices in
Argentina   Austria   Brazil   Chile   Czech Republic   France   Greece
Guatemala   Hungary   Italy   Japan   Poland   Portugal   Singapore
South Korea   Switzerland   Thailand   Turkey   Ukraine   Vietnam

Oxford is a registered trademark of Oxford University Press
in the UK and certain other countries.

Published in the United States of America by
Oxford University Press
198 Madison Avenue, New York, NY 10016

Library of Congress Cataloging-in-Publication Data
Sullins, Donald Paul, 1953–
Keeping the vow : the untold story of married Catholic priests / D. Paul Sullins.
pages cm
Includes bibliographical references and index.
ISBN 978–0–19–986004–3 (cloth : alk. paper)   1. Catholic Church.—Clergy—Family
relationships.   2. Marriage—Religious aspects—Catholic Church.   3. Celibacy—Catholic
Church. I. Title.
BX1912.85.S85 2014
253'.22088282—dc23
2015006 109

1 3 5 7 9 8 6 4 2
Printed in the United States of America
on acid-free paper

To Mary Patricia, LOML; to Archbishop John Myers, who made this book possible; and to Cardinal Bernard Law, who made the Pastoral Provision possible.

Contents

List of Figures

List of Tables

Keeping the Vow

Introduction

Married Priests!?

"Wait—what?! How can that be? *Priests can't be married.*" Carlos, a well-educated traditional Catholic Hispanic man, had just heard me, a Catholic priest, casually refer to my wife. The fact that I am married is common knowledge in the parish I've served for over a decade, but Carlos was new and had not heard. He was serving as lector (reading the Bible lessons) at the Mass I was about to celebrate. His eyes narrowed with suspicion and he took a step backward. "Normally they can't," I agreed, beginning an explanation I had given many times before, "but the Pope has made an exception for men, like me, who used to be Episcopalian priests and have converted. . . ."

"What is an Episcopalian priest?" he broke in, inadvertently lapsing into Spanish.

This explanation, I realized, would have to be more extensive than usual, and the organ prelude for the Mass had already started.

"I'm not the only one," I said, casting about, trying to be reassuring. "There are two other married priests in this diocese."

His eyes only got larger and more quizzical, with a touch of concern. Just then I saw Father Garcia, a canon lawyer from Argentina who was visiting the parish, and asked him to help.

"There are 21 different rites in the Catholic Church, and all of them have many priests that are married except this one, the Latin Rite," I heard him begin, still in Spanish, taking Carlos aside as I turned to the procession with a prayer of thankful relief. A minute later I felt a tap on my shoulder.

"Is there a book I could recommend him," whispered Father Garcia, "that would answer his questions about married priests?"

"No, not really," I said.

Father Garcia looked at me intently. "Then," he said, "you should write one."

This book is the result of that suggestion, and many other encounters and conversations like the one that day. Carlos is not unusual; few Catholics, and certainly fewer non-Catholics, know that the rule of celibacy for Catholic priests is not absolute. To be sure, no Catholic priest, once ordained, is ever permitted to marry, but married men have sometimes been permitted to receive ordination as Catholic priests. At some periods in the long history of the Catholic Church, the ordination of married men appears to have been relatively common, though how common and for how long is a matter of historical dispute. There is no question that the clergy of the Eastern Catholic Churches, continuing an ancient practice of the undivided Church, regularly marry today. In the Western, or "Latin Rite," Catholic Church, the practice is to ordain only celibate men, but there have been rare exceptions. The exceptions are almost always granted to a married priest of another Christian church, almost always Anglican, who has converted to the Catholic faith. In the United States such priests, with their wives and families, have served in Catholic parishes and dioceses since 1981 under a little-known set of canon law norms known collectively as the Pastoral Provision (or Anglican Pastoral Provision). In 2012 more married priests began to be received under a new program established by Pope Benedict XVI. Today there are about 125 Roman Catholic priests in the United States who are married.

Like Carlos, many are curious to learn about married priests. Why did they leave the Episcopal Church? Did they have to go to seminary? What are their views on religious issues, particularly when compared to celibate priests? What do they do for a living? What are their wives like? Perceptive Catholics familiar with Church life wonder how well the married priests are received by other priests, and how a parish or diocese can afford to support them. They also wonder how such tradition-minded leaders as Pope John Paul II and Cardinal Ratzinger, before he became Pope Benedict XVI, came to allow married priests. What role did Church politics play in that development? And, if the door is open, why aren't there many more married priests? Most of all, this small group of married priests raises large and important questions about Catholic faith and policy for many, both Catholic and non-Catholic. If these married converts can be ordained priests, why not married Catholic men? Could the Catholic Church be about to change the requirement of priestly celibacy?

There are also a number of common stereotypes about married priests. It is commonly assumed, for example, that permitting Catholic married men to be ordained would help alleviate the shortage of Catholic priests by attracting many young men to the priesthood. Married men are often seen as better able to relate to what laypersons go through in life, such as the pressure to earn an income, the relationship adjustments and sexual experience of marriage, mortgage payments, time pressures, school tuition, and in-laws. They are thought to be less prone to the scandalous child sex abuse that has been repeatedly discovered among celibate Catholic priests. Are these and similar perceptions true or imagined?

These questions and beliefs about married priests stem from a wide range of personal, historical, sociological, and theological concerns. Few people may be interested in all of them—for example, non-Catholics may not be interested in Catholic Church policy or theology—but all of them share one common feature: they have been necessarily considered in the abstract, as a matter of speculation, in the absence of any concrete information about married priests themselves. Furthermore, these questions and beliefs have never been examined together, but only in an occasional or piecemeal fashion, as part of a larger discussion about some other topic or interest. This volume attempts to make a unique contribution to our understanding of the issues raised by married priests by considering them together in one volume, more or less systematically, and by bringing to bear evidence from the lives and views of married priests themselves.

This book is based on a study of 72 married priests and their wives involving 115 interviews and three surveys over a period of four years (2007–2010). A full description of the research design and methods is presented in the Appendix.

Each of the questions voiced above are examined, to the extent possible, in light of the experience or perspective of these priests and of the relevant historical, sociological, or theological issues involved. The empirical evidence from these priests is sometimes enough to yield a definitive answer to a particular question. More often, it will not provide an answer, but can help to inform the discussion, by fleshing out abstract ideals and convictions about priests and marriage with the actual experiences and lives of the married priests themselves. As befitting men who combined priesthood and marriage in a celibate clerical culture, moreover, their experiences are (as we shall see) often paradoxical, a thick and messy combination of contradictory roles and positions that do not easily fit into the usual categories. By telling their story, I hope to articulate a more fully human perspective on the issues related to the idea of married Catholic priests, and thus to contribute, in a small way, to the understanding of the larger story of the Catholic and American religious experience.

This book also offers a unique perspective in that it is not only written about married priests, but also by a married priest. In many ways, the story of my research subjects is also my own story. I am a Pastoral Provision priest, ordained in 2002 for the Catholic priesthood, 18 years after becoming an Episcopal priest. Very happily married for 29 years, with three children, for the past decade I have taught sociology at the Catholic University of America in Washington, D.C., while also serving as associate pastor (parochial vicar) at the Catholic Church of St. Mark the Evangelist in nearby Maryland. I know what it is like to be a married priest from the inside, as it were, as well as from observation. At the same time, as a trained sociologist, with a background in theology and pastoral care, I am uniquely qualified and situated to engage the wide-ranging factors—sociological, historical, theological, and personal—necessary for a full consideration of the questions and issues raised by married priests.

I am well aware of the methodological difficulties that may be posed by a researcher who is sympathetic, or potentially reactive, to his research subjects. Yet, when Max Weber articulated his ideals for social science research, he called not only for objective or "value-free" inquiry but also "verstehen," that is, insight into the underlying thoughts and motivations of human action.[1] As difficult as it may be for a married priest to try to maintain an objective distance, it would also be difficult for someone who is not a member of this unique group to attain the same level of insight and comprehension into their lives and behavior. Frequently, in the interviews and surveys that form the core of this book, as well as discussions and research initiatives with priests and bishops, I have been able to empathize with and understand the respondent more fully as a result of my own experiences and outlook, even when my perspective was very different from that of the person I was interviewing. None of the factual material or quotations from married priests presented in this book is based on my own experience, though for purposes of interest and color I may illustrate themes with anecdotes from my own experience. In the parts of the book that discuss theological or archival material, I will, as would any scholar, present the range of competing views or perspectives on the topic before arguing for my own perspective or interpretation, which is unavoidably that of a faithful Catholic married priest. Unlike most social scientists, my perspective tends to be right of center—as we shall see in Chapter 1, strong conservatism or traditionalism is typical of married priests—though I am decidedly less traditional than most married priests. I hope to present more liberal views (and more conservative ones), with which I may disagree, in a fair and balanced manner. In these ways I hope that the insight of a knowledgeable insider will add depth and value to the analysis, and will help draw together the disparate themes of this book.

Each chapter of this book is centered on a particular question that people usually ask about married Catholic priests. It is my hope that, as a whole, they will add up to an enlightening portrait of this unusual species and tell us something important about the Catholic Church and its future.

What Are Married Priests Like?

Introduction: Meet a Married Priest

What are married priests like? How do they live and work, and what are their frustrations and satisfactions? How do they compare with ordinary Catholic priests? These questions are the focus of this chapter, which uses national survey data to compare married priests to their celibate counterparts. Of course, generalizations can be misleading or impersonal, especially in my small and diverse sample of married priests. To get a sense of the human dimension that lies behind the numeric tables to follow, come with me as I interview Father Tom, a married priest whose story, though unique, illustrates many of the themes we will consider more broadly later in the chapter.

I AM ATTENDING a service at one of the largest churches in America. As hundreds of people make their way into the spacious, well-appointed sanctuary for an evening Mass, I reflect on the fact that, with over 12,000 members, this Catholic congregation is several times larger than most Protestant megachurches. In addition to its 20 weekly services, eight choirs, and elementary and middle schools, the church also administers a long roster of Bible studies, home groups, outreaches to the needy, and specialized programs for every conceivable class and group of persons. The massive parking lot has section markers, like a sports megaplex, to help you remember where you parked your car. I am impressed by the size and design of the church buildings, a tasteful blend of traditional and modern elements, with striking original artwork and the latest communication and classroom technology. At the service, Father Tom, the pastor and celebrant priest, an unassuming man in his late fifties, delivers a brief, practical sermon, without notes, that is laced with self-deprecating humor. At one point he refers to his own struggles relating to his teenage daughter. No one is surprised, for the long-time pastor of this prominent Catholic Church, in a conservative suburb of the Dallas–Fort Worth metroplex, is a married Catholic priest.[1]

After the service I meet Father Tom and his wife at a local restaurant where they have agreed to be interviewed. After setting up my recording equipment, I ask, "What was it like to come into the Catholic Church?" an open-ended, general question designed to let him set the pace. He begins haltingly: "I announced to my parish at a parish meeting—they had this parish meeting, and I told them that I was leaving. I went through this long lecture. The bottom line was, logically, there's only one way to go here. So, the Vestry met afterwards and basically fired me." There is a long pause. The memory is evidently painful. "They fired me and then the Vestry all resigned. This was on a Saturday." "That must have been quite traumatic," I probe, hearing the anguish in his voice. I can empathize; like many other married priests, I went through a very similar experience. "Oh," he responds, "it was *very* traumatic. *Very.* I *never* want to go through something like that again."

But that isn't the most traumatic part of his story. Father Tom continues that he had thought about converting for years, and kept putting it off, but then, "[A couple of years before that meeting, I preached] a homily in which I claimed to the parish that I had drawn a line in the sand. I didn't say then that I was going to leave, I just said that this needed to be resolved for me, that I just could not continue to live in that way. I had a heart attack at that Mass. It was a wake-up call for me. . . . I realized I was being a little deceptive with them and with myself that I was at the end. [But] that heart attack, that was it: I decided I was not going to die in the Episcopal Church."

When I ask, "What was your greatest loss in converting?" he immediately replies in an anguished tone, "I lost every friend I had." Old friendships, mostly with other Episcopal priests, were abruptly cut off, and he had not been able to regain that kind of fellowship in the Catholic Church. About half of married priests report a similar experience. "We don't fit anywhere. In diocesan gatherings the beginning priests are over here, the archconservative priests have their own table, and the rest are kind of scattered around. I don't fit in as a married man. . . . The priests have been wonderful and accepting, but I've just come to accept that we'll always be kind of on the outside of those relationships." As he speaks, his wife nods emphatically.

"What else (if anything) do you miss in the Episcopal Church?" I ask. He reflects for a moment, then expresses what I will come to learn is a near-universal complaint of married priests. "When I first became Catholic, I was a little bitter about the situation with the music, and it took me a little to get over it. ... In the Episcopal Church we had *wonderful* music, a huge, beautiful classical program, with a professional sounding choir. ... In the Catholic Church it was just a guy sitting at the piano, who was also the cantor. It was horrible, just horrible. Both the style and quality of the music were much lower in the Catholic Church. I just had to lay that at the foot of the cross."

Not surprisingly, another "loss" for Father Tom is that he works much harder than he did in the Episcopal Church. "It just seems that in the Episcopal Church I had more time away from the parish than I do in the Catholic Church. It's just more demanding ... I do 14 Masses a week, plus I do reconciliation every day. I do a Bible study every week. It's a serious study, there are over 2,000 people in it. There may be a list of 20 people in the hospital at a time, I'm talking *serious* illnesses. I have a deacon and an associate to help me, and they're busy all the time. Everyone's busy all the time. I was by myself for a while. So it is just that the demands and rigors of the parish are much greater. There are just more people."

Far from complaining, Father Tom expresses satisfaction at the heavy demands on his time. In a sense, they help justify his decision to convert. "In the Catholic Church I feel like I'm being useful in the world, whereas in the Episcopal Church ... I saw the handwriting on the wall. I saw exactly what was going on, and I said, 'I'm out of here. This is not going to work.' In the RC I have a significant ministry versus working in a dying church."

I ask Father Tom about the other side of the ledger, "What did you gain by converting?" Like almost all the married priests will, Father Tom talks about doctrinal truth. "How does the Church decide on its doctrine and dogma and discipline? Looking more deeply into those, I really felt that the Episcopal Church was just a collection of private opinions. ... I had a need to be intellectually comfortable with what the church that I belonged to believed. I still don't understand everything the Catholic Church teaches, there are things I wonder about; but in the Episcopal Church you weren't required to wonder about things. Everything you wanted to think was just fine, no one was ever going to tap you on the shoulder and say, 'Hey, you've got to teach the truth here.'" I ask Father Tom his own views on behaviors—abortion, contraception, suicide, same-sex relations—that the Church holds to be sinful, though many Catholics disagree. On every issue he is unbending in affirming the official Church teaching. This is typical of a married priest.

I also want to know how others perceive him. Father Tom reflects that he's never been received poorly by a layperson, though sometimes it is awkward when they don't know that married priests exist. "Sometimes I throttle things back. Like in homilies, instead of saying 'I'm seeing my grandchild . . . ,' I'll say, 'Every parent sees their child. . . .' [Because] when I say, 'I'm seeing my child'—then there's always some people who don't know that, and I have to say 'I'm a married priest, the Pope knows about it' and have this big explanation. It gets tiresome."

"Do you avoid displays of affection, like holding hands, when you're at the church?" I follow up. "That hasn't really been an issue because we're both so busy when we're at church. . . . [When I was first ordained, some diocesan leaders] suggested that my wife not even be visible at the church, you know, so as not to detract from the discipline of celibacy. . . . But the bishop has always been very accommodating and welcoming to my wife, and . . . the core members of the parish all know us as a couple, it's not a problem at all. . . . Invisibility has really not been necessary."

FATHER TOM SHARES a lot in common with his fellow married priests. His views are very traditional on both doctrine and the aesthetics of worship. His main regrets and satisfactions about his conversion are the same as those of most married priests. Although he is canonically restricted from holding the title of past, he actually pastors a sizable parish, as do about half of the married priests. And like most married priests, he is uncomfortable with the attention his marital status brings. His location is also typical; about half of all married priests live in Texas, with the highest concentration focused in the Dallas–Fort Worth area.

How do married priests compare to regular (ordinary celibate) Catholic priests? The Appendix presents detailed tables of comparisons (Part VI) and technical information on the related surveys and sampling designs used (Parts I and II). This chapter presents selected findings, grouped broadly into the categories of "objective" and "subjective". The overall conclusion can be stated simply: on the "objective" items like age and length of tenure there is generally little difference between the two groups of priests, whereas on virtually every "subjective" measure of priestly character, belief, and practice, the married priests stand apart from American Catholic priests as a whole.

Objective Conditions
Age

Despite being ordained, on average, about two decades later in life, the married priests are only a couple of years older than the average Catholic priest in the United States. This is due, of course, to the fact that no married Pastoral Provision priests were ordained before 1980. The average age reported by married priests in my 2007 survey was 63.7 years. The average age of priests in a 2001 survey by sociologist Dean Hoge, designed to replicate the 1970 Greeley and Schoenherr survey, was 60.9 years—a difference of 2.8 years. However, since (due to rising longevity and fewer ordinations in recent decades) the average age of priests has been rising steadily for the past 30 years, the true age difference in 2007 was probably at least a year less than this, and likely is still less now.

The average married priest is 49 when he is ordained. This is 13 or 14 years older than the age at ordination of regular Catholic priests, which has been slowly rising.[2] Table 1.1 presents the numbers.[3] As the first column shows, in the past three decades the age at ordination of regular Catholic priests rose from 31 to 36. The middle column shows that married priests ordained during the same time averaged, with some variation, about 50 years of age.

Assuming retirement at 70, then, the average married priest will serve in the Catholic ministry for about 21 years, compared to 33 years

Table 1.1 Age at Ordination and Anglican Tenure, Comparing Married Priests to All US Priests

	US Priests Ordained since 1980*	Pastoral Provision Priests		
		Catholic Ordination	Anglican Ordination	Anglican Tenure
1980–1989	31	48	33	15
1990–1999	33	53	32	18
2000–2009	36	50	—	19

* *Sources*: See note in text.

for regular diocesan priests—a 40 percent reduction in time of service. Many priests, of course, work well past age 70, and married priests are no different. Over half (58 percent) of the married priests age 70 or over still work full-time. A third (33 percent) of them effectively serve as parish pastors. Almost all the married priests who describe themselves as "retired" still work part-time providing assistance with Masses or other parish work.

On the whole, the married priests were not ordained at a particularly young age as Episcopalians, as the third data column of Table 1.1 shows. Their entry into the Catholic priesthood at an older age, it appears, is due almost entirely to time spent in the Episcopal priesthood and the Catholic ordination process, an average of 17 years. The average married priest ordained in the 1980s had served in the Anglican priesthood for 15 years, a figure that has increased to 19 years for the most recently ordained. The minimum Anglican tenure over this time has increased from three to seven years, suggesting that at least part of the increase in average tenure is due to stricter requirements or greater selectivity on the part of receiving Catholic bishops.

Reception and Support from American Catholics

Married priests and their wives reported that they have been personally well received by both priests and laypersons in the Catholic Church. When asked how well they would say they had been received in the Church, virtually all (99 percent of the priests and 100 percent of the wives) responded that they had been received very well or moderately well by laypersons. Almost all (96 percent of the priests and 98 percent of the wives) also reported that they had been well received by other priests.

Despite this, other evidence indicates that opposition to receiving married convert priests exists, though it is not strong. In my 2009 survey of US bishops, over a quarter (27 percent) reported that they have heard objections to the Pastoral Provision from their priests. One in six bishops (17 percent) reported that they do not particularly support the Pastoral Provision, and one in ten (11 percent) believed that the Pastoral Provision should be discontinued. A similar minority (14 percent) of Catholic priests expressed opposition to the Pastoral Provision in Hoge's 2001 survey.[4] A few (8 percent) of the married priests reported having a negative encounter with a priest who disapproved of their status. None reported a serious negative encounter with a layperson. Far more often, both priests and wives reported experiences of support, acceptance, and welcome for them by both priests and laypersons.

Although you might assume—and the Church does—that it would be their marital status that would make it difficult for these priests to relate to their celibate colleagues, in fact the bigger issue is often married priests' doctrinal conservatism and convert status. Marital status cuts both ways. Most American priests support the idea of a married presbyterate, and thus are inclined to warmly welcome a married priest. However, the distinct doctrinal conservatism of the married priests ironically limits support from other priests, since priests who are likely to welcome the fact that they are married are also likely to be put off by their conservatism, and vice versa. Second, relationships formed in seminary and other early formation times often result in lifelong friendships among Catholic priests. Converts like Father Tom—indeed, like all married priests—are not a part of these friendship networks.

Retention

Retention is a primary measure of job satisfaction and suitability. Consistent with their exceptionally high reported happiness, the rate of retention in the priesthood for married priests is far higher than for US priests generally. Table 1.2 summarizes the available data, reporting on survey and archival information for 95 married priests.

Retention rates for all Catholic priests can only be estimated, since defections are seldom reported. Globally, just under 70,000 men have abandoned the priesthood since 1964, compared to a current population

Table 1.2 **Resignations and Defaults, Comparing Married Priests to All US Priests (in Percent)**

	US Priests Ordained since 1980 ($n = \sim14,000$)	Married Priests ($n = 95$)
Percent resigned within 5 years	7	0
Percent resigned within 10 years	10	2
Percent divorced following ordination	0	3
Any negative outcome	> 15	9.5

of just over 400,000 priests.[5] Assuming comparable attrition and mortality for both persisting and defecting priests results in an estimated global defection rate of 15 percent over the past 50 years. The average duration in the priesthood before resigning is 13 years.[6] This estimate of 15 percent defection at 13 years, on average, is consistent with more specific research on US priests, which has found that at least 7 percent of new priests nationwide since 1980 have resigned within five years.[7] By the tenth ordination anniversary, about 10 percent have resigned.[8] The rates are slightly higher for diocesan priests—those who serve parishes—than for those in a religious order.

By contrast, since 1981 only two married priests have resigned, both after five years. Using a generous measure of "negative outcome," interpreted as any situation that could possibly be interpreted as a failure to persist in effective priestly work, a total of 10 married priests, or 9.6 percent, have resulted in any form of negative outcome. This number includes the two resignations already mentioned, one suicide, three divorces, one marital separation, and two cases of persistent refusal to be subject to the supervision of the bishop. Even on this much broader measure, then, married priests are less likely than priests in general to default in ministry.

Unlike celibate clergy, however, every married priest who defaults deeply affects not only his own life in the Church but also that of his wife and (in most cases) his children. For example, among the 10 negative outcomes just mentioned, one of the resignations also resulted in a divorce; in at least two cases the priest's wife, as well as the priest, received financial support from the diocese; and in two cases the priests, allegedly engaged in child sexual misconduct, victimized their own children. For married priests, the ripple effect of troubles is greater than for unmarried priests.

The divorces, while rare, present unique problems. Although the rate of divorce (3.4 percent) is far below that among US married couples, including Catholic couples, the image of a divorced man functioning as a Catholic priest while the Catholic Church does not recognize divorce can be especially scandalous, particularly to celibate clergy and divorced laity. If the priest is functioning as a pastor, experience in Protestant settings tells us that his divorce is likely to affect the congregation. If his wife was a member of the congregation he served, as is almost always the case, their divorce also estranges her from her spiritual home, and can produce split loyalties and conflict among the congregation. The property and support settlements in a divorce can easily result in a legal claim by the wife upon the diocese, particularly if the couple were living in church-supplied housing. Such a claim has in fact been made in one of the three divorces noted above.

A brief look at the causes of clergy resignation suggest some of the reasons that the rate of default is so low among the married priests. Greeley and Schoenherr found that the two strongest predictors of priest resignation, or of priests considering resigning, were difficulty with Church authority and a desire to marry.[9] The latter, of course, is not an issue for married priests. And as we shall see below, they affirm Church authority more strongly than any other group of priests. Their advanced age at ordination also lowers the prospect of defection. Salvini reported that the average age at defection, for all priests worldwide, was 41 years.[10] In Greeley and Schoenherr's data, 90 percent of the resigned priests, compared to only 55 percent of the active priests, were aged 45 or under.[11] By the time they are ordained, at an average age of 49, the married priests are generally much older and more settled in their lives, and have less opportunity to defect, making them thus less likely to default.

Workload

Generally speaking, the workload of married priests is about the same as it is for all US priests. I asked the married priests responding to my survey how many total hours they worked during a typical week, including weekends. The median number reported for a typical workweek was 52 hours. Ten percent reported working more than 72 hours, and an equal proportion fewer than 42 hours. In a 1985 study, US priests as a whole reported a median workweek of 50 hours. A total of 10 percent reported working more than 72 hours, and 10 percent worked fewer than 28 hours. Table 1.3 shows the numbers.[12]

Several other studies have reported longer workweeks for Catholic priests, but these studies either excluded retired priests and/or part-time priests or were confined to pastors, all of which result in a longer average workweek. Looking only at full-time pastors among the married priests ($n = 18$), the average reported workweek was 59.6 hours, which is similar to the findings of these latter studies.[13]

By either method, the number of hours worked reported by the married priests is closely comparable to—though slightly longer than—that reported by regular Catholic priests. The observed difference, at two to three hours a week, is not large, but it is significant because it contradicts

Table 1.3 Priests' Workweek

	US Priests 1985	Married Priests 2007
Hours worked each week		
Median	50	52
10% work more than	72	72
10% work fewer than	28*	42
Days off each week (in Percent)		
Two days	35	14
One day	44	64
No day off	11	22

* Includes part-time workers.

the claim, often made in support of clergy celibacy, that married priests are not able to devote as much time to a parish as are celibate priests.[14]

Regular Catholic priests, however, are able to structure their time to have more days off. Many priests who are pastors can take a day off during the week, but married priests, who are more likely to have Monday-to-Friday work responsibilities, are much less able to do so. Fully one in five (22 percent) of the married priests did not have a weekly day off, twice the proportion for Catholic priests in general. While over a third (35 percent) of all US priests were able to have two days free a week, only 14 percent of the married priests were able to do so. In sum, married priests work about the same amount as most American priests, but they are much less able to take concentrated periods of time for refreshment and renewal.

Geography

Why don't more Catholics meet a married priest? One reason is that, in addition to being rare to begin with, they have been concentrated in only a few US dioceses (see Figure 1.1). The causes and implications of this are explored more fully in Chapter 6, so we'll just focus on the basic data here. Almost three-fourths (74 percent) of US dioceses have never had a married priest. Among the remaining quarter (26 percent) of dioceses who have, most have had just one. Only 10 US dioceses (5 percent) have ordained more than one married priest: Dallas, which has ordained seven

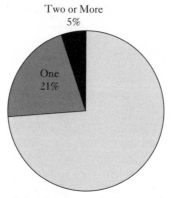

Two or More
5%

One
21%

FIGURE I.I Distribution of Married Priest Ordinations by Diocese (in Percent)

married priests; Fort Worth, Charleston, and Washington, which have each ordained four; Galveston-Houston and New York, which have each ordained three; and Atlanta, Green Bay, Mobile, and Raleigh, which have each ordained two.

As this list of dioceses suggests, for the most part married priests have been a phenomenon of the South, and particularly of Texas. Forty of the married priests serving in the United States, just under half the total, have been ordained in dioceses located in the Southern region as defined by the US Census. One in four married priest ordinations (21) have, like Father Tom's, taken place in the state of Texas. The Dallas–Fort Worth metroplex, with 11 Pastoral Provision ordinations, has the highest concentration of married Catholic priests in the United States.

This geographic imbalance is a result of several factors. First, Southern Episcopalian dioceses tend to have a more socially and theologically conservative and, in Texas, Anglo-Catholic orientation than the US norm. As a result, they tend to produce more priests disposed to consider converting to the Catholic Church, as well as bishops inclined to support them in their conversion. For example, Clarence Pope, the Episcopalian bishop of Fort Worth, supported the incorporation of St. Bartholomew's Episcopal Church into the Catholic Church of St. Mary the Virgin, though the congregation remained intact and retained its church building. Pope later converted to Catholicism. At the same time, both Catholics and Episcopalians in the South are a much smaller minority of the population than elsewhere in the country. In terms of religious culture, Texas is a Baptist domain in much the same way that Massachusetts is a Catholic domain. Consequently, conversion between Episcopalians and Catholics does not create stress for the dominant religious culture in the South, as it might in other parts of the country. Finally, Catholic dioceses in the South often have fewer priests to serve the faithful, so their bishops may be more open to creative solutions, such as using married priests.

Views, Beliefs, and Practices
Priestly Role and Function

How do married priests understand their roles? How do they compare to celibate priests? We have consistent data on five such questions.

The top two items in Table 1.4 express core elements of the Catholic understanding of the priesthood: that a priest's primary role is presiding at the Eucharist, and that a priest is fundamentally different from

Table 1.4 Issues in the Priesthood (in Percent), Comparing Married Priests (2007) with US Priests in 1970 and 2001

How much do you agree or disagree with each of the following statements?	Percent Responding "Agree Strongly" or "Agree Somewhat"		
	US Priests 1970	US Priests 2001	Married Priests 2007
I feel that I am most a priest when I am "saying Mass" (presiding at Eucharist) and hearing confessions.	69	77	81
Ordination confers on the priest a new status or a permanent character which makes him essentially different from the laity within the Church.	70	83	92
Celibacy should be a matter of personal choice for diocesan priests.	53	52	34
The Catholic Church needs to move faster in empowering lay persons in ministry.	—	70	26
I think it would be a good idea if the priests in a diocese were to choose their own bishop.	—	43	4

Wording of questions is slightly different between surveys. Data show diocesan priests only.

a layperson. This understanding of the priesthood, which may properly be called a sacramental one, is affirmed by at least two-thirds of priests, and has grown stronger in recent years. Notably, the married priests affirm this Catholic understanding of the priesthood more strongly than do regular Catholic priests, even the younger or more recent sample of priests. We will see this pattern repeated on almost every issue of Catholic doctrine or morals: the views of priests 40 years ago are the least consonant with formal Catholic teaching, the most recent views of priests are more in conformity, and the views of the married priests are even more so. Nonetheless, on these issues of priestly role, the self-understanding of the married priests, albeit more extreme, is in line with that of all Catholic priests.

On the other hand, for the bottom three items of Table 1.4, the views of the married priests depart sharply from those of regular Catholic priests. These items relate to perceived or proposed changes in the Church's structure or authority. The large differences reflect the particular experience of the married priests as former Episcopalians. Generally, the married priests were concerned that the Catholic Church would not repeat what they judged to be failed or problematic policies of the Episcopal Church. Ironically, only a third (34 percent) of married priests, compared to a majority (52–53 percent) of regular priests, support optional celibacy for priests. This view reflects their experience as married priests in counterintuitive ways. We will consider this at length in Chapter 7.

More than two-thirds (70 percent) of regular priests, but only a quarter (26 percent) of married priests, agreed with the statement "The Catholic Church needs to move faster in empowering lay persons in ministry." Married priests noted that they disagreed not because they opposed the participation of laypersons in the Church, but because they felt the Church was already moving very fast in empowering lay involvement and risked being overwhelmed by the changes. However, lower support for this item is also consistent with the married priests' higher support for a sacramental view of the priesthood.

Strikingly, only a negligible number (4 percent) of the married priests, but 4 in 10 (43 percent of) regular priests, were in favor of having priests elect their diocesan bishop. Many married priests made clear that their answer reflected their experience in the Episcopal Church, in which bishops who upheld unpopular positions on moral or doctrinal matters were unlikely to be elected. This politicization of Church positions and policy was, in their view, a large part of the reason that the Episcopal Church was unable to withstand the cultural forces that were eating away at traditional Church teachings. One married priest in the Northeast, with long tenure as an Episcopalian and a degree in sociology, commented, "Lord. Disagree strongly. I've seen what people will pick. I was in an Episcopal diocese when that happened, and oh my goodness. A good guy to play golf and gin rummy with, but I wouldn't trust my dog to him theologically. . . . I want somebody who's on the throne of Peter." Another married priest, who grew up in strict Calvinist churches, related his emphatic opposition explicitly to his conversion choice: "I strongly, strongly, strongly disagree with that. . . . It's congregationalism. If I'd have wanted to be a congregational minister, I would have gone there."

In sum, the married priests are similar to regular Catholic priests in their understanding of priestly role and identity, but on issues relating to church structure and discipline, their views are strikingly different in ways that reflect their unique experience.

Morale

Sources of Satisfaction

I wanted to assess what aspects of their jobs bring married priests the most satisfaction. Following previous surveys, I asked about six specific items. The results are shown in Table 1.5, listed from most important to least important. Every item follows the pattern already observed for the items relating to the priestly role, with the 1970 responses at one extreme, the Pastoral Provision responses at the other, and the 2001 responses in the middle.

Since 1970, for regular priests, the importance of two, and probably three, items has increased, while the importance of three others has declined. (Item 2 was not asked in 1970, but the high 2001 responses on this item make it unlikely that its importance would have been higher in 1970 if it had been asked.) These apparently simple changes over time, however, reflect a complicated interaction between life course changes in satisfaction and the age structure of the presbyterate.

For regular priests, the sources of satisfaction are substantially different for older priests than for younger priests. Figures 1.2 and 1.3 show the age trends for priests in 2001 and 1970. For every item, the responses of older and younger priests are significantly different. The age trend for spiritual security from responding to the divine call, respect that comes to the priestly office, and the opportunity to work with many people is

Table 1.5 Important Sources of Satisfaction (in Percent),* Comparing Married
Priests (2007) with US Priests in 1970 and 2001

How important is each of the following as a source of satisfaction to you?	Priests Responding "of Great Importance"		
	US Priests 1970	US Priests 2001	Married Priests 2007
1. Joy of administering the sacraments and presiding over the liturgy.	83	94	100
2. The satisfaction of preaching the word.	—	80	96
3. Opportunity to work with many people and be a part of their lives.	73	66	60
4. Spiritual security that results from responding to the divine call.	44	51	59
5. Respect that comes to the priestly office.	25	29	10
6. Engaging in efforts at social reform.	21	20	19

* Showing diocesan priests only.

generally similar among both groups of priests, 30 years apart. Both in 1970 and in 2001, older priests derived greater satisfaction from the security and respect they felt, and less from the opportunity to work with many people. Thus, a large part of the apparent change over time for these items is simply an artifact of the fact that younger priests comprised a much larger proportion, and older priests a much smaller proportion, of the presbyterate in 1970 than in 2001. In 1970, 25 percent of priests were younger than 35, and 13 percent were older than 60. By 2001, only 4 percent of priests were under 35, and half (50 percent) were over 60 years of age.

The age trends for satisfaction from administering the sacraments and social reform efforts, however, have reversed over the course of 30 years. In 1970, the youngest priests derived the least satisfaction of any age group from administering the sacraments and the greatest satisfaction from social reform efforts; in 2001 it was just the opposite. If, as Greeley and Schoenherr suggested, the 1970 findings indicated that younger priests received less satisfaction from their religious role and more from their social role, we would have to say that three decades later the situation was

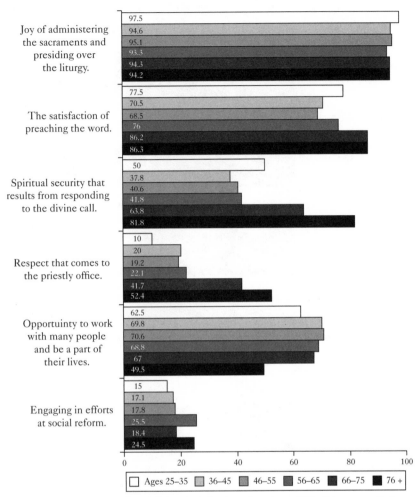

FIGURE 1.2 Sources of Priestly Satisfaction by Age (US Diocesan Priests, 2001–2002) (Percent Responding "of Great Satisfaction")

reversed. At any rate, these changes are not simply due to changes in the size of age cohorts.

Despite these differences and trends, there is one striking similarity among the priests' responses in Table 1.5. Although the proportions are different, the relative rankings of the sources of satisfaction for all three groups of priests are identical (with one exception: 5 and 6 are reversed for the married priests). This suggests that, despite all the other differences, the overall structure of satisfaction—that is, the way that all of the sources collectively contribute to the priest's total satisfaction—is similar and relatively stable for all three groups.

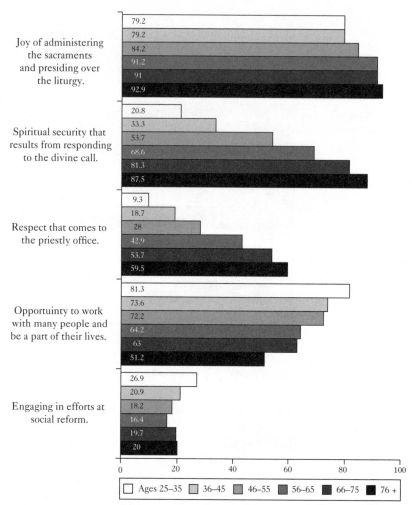

FIGURE 1.3 Sources of Priestly Satisfaction by Age (US Diocesan Priests, 1970) (Percent Responding "of Great Satisfaction")

What accounts for this? By digging deeper into the data, we can see that there are three underlying factors. The top two items, "the joy of administering the sacraments and presiding over the liturgy" and "the satisfaction of preaching the Word," are related to priests' liturgical role. Items 4 and 5, "spiritual security that comes from responding to the divine call" and "respect that comes to the priestly office," also share a common dimension: the recognition of one's esteem by God and others. Items 3 and 6, "opportunity to work with many people and be a part of their lives" and "engaging in efforts at social reform," both reflect communal or social engagement.[15]

The effects discussed here are based on the underlying dimensions, but they can also be discerned, in most cases, by a close examination of the percentages reported in Figure 1.2. For most diocesan priests, liturgical role satisfaction is the most important of the three dimensions. As Figure 1.2 shows, this is particularly the case with regard to presiding at Mass. Overall, 94 percent of US priests report the joy of administering the sacraments to be of great importance to their satisfaction as priests. Paradoxically, because this is such a high and ubiquitous source of satisfaction, it does little to explain the differences between more satisfied and less satisfied priests. Recognition and social satisfaction are of about equal weight overall, one or the other being more important for some priests and less important for others. The importance of all three dimensions of satisfaction varies greatly by the age of the priest.

For all US diocesan priests in 2001, liturgical role satisfaction declined with age. This is probably related to the growing sacramentalism, discussed above, of more recent ordination classes, since in the 1970 data liturgical role satisfaction increased with age. Recognition satisfaction increased with age, probably an enduring aging effect, since the trend was almost identical in both 2001 and 1970. As priests grow older, they derive more satisfaction from recognition or affirmation by God and the laity.

Perhaps younger priests are more interested in recognition by peers. Satisfaction from social engagement is highest for priests in the middle of their careers, but lowest among the youngest and oldest priests. This may relate to the greater liberalism of priests in their fifties and sixties, discussed above, or it may reflect the fact that these priests, pastors in mid-career, are at the height of their ability to affect communal and social change. Those who have more influence have more opportunity to derive satisfaction from wielding it. The net effect of these trends is that, among the youngest priests, liturgical role satisfaction is high, but satisfaction due to recognition and social engagement is low; among the oldest priests, recognition satisfaction is high, but liturgical role and social engagement satisfaction is low. For those in middle age or mid-career, social engagement satisfaction is high, and liturgical and recognition satisfaction is moderate.

The structure of priestly satisfaction is quite different for married priests. Unlike regular priests, for whom, as we saw above, celebrating the liturgy and preaching are two expressions of a single liturgical role, married priests see preaching as distinct from the satisfaction of celebrating the liturgy. This is consistent with their Protestant background, which does not strictly associate preaching with sacramental worship. In many Protestant worship settings, preaching displaces communion entirely, and is not reserved to sacramentally ordained persons.

Preaching has a unique importance for the married priests for several reasons. As persons trained and formed in a religious culture that is more oriented to preaching in worship, they often find that they are considered comparatively good preachers in the Catholic setting. One married priest, trained in a Presbyterian seminary, frankly observed, "You know as well as I do, the preaching in the Roman Catholic Church is pathetic. So any of us that can stand up there and preach a sermon, which we all can, the laymen just gush all over you. I've got laymen who say I'm the greatest preacher they ever heard. Well, you know, I'm not the greatest, but I'm probably the greatest *they* ever heard."

Preaching is also of unique importance to these priest converts because it is an opportunity to communicate the doctrinal essentials of the faith that formed the basis, in most cases, of their own conversion, and which many American Catholics do not seem to know well. One married priest, who teaches theology in a Catholic school, observed, "To me, given my limited [engagement in] parish congregational life, preaching has to become more important, because this is the only time you get to talk to them. . . . I will preach stuff at a daily Mass at church, and I will have life-long Catholics say, 'Gee, I never heard it said like that before.' In one way, that's gratifying; in another way, it's alarming."

Respect for the priestly office is only weakly related to satisfaction for the married priests. As shown in Table 1.5, only 10 percent of them report that it is of "great importance" to them. Married priests see the remaining three items—spiritual security from responding to the divine call, opportunity to be a part of the lives of many people, and social reform efforts—as related. This suggests that, for the married priests, priestly satisfaction is less related to their status as priests and more related to priestly functions themselves. Whether or not they receive recognition, feel secure, or succeed in changing society is less important than their ability to do the unique things that a priest does. This no doubt reflects the unique character of these men as priest converts. Each of them voluntarily relinquished the social attributes of priesthood—the elements of the third dimension, which they already had as Episcopal priests—in order to perform what they perceived to be more authentic priestly functions, in preaching and celebrating the sacraments. It is thus not surprising that, as Catholic priests, they now derive unique satisfaction from the enactment of those functions.

Happiness

Married priests reported very high levels of personal and professional satisfaction, notably higher than the already high levels reported by priests generally. As a global measure of happiness, I asked a question that has been used on many opinion surveys, including all former surveys of Catholic priests: "Taking all things together, how would you say things are these days? Would you say you are very happy, pretty happy, or not too happy?" (see Appendix, Table A.5). On this question the married priests report an exceedingly high level of happiness; fully two-thirds (66 percent) of them report being "very happy." It is hard to find a comparable group that also reports their level of happiness to be this high. Only one-third (33 percent) of Americans over the past decade have reported that they are "very happy" on the US General Social Survey (GSS). Married Americans and persons who are very religious are somewhat happier than others; among married persons who are very religious, 48 percent reported themselves to be "very happy" on the GSS. Similarly, just under half (46 percent) of US priests in 2001 described themselves as "very happy"; this proportion is higher than that of priests in the past, although still much lower than that of the married priests. In the 1970 Greeley and Schoenherr survey, only 28 percent of US priests described themselves as "very happy"; by 1985 this had risen to 37 percent.

Other measures of happiness or satisfaction reported a similar pattern of responses. Two-thirds (66 percent) of US priests in 2001 said that if they had to make the choice again, they would definitely become a Catholic priest. Only half (50 percent) of priests responded this positively in 1970. By contrast, 9 in 10 (89 percent) of the married priests, with no differences by age, said they would definitely make the same choice to become a Catholic priest. Among regular priests, but not the married priests, older priests are more definite in this response than younger priests; the trend was much steeper in 1970. Among regular priests, pastors and those ordained for a shorter time tended to report somewhat lower happiness than the alternatives; but this was not the case among the married priests.

Why are the married priests consistently so much happier than regular Catholic priests? Our data cannot support firm conclusions on this point, but do suggest a couple of likely possibilities. It is possible, for example, that their higher happiness is due simply to the fact that they are married. Just as, in general, married men are happier than unmarried men in comparable circumstances, so perhaps married priests are happier than unmarried ones, all other things being equal. In studies of Protestant clergy or religious leaders, married ministers are usually happier than unmarried ones by about 7–10 percentage points.[16]

It would also seem plausible that happiness, for a priest, would be affected by his perceived relationship with God. Indeed, for the married priests, happiness is related to their spiritual or devotional life, but spirituality, for several reasons, does little to help us understand their happiness. To get a sense of the priests' spiritual state or growth, I asked each priest the following question: "Compared to a year ago, would you say that today you are closer to God, further away from God, or about the same?" Overall, just over half (53 percent) of the priests reported feeling closer to God; only 6 percent felt further away from God, and 39 percent felt about the same (Appendix, Table A.6). The sense of feeling closer to God has a strong effect on happiness: 79 percent of those who felt closer to God reported being very happy, compared to only 64 percent of those who did not feel closer to God. However, the effect of happiness on closeness to God is even stronger: 61 percent of married priests who reported they were "very happy," but only 38 percent of those less than very happy, reported feeling closer to God than they did a year ago. Since these are both subjective self-assessments, we cannot know whether feeling closer to God leads to being happy or whether being happy leads to feeling closer to God. Furthermore, very little of the comparative research on priests has addressed matters of devotional practice or prayer, and none has also measured spirituality. Thus, we are unable to make comparisons or draw inferences from the characteristics of priests in general on this important topic. I will discuss the spirituality and devotional practices of the married priests more fully later in this chapter.

It is also likely that, as with their orthodoxy, the greater happiness of these priests reflects some of the dynamics of conversion. Our findings above on the unique structure of their sources of satisfaction support this idea. Most Catholic priests were already Catholic before entering the priesthood. For the married priests, it was the other way around. Their satisfaction as Catholic priests, then, may reflect their particular satisfaction in being Catholic over and above the satisfaction they share with all priests. This satisfaction may well also include an element of self-justification.

To the extent that overall happiness reflects priestly satisfaction, the married priests, despite their differences from other priests in assessing the importance of sources of satisfaction, generally gain happiness from the same source as other priests. To say that something is important as a source of satisfaction, of course, does not mean that one is actually able to derive such satisfaction in his present circumstances. As noted above, for all priests the joy of celebrating the sacraments is most strongly associated with overall happiness. Of the regular priests' three dimensions of satisfaction identified above, only liturgical role satisfaction—that is, celebrating the sacraments and preaching—is positively correlated with the priests' self-reported happiness. Recognition and social satisfaction have little relationship to current happiness, and satisfaction from engaging in efforts at social reform is *negatively* related to happiness. Regular Catholic priests who consider this an important source of satisfaction may experience more frustration than fulfillment from doing so.

For a married priest, celebrating the sacraments is also strongly and uniquely associated with happiness. Satisfaction from preaching, however, as distinct from celebrating the liturgy, is negatively associated with happiness. This may reflect disappointment at the more restricted or less central place of the homily in Catholic worship as compared to sermons in the Episcopal Church. The social attributes of priesthood reflected in their third dimension of satisfaction have a weak relationship with happiness.

Usefulness and Challenge

Like Father Tom, another important source of happiness for married priests is the feeling of being useful in the Catholic Church. For all Catholic priests, we would expect the conditions and challenge of work assignments to have a particularly strong effect on their sense of satisfaction or happiness, since they make an unusually strong personal commitment to their vocation and the institution in which they both live and work. A study of the careers of Catholic diocesan priests found that challenging work, autonomy, and positive relations with other priests were among the most important factors for a priest's happiness and career satisfaction.[17] To test this question, I asked the married priests about their work, working conditions, and how well they felt that their skills and abilities were being used, using standard questions that had been asked on other surveys.

To measure their sense of usefulness, I asked the married priests: "How well do you feel your skills and abilities are being used in your present assignment?" Possible responses were "a great deal," "fairly much," "to some degree," "comparatively little," or "not at all." Despite concerns that the married priests may not be well utilized, nearly half (44 percent) of them, slightly more than regular priests (40 percent), responded that their skills and abilities were being used a great deal in their present assignment.[18] See Appendix, Table A.5.

Consistent with prior research, I also found that the sense of usefulness was strongly related to happiness for both groups of priests. The correlation is a little stronger for the married priests (.40) than for US priests in general (.30). Figure 1.4 illustrates the effect, showing the difference in happiness for priests reporting that their skills are being used a great deal and those who feel their skills are being used comparatively little. Although happiness is higher overall for the married priests, for both groups of priests about a third (33 percent) more who feel their skills are being used a great deal report that they are very happy, compared to those whose skills are comparatively little used. Other differences in happiness between the two groups, and how they are measured, are discussed further later in the chapter.

Research has found that pastors are generally less happy than priests who serve in other roles. The pastoral role is diffuse, subject to competing

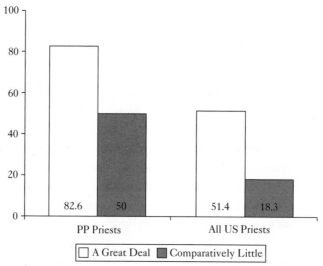

FIGURE 1.4 Priests' Reported Happiness by Usefulness, Comparing US Diocesan Priests (1993) with Married Priests (Percent "Very Happy" among Priests Reporting That Their Abilities Are Being Used "a Great Deal" and "Comparatively Little")

pressures from parishioners and superiors, and increasingly involves administrative duties that most priests do not find fulfilling. Although married priests are restricted from serving as pastors, about a third (30 percent) of them serve as de facto pastors, functioning as the sole or senior pastor of a parish but without the canonical title of pastor. In the 2001 US priest data, those with an administrative or educational apostolate outside the parish were more likely to affirm that their skills were being used a great deal or fairly much (83 percent) than were pastors (73 percent). This is also true for the married priests: those who were serving effectively as pastors were *less* likely to report that their skills were being used a great deal (47 percent) than those serving in other jobs (59 percent). Seven percent of effective pastors, but no non-pastors, among the married priests reported that they were "not too happy." As we will discuss elsewhere, many US priests and bishops question the policy restricting married priests from serving as pastors more regularly. But a change in policy would likely not increase married priests' happiness.

Devotional Practices

During the interviews I asked the married priests about their spiritual and devotional practices (see Appendix, Table A.6). This seems an obvious set of issues to address with priests, and was included in Greeley and Schoenherr's original study; however, recent surveys of priests have seldom concerned themselves with such issues. A notable exception is a set of two related surveys by Hoge of priests who were ordained during the years 1981–1985 and 1996–2000. Since these periods fall within and roughly bracket the years during which the Pastoral Provision priests were ordained, that is, 1981–2006, Hoge's findings form a reasonable basis of comparison on these issues. Due to differences in the wording of questions, the comparisons are not exact. The results are shown in Table 1.6. Items in the table are listed from most to least practiced devotions by the married priests. The comparison reveals two broad facts about the devotional life of the married priests. First, following the pattern we have already seen on other issues, they have high levels of personal devotional practice, higher than that of their contemporaries and roughly comparable to that of recently ordained priests. Second, their devotional practice appears to be subject to greater opportunity constraints than is the case for most Catholic priests.

Table 1.6 Devotional Practices of Catholic Priests, Comparing Married Priests (2007) with US Priests in 1990 and 2005

	A Priests 1990[*]	B Priests 2005[*]	C Married Priests	Difference (C–B)
How often do you. . . .				
Pray the Liturgy of the Hours (breviary)? *(% daily for all or some of the hours)*	38	62	82	20
Practice a devotion to a particular saint? *(% weekly or more often)*	—	37	48	11
Pray the Rosary? *(% weekly or more often)*	—	58	68	10
Receive the Sacrament of Reconciliation (confession)? *(% monthly or more often)*	24	50	47	-3
Practice Eucharistic Adoration? *(% weekly or more often)*	—	52	46	-6
Celebrate Mass? *(% daily)*	62	68	61	-7
Meet with a spiritual director? *(% monthly or more often)*	31	37	22	-15
Make a retreat? *(% yearly or more often)*	—	94	69	-25

[*] Diocesan priests ordained 5–9 years.

Source: Hoge (2006): 80–81. See note 35.

Table 1.6 suggests that US Catholic priests have been growing more active in their devotional practices in recent years.[19] For all the devotional practices measured in both periods, priests ordained in 1996–2000 report higher participation than those ordained 15 years earlier. This pattern is similar, and probably related, to the pattern of growing conformity among more recently ordained or younger priests that we have already observed. In most religious settings, not surprisingly, those who consent more strongly to a religion's teachings are also more likely to observe its practices. Substantial research has demonstrated this link between belief and practice among American Protestants. Here there appears to be a similar link among Catholic priests.

The Liturgy of the Hours, also known as the Divine Office or the breviary, is a set of forms for daily prayer tracing back to third-century monastic practice. It includes short forms, or "offices," for Scripture reading and prayer, designed to be observed every few hours throughout the day. Today these offices form the framework for the prayers of most Catholic religious orders, but priests outside the orders are also encouraged to participate, either in common or individually, in as many offices as feasible, and are enjoined by custom and canonical obligation to participate daily in at least the two main offices, observed at morning and evening. Canon Law also obliges every Catholic priest to make a retreat annually. These devotional practices, then, are in some respects definitive or uniquely characteristic of Catholic priests; that is, the level of their observance among priests is suggestive not only for understanding their personal spirituality but also regarding matters of priestly identity and participation.

Married priests report far higher regular participation in the Liturgy of the Hours than do Catholic priests in general. Four-fifths (80 percent) of the married priests surveyed reported that they recite all or some of the hours every day. This is one of the highest rates of compliance with this rule of devotion found among any group of priests. Greeley and Schoenherr's 1970 survey found, by contrast, that only just over half (54 percent) of diocesan priests prayed all or some of the hours daily, commenting that "the widespread disregard of the obligation of the breviary is rather a striking phenomenon."[20] By 1990, observance of this central priestly devotion, at 38 percent, was even lower, but by 2005, when 62 percent of recently ordained priests reported praying the hours, it had recovered. These proportions are for priests ordained less than 10 years; compliance is likely much lower among all priests.[21] In Greeley and Schoenherr's study, compliance with the breviary was highly correlated with age, but in the opposite direction: ranging from just 28 percent of priests age 35 or under to 86 percent of those over 55. Married priests are also more likely than the average Catholic priest to pray the rosary or to pray to a particular saint. These reflect common practices among Anglo-Catholic Episcopalians, which they now continue as Catholics.

Unlike the top three items in Table 1.6, the next three items—Eucharistic Adoration, celebrating Mass, and going to confession—involve an element of opportunity as well as desire. Since many married priests do not serve as pastors or in parish settings full-time, their opportunities to engage in these devotions or sacraments are somewhat more limited than for priests in general. Nonetheless, the married priests practice Eucharistic Adoration and celebrate Mass at about the same frequency as other newly ordained priests. The same is true for going to confession, although both married priests and newer priests reported more frequent confession than earlier cohorts of priests. Daily Mass celebration is comparable, but slightly less common, among married priests than among priests in general. It should be noted that married priests do not normally make a commitment to daily Mass celebration as an act of devotion, as many regular priests do.

Married priests make far less use of retreats or regular spiritual direction than do regular Catholic priests. Only a fifth (22 percent) of the married priests reported meeting with a spiritual director at least once a month, compared to almost twice that proportion (37 percent) among all priests. Likewise, the proportion of married priests making an annual retreat was a fourth (25 percent) lower than among all priests. It is not clear why this is the case, since these practices are common among Anglo-Catholic Episcopalians. Perhaps, as with Adoration, confession, and Mass, the married priests confront greater practical difficulties in making use of these devotions. Unlike virtually all Catholic pastors, many married priests do not have allowances of time and funds provided for them to take an annual retreat. Many of the married priests, in responding to these questions, expressed difficulty in finding a spiritual director who could relate to their unique life experiences and status. The same schedule constrictions that, as we shall see in later discussion in this chapter, make it more difficult for the married priests to take a day off may also be reflected here. Scheduling a week away or taking on a monthly spiritual direction meeting may simply be much more difficult in the face of multiple family, parish, and work demands.

Those who persist in finding a spiritual director, however, find it well worth the while. The subjective sense of being closer to or further away from God, which we saw earlier is associated with the married priests' reported happiness, is strongly affected by the priest's devotional practice. Table 1.7 shows the results. For each item in this table, the first column compares the percent responding "closer to God" among those who followed the practice regularly to those who did not. The second (rightmost) data column reports the difference between the two groups, showing thereby the effect of each spiritual practice on the priests' sense of growing closer to God. Items are listed in descending order of the size of this effect.

As these findings make clear, regular spiritual direction has the strongest effect of any spiritual practice on the spiritual growth of the married priests. Four in five (80 percent) of the priests who met with

Table 1.7 Effect of Spiritual Practice on Felt Closeness to God (in Percent)

As compared to this time last year, would you say you are closer to God, farther from God, or about the same?	Percent Responding "Closer to God"	Effect of Discipline
How often do you meet with a spiritual director?		
Monthly or more often	80	+32
Less than monthly	48	
How often do you receive the Sacrament of Reconciliation?		
Monthly or more often	70	+27
Less than monthly	43	
How often do you celebrate Mass?		
Daily or more often	62	+20
Less than daily	42	
How often do you pray the Rosary?		
Weekly or more often	58	+20
Less than weekly	38	
How often do you practice Eucharistic Adoration?		
Weekly or more often	59	+15
Less than weekly	44	
Do you regularly pray the Liturgy of the Hours?		
Every day	51	−19
Less than every day	70	

a spiritual director at least once a month reported feeling closer to God than they were a year ago; but less than half (48 percent) of those who did not have regular spiritual direction had grown closer to God, a difference or effect of 32 percent. Confession at least once a month, with a difference of 27 percent, had almost as strong an effect. Daily Mass celebration and weekly rosary and eucharistic adoration also increased the proportion feeling closer to God by 15–20 percent.

Moral and Doctrinal Conservatism

Although the promotion of belief in religious teachings is arguably one of the central tasks of religious leadership, surprisingly little research in past decades has examined the beliefs of Catholic priests. In order to profile the doctrinal and moral convictions of the married priests, therefore, it is necessary to build a similar profile of all Catholic priests to use for comparison. In addition to showing the characteristics of the married priests, then, this section of the chapter also presents some new information about the moral and doctrinal views of Catholic priests generally.

One might expect that married Catholic priests, as exceptions to the rule of priestly celibacy, would be less likely to agree with other Church teachings. After all, most of the pressure to relax the celibacy requirement has come from liberal Catholics. But this presumption could not be further from reality.

To measure their views on such issues, I presented the married priests with a series of nine actions. For each item, I asked, "Do you think [this action] is always, often, seldom, or never a sin?" The nine actions were carefully chosen as ones that are proscribed as sinful in Catholic moral teaching, as expressed in the Catechism of the Catholic Church, but on which there is widespread dissent among American Catholics: abortion, human cloning, fetal stem cell research, homosexual practice, extramarital sex, suicide, masturbation, artificial birth control, and condom use for AIDS defense. These questions were developed by survey researchers at the *Los Angeles Times* for a 2002 national survey of Catholic priests, thus permitting comparison of the married priests with all regular US priests. The findings are presented in Figure 1.5., with more detailed responses shown in Appendix, Table A.8. The items in this figure are listed in descending order of agreement with Church teaching by the married priests.

As a point of reference, Figure 1.5 also reports the views of active lay Catholics for those issues for which comparable data were available. The majority of those who identify themselves as Catholic on opinion surveys have only a distant attachment to the Catholic Church, are not very active in the practice of their faith, and express views on most issues that are not very different, on average, from those of all Americans, Catholic or not. By contrast, Catholics who are active in their faith, for example by being registered in a church, attending Mass regularly, or sending their children to a Catholic school, are much more in agreement with the Church's teaching and thought than is the American population at large. Figure 1.5 uses weekly Mass attendance to define active Catholics; by this standard, about one-fourth of all American Catholics are active, that is, attend Mass at least once a week. Roughly speaking, the active Catholics reported in Figure 1.5 are about 20 percent more likely than inactive Catholics to conform to Catholic teaching.

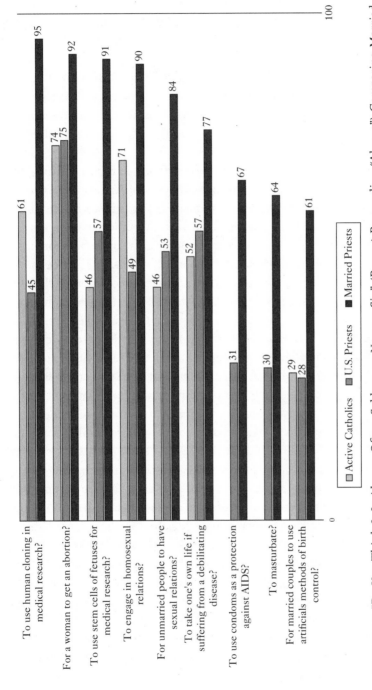

FIGURE 1.5 "Do You Think It Is Always, Often, Seldom, or Never a Sin" (Percent Responding "Always") Comparing Married Priests, Regular US Priests, and Active Catholics

Figure 1.5 clearly documents the striking doctrinal orthodoxy or moral conservatism of the married priests. For every item in the chart, a substantially higher proportion of the married priests than of either regular priests or of active Catholics affirmed that the action was always a sin. On most issues, the proportion of regular US priests affirming that the action in question is always a sin is (1) similar to that of active lay Catholics or Catholic males, (2) thus higher than that of nominal Catholics and/ or the US population (not shown), and (3) lower than that of the married priests.[22] A closer examination of the specific moral issues involved will clarify and nuance these general observations.

Principled opposition to elective abortion, a highly controversial issue, is one of the most well-known features of Catholic moral teaching. Abortion is one of the few sins considered so heinous by the Church that procuring one incurs an automatic excommunication. Yet less than one-fifth of American Catholic laity consider abortion to be wrong in all circumstances. In Gallup tracking polls in 2006–2008, three-fourths (74 percent; shown in Figure 1.5) of Catholics who reported that they attended church regularly did not think that abortion was morally acceptable.[23] Likewise, three-quarters (75 percent) of Catholic priests responded that abortion is always a sin.[24] However, the married priests exceeded this relatively high level of agreement with the Church's teaching by one-fifth: almost all (92 percent) of them agreed that abortion is always a sin. For both US priests and married priests, support for the Church's teaching on this item was higher than for any other item measured.

Consistent with its stance on abortion, Catholic moral thought also opposes human cloning and the use of fetal stem cells, both of which involve destroying human embryos, for scientific research. There are no data on how Catholics feel about human cloning, so Figure 1.5 reports the opinion of all Americans: an estimated three-fifths (61 percent) oppose "the cloning of human embryos for medical research."[25] A small majority (45 percent) of regular Catholic priests nationwide,[26] but almost all (95 percent) of the married priests, responded that human cloning for medical research was always sinful (Figure 1.5, second item). The survey of regular Catholic priests did not specify "human cloning," just "cloning," so it very likely understates the true opposition of Catholic priests. The results for embryonic stem cell research are similar. Three-fifths (57 percent) of US Catholic priests affirmed that using fetal stem cells for research was always sinful. This is well below the 91 percent of married priests who did so, but well above the 46 percent of active Catholics who, in Gallup polls, did not think that fetal stem cell research was morally acceptable (Figure 1.5, third item).[27] Contextualizing the issue by mentioning embryos and medical research is important when assessing opinion about cloning; when simply asked if they favor or oppose human cloning, nine in ten Americans respond that they oppose it.[28]

Half (49 percent) of Catholic priests nationwide said that to engage in homosexual relations is always sinful (Figure 1.5, fourth item). The specification of "homosexual relations" is important to the question. Catholic teaching makes a distinction between homosexual orientation and behavior, holding that, while homosexual orientation is not in itself sinful, it is disordered or unnatural, with the result that all homosexual relations are thereby sinful. Despite media portrayals of general acceptance of homosexual relations in American culture, the views of the priests are actually more tolerant than those of lay Catholic males, or American males generally, about three-fifths of whom hold that homosexual relations are always wrong. The proportion of regularly worshipping Catholic males who report that they believe homosexual relations are always wrong is even higher, at 71 percent.[29] This group is more liberal, in turn, than regularly worshipping Protestant males, 87 percent of whom believe that homosexual relations are always wrong.[30] On this item priests have lower agreement with Catholic teaching than do lay Catholics. This is probably due, in large part, to the fact that the proportion of priests who themselves have a homosexual orientation is much higher than among lay Catholic males. In the *Los Angeles Times* survey, 15 percent of US priests reported their sexual orientation as either homosexual or more on the homosexual side; the comparable proportion among US Catholic males (or all US males) is, generously, under 3 percent.[31] Not surprisingly, persons of a homosexual orientation are much less likely to characterize homosexual relations as sinful. Only 13 percent of the homosexual priests, compared to 60 percent of heterosexual priests, thought homosexual relations were always sinful.

In striking contrast, 9 in 10 (89 percent) married priests agreed that homosexual relations are always sinful. The 41-point difference between married priests and all US priests on this issue is the largest for any moral issue (except cloning, which, as noted above, doubtless understates the opposition of US priests). One might be inclined to attribute this difference, in part, to the fact that the married priests are married. Married men are both much less likely to have a homosexual orientation than are unmarried men and more likely, by about 20 percentage points,

to say that homosexual acts are always wrong than are unmarried heterosexual men.[32] The strong opposition of the married priests may also
be prompted by a reaction to the movement toward greater acceptance
of homosexual practice in the Episcopal Church. However, among the
married priests, those ordained in the 1980s, when homosexuality was
a much less salient issue, are much more likely to consider homosexuality always sinful (at 95 percent) than are priests ordained since 2000 (at
73 percent).

Over half (53 percent) of regular priests agreed that sexual relations between unmarried persons is always a sin (Figure 1.5, fifth item).
Following the familiar pattern, the proportions expressing similar
responses are much higher among the married priests (84 percent) and
somewhat lower among active lay Catholics (46 percent).[33] As with other
issues, regular Protestant churchgoers are more proscriptive about extramarital sex than Catholics, or even than the US Catholic priests; 70 percent of this group does not feel that sex between unmarried persons is
ever morally acceptable.[34]

Three-fifths (57 percent) of Catholic priests responded that it is
always sinful to take one's own life if suffering from a debilitating disease (Figure 1.5, sixth item). This is somewhat more restrictive than the
view of regularly worshipping Catholic males, half (49 percent) of whom
opposed the right to suicide in response to a similarly worded question
on the General Social Survey.[35] Both priests and active Catholic males are
more liberal than Protestant males, however, 65 percent of whom opposed
the right to suicide if suffering from an incurable disease. The married
priests are even more strict; three-fourths (77 percent) of them responded
that suicide in the face of a debilitating disease was always a sin.

The bottom three items in Figure 1.5, concerning AIDS prevention,
masturbation, and artificial contraception, are distinct from the other
issues measured. The response proportions for these items are similar
to each other, but noticeably lower, as a group, than the responses for
the six items above them. Less than one-third (28–31 percent) of all US
priests agreed that these three items are sinful. Although almost twice
that proportion of married priests responded that they are always sinful
(61–67 percent), among both groups agreement with the Church's formal teaching is lowest for these items. Unlike the other six items measured, these actions all have to do with the moral nature of the sexual act,
specifically on whether a sexual act that precludes procreation is sinful.
Acceptance of this principle has been particularly low among American

Catholics since it was controversially reaffirmed in the 1968 encyclical *Humanae Vitae*. As Figure 1.5 reports, in a less strictly worded question about Church policy in a 2005 poll, less than one-third (29 percent) of committed Catholics supported the Church's proscription on birth control.[36] In a more direct question about the morality of contraception asked in a 2003 survey, only one-fifth (20 percent) of Catholics who described themselves as very religious thought that artificial birth control was "morally unacceptable."[37]

While agreement with the sinfulness of these three actions is very low among Catholics, among Protestants it is negligible, in contrast to most of the top six items of Figure 1.5, for which Protestants hold stricter moral positions than Catholics. The idea that a sexual act that does not preserve the procreative end of sexual relations is sinful is not a feature of Protestant doctrine, nor is opposition to birth control a moral issue for most Protestants. I was unable to find comparable data for Protestants on masturbation or using condoms for AIDS defense. In the survey just cited above, in which 20 percent of very religious Catholics opposed artificial birth control, the corresponding proportion for Protestants was less than 3 percent.

We have seen that the married priests are far more likely to agree with the Church's position on all nine of these moral issues than are Catholic priests or active Catholic laypersons nationwide. As another general indicator of their moral views, I asked the priests to rate the Pope's views on moral issues as generally too liberal, too conservative, or about right. In the 2002 survey, 33 percent of US diocesan priests felt that the Pope was too conservative on moral issues; only 6 percent of the married priests shared this opinion (Appendix, Table A.8). On the question of whether faithful Catholics must follow all the Church's teachings, most (57 percent) of the married priests, but only one-third (35 percent) of all Catholic priests, felt that Catholics must follow all the Church's teachings to be faithful (Appendix, Table A.9).

The views of the married priests are so strongly supportive of Catholic teaching that some may characterize them as representing an automatic or unthinking adoption of formal Catholic teaching. It is also possible that, on a survey commissioned by Church authorities, the respondents may have overstated their orthodoxy. However, while all the items in Figure 1.5 express actions proscribed by Catholic teaching, not all of them receive full or equal support from the married priests. The distribution of support for the items among married priests, in fact, is consistently about 25 percent higher than that of all Catholic priests. The range of support from the highest to lowest item is lower for the married priests, at 34 percent, than for all Catholic priests, at 47 percent, suggesting that the married priests may be somewhat more ideological, but there is still a wide range of response.

Conservative Converts

Why do the married priests exhibit such high levels of conformity with Catholic doctrine? For the most part, it is because they are converts. Conversion from Protestantism induces, predicts, or selects for Catholic orthodoxy in several ways. One married priest who has served for many years in a liberal urban diocese in the Northeast told me, "These are all things upon which the Church's teaching is clear. So it's baffling to me that people could say otherwise. That's the kind of Catholics we are. I mean, if you wanted to disagree with the Church, why not be an Episcopalian? We have had people say, 'Why would you want to leave the Episcopal Church?' You know, 'I'm only Catholic because I'm Italian.' [laughter] And people are serious, when they say things like that." It is precisely because they came to a prior understanding that is congruent with Catholic teaching on many moral and doctrinal issues that most of the married priests have joined the Catholic Church.

For these priest converts, the formal expectation of conformity to Catholic Church teaching is clearly seen as desirable, in contrast to the free-thinking sensibilities of the Episcopal Church. Another married priest, a professor in a Catholic educational institution, described his identification as a priest with formal Catholic teaching as "liberating" for his preaching. He explained, "When I climb up into the pulpit, I don't have to issue a lot of disclaimers, saying this is the only Anglican pulpit that you're likely to hear what I'm about to say. Getting up into the pulpit and realizing that I'm declaring the Catholic faith of the Catholic Church to a Catholic congregation, with no complications, that was very gratifying. I didn't have that in Anglicanism. I think that's a great plus."

Clergy conversion also serves as an effective selection mechanism. Potential priests with less strong convictions are less likely to persist in the conversion process. But the stronger moral stance of the married priests doesn't just reflect what they left behind; it also reflects what they brought with them. As we have seen, on many issues, active American

Protestants are more conservative—that is to say, more in conformity with the teaching of the Catholic Church—than are active American Catholics. On most moral issues, of course, conservative Protestant denominations and the Catholic Church have the same or very similar moral stances. But Protestants are more conservative on some moral issues, such as abortion or suicide, even when their church bodies adopt more liberal positions than does the Catholic Church. On the other hand, this is not true of Episcopalians, who are among the most liberal Protestants as a group, and who are decidedly more liberal than Catholics on all of the moral issues examined. For example, only 40 percent of Episcopalians believe it is always a sin to obtain an abortion, and only 36 percent say that homosexual relations are always sinful.[38] The married priests, most of whom grew up as highly religious conservative Protestants (see Chapter 4), may reflect something of this characteristically Protestant heightened moral sensibility.

Like Newer Priests

From another perspective, however, the conservatism of the married priests is not a point of contrast with their peers in the US presbyterate, but rather a point of similarity. A sample of all US priests is like a snapshot that includes priests of all ages and number of years ordained. As prior research has shown, however, since the 1970s annual ordination classes of priests have been growing more conservative.[39] Thus priests ordained more recently are, like the married priests, more conservative than those ordained in the 1970s, and by the same token, less different from the married priests. Figure 1.6 shows the strength of this trend, comparing the moral views of married priests with all US diocesan priests ordained in successive decades since the 1970s. As the figure shows, priests ordained more recently are in greater conformity with Church positions, and thus more similar to the marrieds priests, than those ordained earlier. (Due to the inaccuracies noted earlier, the data for human cloning are not shown, but there is also a similar trend on this issue.) For seven of the eight items (all but abortion), there is no statistically significant difference between the views of the married priests and regular US priests ordained since 2000.[40]

Although married priests (and recently ordained priests in general) have much more conservative views than priests ordained in the 1970s (and earlier), their views are almost identical to priests who are being ordained today. This suggests that the differences in opinion on moral issues will substantially diminish going forward. At this point in time,

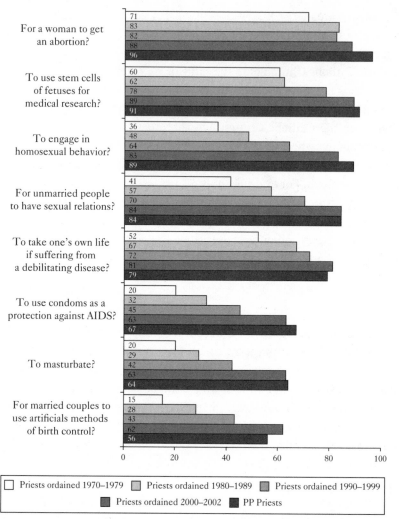

FIGURE 1.6 Priests on Moral Issues, Comparing Pastoral Provision Priests with US Priests by Decade of Ordination (Percent Responding "Always a Sin")

however, married priests are in the paradoxical position of having a moral outlook that is very similar to that of priests 20 to 30 years their junior, but very different from priests their own age.[41]

This affinity between the newest priests and the married priests alters the question posed earlier. Instead of (or in addition to) asking why the married priests are more conservative than all US priests, we could ask why both the married priests and the newest priests are more conservative than priests ordained three and four decades ago. As I have recently shown elsewhere, the formation processes for American priests—pre-seminary, seminary, internships, diaconate, and so on—appear to have become more oriented to orthodoxy since the 1970s, instituting procedures or norms that have favored more conservative candidates in recent years and/or that favored more liberal candidates in earlier years.[42] This influence would also account for the unique views of the Pastoral Provision priests relative to their contemporaries, since they are the products of a functionally separate screening and approval process that, with more direct oversight by the Vatican, may have enacted different, more conservative norms than was or is typical in the United States.

The Other Married Priests

Mention should be made of the views of the married priests toward another group with whom they are often contrasted: men who have left the Catholic priesthood in order to marry. The number of resigned priests is not trivial: an estimated 25,000 American Catholic priests, most subsequently married, have been laicized since the 1960s. Many of these men would understandably like to return to some level of priestly ministry, if possible. For them, and for those who advocate for them, it is difficult to reconcile the fact that they are excluded from the priesthood for deciding to get married while the Church is accepting another group of married men to serve as priests. "Every time the church allows a person from outside our tradition to serve, it's a harsh and sad reminder to those born Catholic that they're still second-class citizens," commented a representative of Call to Action, a progressive Catholic reform group, on the occasion of a recent Pastoral Provision ordination.[43]

Catholic teaching makes a sharp distinction between a man who has been ordained who seeks to marry, which has never been permitted, at least since the Apostolic Era, and a man who has been married who seeks to be ordained, which has often been permitted.[44] Citing this distinction, Catholic leaders typically respond to progressive Catholic critics that Church policy is not inconsistent when it insists that resigned priests not be permitted to return to priestly ministry as married men. To the Call to Action statement above, for example, a spokesman for the Catholic bishop involved responded, "They knew the rules going in, and they had the option to make the decision then."[45]

The Pastoral Provision priests themselves are inclined to be sympathetic toward the resigned married priests. Most (54 percent) of them, responding to a question on the issue, agreed that it would be good thing if there were a way that priests who resigned from the priesthood to get married could return to active ministry. Despite their strong conservatism on other issues, this support is actually a little *higher* than the average among US priests, which was 49 percent in 2001 and 48 percent in 1970. Notably, their support is much higher than that of the youngest and oldest priests (at about 30 percent) to whom the Pastoral Provision priests are most similar on doctrinal issues.

On this issue, it appears, the position of the married priests is not primarily informed by principle. As noted above, only a third (34 percent) of them support optional celibacy as an idea, a much lower proportion than that of all US priests (52 percent). Strikingly, no Pastoral Provision priest recommended becoming Episcopalian as an option for resigned married Catholic priests. Rather, as the only other group of persons in the Church with the experience of both marriage and priesthood, the married priests of the Pastoral Provision typically expressed empathy and understanding for the resigned priests. One priest, who had worked through his own marital struggles, reflected:

> I don't point the finger at anybody who tried to live the celibate life and discovered that it was impossible for them, or else, very humanly, fell in love with somebody and decided that, I'd much rather live a married life than continue in this vocation. So I have sympathy for these people.

The married priests sympathized with the loss felt by the resigned priests. As one married priest said, "I can well imagine how much they must miss being a priest and functioning as a priest." But they also felt it was a loss for the Church: "I know several men who have left the priesthood to marry. I think the Church is cheated by not allowing these men to return to minister."

Even those who opposed regularizing the resigned priests on principled grounds often tempered their views with sympathy and respect for the resigned priests. This ambivalence is clear in the remarks of the following priest, a strong Anglo-Catholic who has been married 40 years:

> I would not be in favor of readmitting [priests who resigned to get married]. ... I think it's a can of worms. Thirty-five thousand Corpus Christi [*sic*] priests out there—and they're great guys. I've

met a lot of them, working in the Church. Doing great things. But
I think it's a slippery slope.

While the theological distinction between the two groups of priests is
comprehensible, and canonically dispositive, it certainly does not follow,
and should not be taken to imply, that the Pastoral Provision priests are
superior to or more faithful than the resigned married priests. The processes of discernment and adjustment for the two groups of men appear
to be very similar. It is true that priests or former priests who left to marry
broke a preexisting vow of celibacy in order to become married; but the
Pastoral Provision priests broke a promise of fidelity to their bishop in
order to become Catholic. Both chose to renounce their vocation and call
for the sake of an ideal. Both had to struggle with the sacrifice of loss
of career and income, and the journey to a new identity; and both have
struggled, in their own way, with the potentially conflicting roles of husband and priest.

Conclusion

So, what are married priests like? In many ways, they are similar to all
priests. They are about the same average age as all priests but have shorter
tenure in the priesthood and are thus less likely to defect. They work just
as hard as celibate priests, on average, but have fewer full days off. Fewer
serve as pastors due to canonical restrictions.

In their views and religious practice, the married priests, we might say,
are not only like all priests, but strikingly more so. Their average satisfaction, happiness, and sense of being well-utilized exceed the already high
levels of regular Catholic priests. In their moral and doctrinal views, the
married priests are notably and consistently stronger in agreement with
the formal teachings of the Catholic Church than are priests in general,
who in turn are more in agreement than are Catholic laypersons.

The strong and reliable conservatism of the married priests suggests
that their priesthood may have a different emphasis, or reference role,
than that of regular Catholic priests. One of the root understandings of
priesthood in the Judeo-Christian tradition is that of a mediator, someone who stands or goes between God and his people. Like the brothers
who were Israel's first religious leaders, the priest is called, like Moses,
to declare God's will to the people and, like Aaron, to offer prayers and

sacrifice for the people's sins. In this dual dynamic, the priest alternates between the roles of a prophet—representing God to the people—and an intercessor—representing the people to God. In the Catholic Mass these roles are exercised in the two parts that comprise every Mass: the Liturgy of the Word, in which the priest expounds the word of God in the homily, and the Liturgy of the Eucharist, in which he offers up to God the Church's prayers and the paschal sacrifice of Christ. In accordance with this ancient understanding, only priests are permitted to preach and to preside at Eucharist during the Catholic Mass, since these roles are understood to be uniquely expressive of the priesthood.

In the American Catholic Church the mediating role of priests takes on a special resonance with regard to moral and doctrinal issues, as priests often find themselves in a conflicted middle between official Church tenets—which are clear, specific, and generally claim divine authority—and the beliefs of American Catholics, which are often very different. For a priest this conflict is a serious matter since, called to identify both with Christ as prophet and with his people as intercessor, it goes to the core of his dual identity. The difficulty is not merely intellectual. There are strong personal and social forces at work tempting priests to resolve the tension either in favor of denying the truth of Church teaching in order to fully affirm the people, or in favor of denying the faithfulness of the people in order to fully accept the Church's teaching. The jarring incompatibility of the authoritarian impulses of the hierarchy that defends Church teaching and the democratic sensibilities of American Catholics who dispute it only adds to the strain.

In the midst of this tension, the married priests clearly lean, not without incongruity or qualification, toward the prophetic end of the spectrum. As we have seen, in contrast to American priests as a whole, they hold beliefs and opinions that are in much closer conformity to the formal teaching of the Catholic faith, and the difference is most visible with regard to moral and ethical issues that are often the subject of conflicted discourse in American society or American Catholicism. In large part, their strong conformity results from the experience and challenges of conversion, which we will examine in detail in the next two chapters.

Married priests, however, share their more prophetic tendency with today's younger priests, whose doctrinal and moral convictions are much more in conformity with Church teaching than are those of older priests.[46] As a result, the married priests occupy a unique place in the American presbyterate. As older priests, they are similar to their contemporaries in terms of age, life experience, work practice, and pastoral sensitivity. As recent ordinands, they are more like younger priests in their moral and doctrinal views, devotional practice, and their satisfaction and happiness in the priesthood. In their unique combination of pastoral experience with reliably high conformity to Church teaching, their priestly function may be, at best, more integrated than that of either younger or older priests. In these respects the married priests may be described, for better or for worse, as more Catholic than native Catholic priests.

How Did They Come to Be Married Priests?

"WHAT WOULD I HAVE to do to become a married priest?" I often get this question from a young man in a Catholic setting. He may just be curious, of course, but more often he is considering the possibility of becoming a priest and, like all young men in that position, weighing that vocation against the possibility of marriage and family. The prospect of serving as a priest while circumventing the rigors of celibacy is understandably attractive. One young man told me, "You [married priests] are cheating"— before asking how he could become one, too.

Unfortunately, if the questioner is already Catholic, the short answer to the question is that it is not possible for him to become a married priest: marriage after Catholic baptism makes a man ineligible for ordination. The married priests described in this book all were married before they became Catholic. The longer answer to this question, which explains the history and background for this requirement, and what men who are eligible—potential convert priests who are already married—have to undergo in order to become a married priest, is what this chapter is about. How did the Pastoral Provision get started?

The term "pastoral provision" refers to a privilege or accommodation that is made for pastoral reasons, to remove barriers or to help facilitate the spiritual growth of a person or group. The decision establishing the set of policies and permissions that have come to be known as the Anglican Pastoral Provision (or simply Pastoral Provision, in capitals) allowed Anglican priests to retain certain cultural practices—particularly their wives and the traditional Anglican liturgy—to smooth their entry into the Catholic faith. How is it that the Catholic Church came to make an accommodation for Anglicans that is (from the perspective of the Church and those of us who have benefited from it) so generous? And why only for Anglicans, not other Christian denominations or those born Catholic?

The 1980 decision reflected a unique confluence of trends both within and outside the Catholic Church. Conceived as an ecumenical initiative in the spirit of Vatican II, the story of the establishment of the Pastoral Provision revolves around the centuries-old forces separating Catholicism and Anglicanism, the particular cultural situations of both churches in the 1970s, and the particular interest and persistence of one man: Bishop Bernard Law.

Vatican II and Ecumenism

Since the mid-1800s a small but steady stream of Anglo-Catholic and evangelical Anglican clergy, inspired by John Henry Newman, made their way to Roman Catholicism. Yet the Church did not meet them halfway. Married Anglican priests who converted and wished to be ordained were required to separate from their wives, who were expected to enter a religious order; not surprisingly, almost all the Anglican clergy who converted during this period were, like Newman, already committed to celibacy. Anglican clergy conversion was made even more difficult when in 1896 Pope Leo XIII declared Anglican orders to be "absolutely null and utterly void."[1]

During this period the Catholic Church was reacting against modernizing trends that had begun to take root in many Protestant churches. Beginning in 1910, Catholic clergy and scholars were required to take an Oath Against Modernism, in which they repudiated relativism, religious pluralism and development, and text-critical Bible scholarship. The difference between Catholic and Protestant was understood as a difference between truth and error; fellowship or dialogue with Protestants as if they were legitimate Christian believers was explicitly prohibited. The notion of facilitating Anglican clergy conversions was hardly compatible with the Church's stance during these years. But this was about to change dramatically.

In 1962 Pope John XXIII called the Catholic bishops of the world to the Vatican for a Council. He is reported to have said that he wanted to "open the windows" of the Church to let in some fresh air. He officially described the purpose of the Council by means of the Italian word *aggiornamento*, literally, to bring the Church up to date with the modern world. Vatican II, which produced 16 major teaching documents over a period of four years, introduced a wide variety of ecclesiastical reforms that attempted to change the tenor and emphasis, though not the underlying truth-claims, of the Church's engagement with modernity. The culminating document of the Council, issued on December 7, 1965, was a comprehensive pastoral and theological exposition of the Church titled "The Church in the Modern World."[2]

In addition to instituting major reforms directly, the Council also proposed many reforms for other agencies in the Church to consider and implement, and articulated a new openness to innovative change, an attitude that became known as the "spirit of Vatican II." To a considerable extent, it was this that made the Pastoral Provision possible.

In several groundbreaking provisions, the Council set forth a new, more positive stance toward non-Catholics. There was a new emphasis on religious freedom and the freedom of conscience, even for those who disagreed with the Catholic faith. The Catholic Church no longer sought to be the only or the dominant religion in a country, but advocated equal freedom for all religions in every country. The Council documents spoke of other faiths appreciatively and with respect, acknowledging that many of them taught things that were true and that their followers could find salvation.

This new openness applied even more strongly to Protestants. In sharp contrast to the Church's former practice of condemning the errors of Protestants, Vatican II adopted a new policy of ecumenism—that is, reaching out to Protestants as fellow Christians to build positive fellowship and dialogue. Throughout the Council documents, Protestants were referred to as "separated brothers," and the common features that Protestants shared with Catholics were emphasized and commended. The Decree on Ecumenism affirmed that ". . . Catholics must gladly acknowledge and esteem the truly Christian endowments from our common heritage which are to be found among our separated brethren" and admitted that Catholics had "fail[ed] to live by [the truth and means of grace] with all the fervor that they should."[3] For the first time in Catholic discourse, Protestant communions were called "Churches," and the Council acknowledged and asked pardon for the Catholic Church's own sins leading to the schism with Protestants.

Although affirming that much truth and sanctity could be found (in a partial way) in the Protestant churches, the Council did not shrink from asserting that the most complete expression of the Christian faith resides only in the Catholic Church. But the change of language and image was telling: the difference between Catholic and Protestant was no longer between truth and error but between whole and part. Individual Protestants who found their way to Catholic faith and affiliation had to change only some—how much depended on their denomination—of their beliefs, and were fulfilling, not repudiating, the Christian faith they already possessed: a view summed up as an "ecumenism of return." Protestant communions that no longer practiced holy orders or the sacraments (such as Baptists and Pentecostals) were the furthest from Catholicism; those who had retained sacraments and orders in some part (such as Lutherans and Episcopalians) were much closer. Among this latter group, the Council observed, "the Anglican Communion occupies a special place."[4]

Among the reforms initiated by Vatican II was a restoration of the ancient office of permanent deacon—that is, ordained clergy who were not priests or in full-time ministry, but who performed important ministerial and evangelistic functions part-time while working in a secular career.[5] For the first time, married men were permitted to serve as deacons, who officiated at weddings and baptisms, preached homilies during the Mass, and wore clerical collars like those of priests. The permanent deaconate proved to be highly popular in the United States, and deacons were universally well-received and well-regarded. By 2007 more than 15,000 married deacons, in every diocese, were serving in Catholic parishes in the United States, exposing almost all American Catholics and priests to a positive example of a married man in Catholic holy orders.

In 1967 Pope Paul VI, citing the Council's decision to permit married deacons, published a suggestion that directly prefigured the Pastoral Provision. In an encyclical on priestly celibacy, he proposed that "a study may be allowed of the particular circumstances of married sacred ministers of Churches or other Christian communities separated from the Catholic communion, and of the possibility of admitting to priestly functions those who desire to adhere to the fullness of this communion and to continue to exercise the sacred ministry. The circumstances must be such, however, as not to prejudice the existing discipline regarding celibacy."[6]

The Failure of Dialogue

In 1968, spurred by the ideals of Vatican II, following a joint declaration of Pope Paul VI and the Archbishop of Canterbury Michael Ramsey (leader of the Church of England and symbolic head of the Anglican Communion), an Anglican–Roman Catholic International Commission (ARCIC) was formed. The church leaders called for "a serious dialogue founded on the Gospels and on the ancient common traditions [that] may lead to that unity in truth for which Christ prayed."[7]

Over the next 15 years ARCIC produced three "Agreed Statements" on the central theological issues of the Eucharist, ordination, and Church authority, culminating in a widely read Final Report in 1982. In the eyes of many observers, and certainly of those closest to the dialogue process, substantial progress was made toward a greater level of unity between Catholics and Anglicans. The Anglo-Catholic goal of corporate reunion with Rome seemed, for a time, to be within reach.

But just as it seemed to come into view, it suddenly evaporated. In September 1976, the Episcopal Church (the Anglican Church in the United States) elected to amend its canons to permit the ordination of women as priests. This action placed two serious obstacles in the path to unity. First, it directly contradicted Catholic doctrine and practice. In an exchange of letters prior to the Episcopal Church's action, Pope Paul VI wrote to the Archbishop of Canterbury, Donald Coggan, that "a new course taken by the Anglican Communion in admitting women to the ordained priesthood cannot fail to introduce into [the ARCIC] dialogue an element of grave difficulty . . . ," and expressed sadness at the possibility of "so grave an obstacle and threat on that path [to unity]."[8] In the polite language of ecumenical discourse, such a statement expressed the strongest possible opposition. The Catholic Congregation for the Doctrine of the Faith (hereafter CDF; also sometimes called the Sacred Congregation for the Doctrine of the Faith, the Pontifical Council for the Doctrine of the Faith, or the Holy Office) observed, in a later commentary, that the ordination of women "was formally opposed to the 'common traditions' of the two Communions," and that "the obstacle thus created was of a doctrinal character."[9] This position was no surprise to Anglicans. Archbishop Coggan had written to Paul VI on the matter in the first place because, he said, "we are aware that action on this matter could be an obstacle to further progress along the path of unity."[10] Michael Ramsey, Coggan's predecessor as Archbishop of Canterbury, had strongly opposed the ordination of women, due in part, as Stanford notes, to his "realization that any move in the direction of women priests would damage the relations he was fostering with Rome."[11]

The ordination of women as priests (and, later, the ordination of women and homosexuals as bishops) not only impeded unity with Rome, it also impeded the unity of Anglicans with each other. As the prominent ecumenists Mary Tanner and Andrew Faley have recently recounted, "Anglicans' initial enthusiasm and hope [for unity with Rome] waned, partly due to ... the threat to internal unity posed by the pressure to allow the ordination of women."[12] Though often unacknowledged, this problem of Anglican unity posed an even more intractable obstacle to Anglican–Roman Catholic unity than did the underlying issues, because it was rooted in the institutional arrangements of Anglicanism itself.

The Anglican Communion is not a single church or even a denomination, but a loose fellowship of 44 autonomous national churches, mostly located in former British colonies. There is no single authority to which they are subject; the Archbishop of Canterbury holds an honorary and symbolic leadership role, but has no juridical authority outside the Church of England. While the Anglican churches share a common culture, ethos, and history, they are free to disagree on matters of doctrine and practice—and with the loss of the British Empire as a unifying force, they increasingly do so. This institutional arrangement may be beneficial in many ways for the member churches, but it has the disadvantage of making a common initiative on which there is not substantial consensus, such as movement toward unity with Rome, virtually impossible.

Anglicans favorable to unity with Rome faced the dilemma that to heal that schism might create one with their fellow Anglicans. From the Catholic side, it was difficult to know whether one's partner in the dialogue toward unity represented an Anglican consensus or a minority position. To this day, the Anglican Communion has not resolved the issue of the ordination of women (or homosexuals); various provinces have each determined to go their own way. The result for ecumenical efforts following 1976 was that, as Tanner and Faley summarize, "both within the Anglican communion and in its previously hopeful ecumenical journey with Roman Catholicism, there was a sense of going nowhere."[13] It was out of this experience of disappointment that, beginning in 1977, some groups of Anglo-Catholic Episcopalian clergy approached Roman Catholic authorities about becoming ordained as Catholic priests.

Rome Opens the Door

The most active group of Episcopal priests to seek Catholic ordination was the Society of the Holy Cross (abbreviated as SSC, from its Latin name "Societas Sanctae Crucis"). The SSC is a fraternity of Catholic-minded Anglican priests founded in London in 1855 in the wake of the Oxford Movement. Committing themselves to a disciplined rule of life based in Catholic spiritual practices such as Eucharistic adoration, confession, and the Divine Office of daily prayers, priests of the SSC pledge themselves both to reform Anglicanism in a Catholic direction and to pray and work for "reconciliation with the Holy See."[14] On December 1, 1976, a synod of American SSC priests delegated the Provincial Vicar of the North American Province, the Reverend James Parker, to inquire whether properly disposed married Episcopalian priests might be received into the Catholic Church while retaining both their marriage and their priesthood. At the time there were about 80 SSC priests in the United States.

Working with Bishop Bernard Law, executive director of the Committee for Ecumenical and Inter-religious Affairs of the US National Conference of Catholic Bishops (NCCB), and Archbishop Jean Jadot, the Pope's US representative, Parker and others spent almost four years advancing a series of proposals and revisions through the committees of the American bishops and the Vatican bureaucracy.[15] Along the way, two other Anglican groups joined the SSC with similar or parallel petitions: the Evangelical and Catholic Mission (ECM), another group of Episcopal priests; and a group of breakaway Episcopal parishes calling themselves the Pro-Diocese of St. Augustine of Canterbury (PDSAC). Finally, on June 20, 1980, the norms of the Pastoral Provision were approved by Pope John Paul II, and were communicated by way of letter to Archbishop John Quinn, president of the NCCB, on July 22.[16]

The decision provided that "reordination of the Episcopalian clergy, even those who are married, shall be allowed" after approval of the candidate by the CDF.[17] Each candidate must make a profession of faith and undergo any necessary theological or catechetical preparation. The married priests were to be ordained but could not become bishops or remarry if widowed. It was a temporary, one-time exception to the rule of celibacy; future priests from reconciled former Anglican parishes could not be married. "Special care," the letter insisted, "must be taken on the pastoral level to avoid any misunderstanding regarding the Church's discipline of celibacy."[18] The document also approved the use of Anglican liturgical elements by former Anglican priests for former Anglican converts only. Any liturgy celebrated outside this group would have to conform to the regular Roman Rite.

As a general principle, the "admission of these persons, even in a group, should be considered the reconciliation of individual persons," and not as an ecumenical unification or merger.[19] Reconciled Anglicans would be incorporated into existing dioceses under a local Ordinary bishop, rather than as a separate Anglican jurisdiction. But this was not intended to exclude the possibility of establishing some other type of jurisdiction for reconciled Anglicans in the future.

The decision communicated by this short letter was, ironically, a characteristically Anglican resolution: compromising, vague, and subject to competing interpretations. On the two questions that had been presented to the CDF and the US bishops—whether married Anglican ministers could be ordained as Catholic priests, and whether parishes of Catholic-minded Anglicans could form their own diocese or similar jurisdiction—there was a split decision. Priests and parishioners could reconcile with the Catholic Church as individuals, but the vision of a corporate reunion of parishes that retained a collective Anglican identity was rejected (though not permanently).

In large part, the limited and qualified nature of the decision reflected the concerns of Catholic leaders that neither the rule of clergy celibacy nor ongoing Anglican ecumenical dialogue would be compromised by their action. The married priests were being received under a very narrow, limited, and temporary exception to the rule of celibacy, and not as a precursor to a change in the rule itself; and they were being received as individual converts, not as a bloc that might complicate ecumenical relations with Canterbury. A cover letter to Archbishop Quinn accompanying the decision reinforced these concerns, cautioning him to be careful about "the sensitive areas of ecumenism and celibacy" in publicizing the provision.

Despite this, the announcement of the Pastoral Provision was met with widespread publicity, to the jubilation of many American Catholics and the concern of the Vatican and many Protestants. "The First Married Priests" announced the headline in *Newsweek*, over a story that reported that "[t]he unexpected announcement seemed to be a first step toward a married Catholic clergy."[20] "Married Anglican priests could become Roman Catholic priests and remain married," reported the Associated Press.[21] In a sharp break with the CDF, Archbishop Quinn's office fanned the flames.

His spokesman, Father Miles Riley, called the decision "a foot in the door," and Quinn himself described the decision as "precedent-setting."[22,23]

Heightening ecumenical concerns, Quinn stated that the new policy set a precedent in providing for "a continuing 'organizational structure and common identity' of the newcomers with the Roman church," despite the fact that the provision had explicitly rejected doing this.[24] The CDF, reportedly upset at the tone of the announcement, "replied angrily [to reporters' questions]: "We know nothing about it. Ask Archbishop Quinn—he has all the answers."[25]

The misunderstanding was amplified by the fact that Archbishop Quinn did not mention the involvement of the SSC or ECM in seeking the provision, but only the PDSAC. Archbishop Quinn may have been respecting the desire of the first two groups to avoid publicity; on the other hand, the PDSAC actively sought publicity, and their statements magnified their involvement. "[W]e are the only identifiable entity involved in this," Father Barker, a PDSAC representative, told the press, relating a dramatic story of slipping into the Vatican to present a sensitive petition to reconcile Anglicanism with the Pope.[26] In response, the president of the World Council of Churches commented, "There's no question but that [the decision] will have a damaging effect" on ecumenical dialogue.[27] Liberal Episcopalian bishops William Swing and John Spong publicly denounced the decision, and the latter called for an end to further dialogue with the Catholic Church.[28]

Successful Conclusion, Disappointing Beginning

In a startling act of ecumenical accommodation, the Catholic Church had chosen to contravene one of its most controversial and definitive rules in order to receive married men as priests. The decision was enabled by an unusual congruence between liberal and conservative forces in the Catholic Church. Certainly some would consider it ironic that the Episcopal Church's acceptance of the ordination of women led to the Catholic Church's acceptance of the ordination of married men. However, though both actions were goals of American Catholic progressives in the 1970s, in Catholic thinking they are hardly comparable. The male-only priesthood is a matter of theological principle and universal and unbroken practice, while the celibate priesthood is a matter of varying discipline, which has always had exceptions and is not universal today. The cause of the Anglican petitioners appears to have fostered a unique coalition among the bishops in the 1970s. Conservatives supported receiving these Anglican priests, who objected strongly to ordaining women, despite their being married. Progressives supported receiving these Anglican priests because they were married, despite their objection to the ordination of women.

All of these forces may have come to naught, however, but for the commitment and leadership of one man: Bishop Bernard Law. Although the impetus that led to the Pastoral Provision clearly came from disaffected Episcopalians, American Catholic leadership was quick and welcoming in responding to their concerns; and none was so responsive or so welcoming as Bishop Law. From his early contact with Father Parker and the SSC to his eventual acceptance of the responsibility to develop and administer the policy as the first Ecclesiastical Delegate (ED), Law actively guided and shepherded the process to its successful conclusion. Within four months of Parker's April 1977 meeting with the Apostolic Delegate—an appointment Law had arranged—Law had brought together representatives of disparate groups of dissidents, including two Episcopalian bishops, to produce a consensus draft petition that became the basis for NCCB preliminary action only a month later, and produced a decision from the US bishops in little more than a year. Given the novelty and complexity of the issues, and the highly deliberative nature of church decision-making processes, this was remarkable progress to make in such a short time. Although many parties contributed to the progress of the question, it was Law's commitment that was paramount. When, in mid-1979, it seemed that the process had stalled, it was Law who single-handedly prodded both the CDF and the leadership of the American hierarchy to resume their consideration of the question.

But it was more than just an impressive feat of management. Law possessed both the knowledge and the authority to make the efforts of these Protestant postulants intelligible to Catholic leaders. The SSC, ECM, and PDSAC explored the idea of becoming Catholic in a typically Protestant manner—that is, individualistic and disordered. Law received their concerns, from the start, in a typically Catholic manner—that is, collective and ordered. Without Law's leadership, there is every possibility that the separate petitions would not have persisted, foundering and fragmenting through competition and minute disagreements. Law held the concerns of the petitioners together and demonstrated the patience and persistence to present them successfully to the magisterium in Rome.

While the conclusion of the petition was successful in principle, the experience of reception was hugely disappointing in practice. When the Pastoral Provision decision was announced, most observers expected the first ordinations to occur within a year; but that was not to be. As delays mounted and the very limited nature of the new policy became clear, the initial jubilation among its supporters and the concerns about celibacy and ecumenism among its detractors all subsided. The delays were simply procedural and endemic on the part of the CDF; at the same time, it is possible that they felt the August announcement to be premature. It was not until early 1981 that the Congregation named an ED—Bishop Law—to administer the new policy, at which time the CDF released its own public announcement. Following this action, procedures and policies that had been left unclarified in the original decision had to be settled, arrangements made for processing and reviewing dossiers, and a process of theological assessment and formation established. Law turned to Father Parker for help, naming him his executive secretary to help establish and administer the Pastoral Provision office. During this time Cardinal Seper retired, and the new Prefect of the CDF, Cardinal Joseph Ratzinger, who would later become Pope Benedict XVI, took office. It took almost two years before the first petitioning priest, Father James Parker himself, was finally ordained, on June 29, 1982.

If the initial publicity surrounding the Pastoral Provision implied more structure than was intended by the new policy, it also anticipated far more participation than eventually occurred. The PDSAC alone reported that it had 63 priests and over a thousand laity prepared to reconcile with Rome, but it was not the only group to forecast sizable numbers. Throughout the petition process, everyone was convinced that the few persons inquiring were the vanguard of a much larger movement. In early 1977, at the very beginning of the process, the Ad Hoc Committee reported to the bishops that it was "quite realistic" that over a thousand Episcopal clergy and as many as 300,000 laity would be highly sympathetic to being received into full communion with the Catholic Church.[29] Parker was convinced, at first, that all or almost all SCC priests, and later, that a substantial portion of them would convert to Rome.

All of these estimates proved highly inflated. The expected flood of applicants turned out to be a trickle. The much-heralded PDSAC turned out to be more promise than substance, yielding only three parishes and the same number of priests. In the five years following the August 1980 announcement of the Pastoral Provision, just 27 married men were ordained as Catholic priests; the subsequent five years saw only an additional 17. But for those who had worked so hard to achieve a favorable decision, the expectation of large numbers was hard to relinquish. Even as late as December 1982, observing that only 24 priests and three parishes had yet submitted petitions, Law commented, "There are reasons to believe that after [the first group] there may be an increase of requests in this matter."[30] Twenty-five years later, however, the total of married priests ordained had only reached 84.

The reasons that the numbers have been so small will be discussed in Chapter 6. One factor has been the long and often frustrating process of transition and screening that potential married priests must go through.

What Does a Man Have to Do to Become a Married Priest?

For a layperson, switching religions is easy: the convert simply disassociates himself from the old church and commits to a new church, to which he or she is gladly welcomed; but when a clergyman converts with the prospect of continuing as a clergyman in the new religion, things are much more complicated. The new religion will become not only his place of worship but also his employer, and like any employer, must consider his qualifications and experience and determine whether or not it wants to take him on. If it does, there follows a process of matching the converting clergyman with a suitable position and often providing for his compensation or support, according to the particular norms and practices of the religious group. For the Pastoral Provision priests, converting to the Catholic faith involved a multiyear process of ecclesiastical and diplomatic review by the Vatican curia, the world's oldest and perhaps most complex bureaucracy; psychological and theological assessment by a US administrative bishop; and vocational support and placement by a receiving diocese.

Observers are often surprised—either happily or with dismay—to learn that the Church's scrutiny of the convert married priests has been extensive and rigorous, often involving remedial study or mentoring before ordination is approved. There are essentially two evaluative processes. First, the priest's credentials and qualifications for Catholic priesthood and for exemption from the requirement of celibacy are reviewed and approved by the CDF in the Vatican. The depth of this review and import of the approval may be inferred from the fact that, until he was elected Pope in 2005, almost every Pastoral Provision rescript (the document waiving celibacy) was personally signed by Cardinal Joseph Ratzinger. Second, every priest has to be certified for theological and pastoral competence by a committee of American theologians and seminary professors. This process involves local, national, and international authorities.

Decision and Delay

For many of the priest converts, the review and assessment process comes with an element of deflation and frustration. With only a couple of exceptions, every Pastoral Provision priest initially contacted the Catholic diocese in which he would eventually be ordained only after he had made a firm decision to convert. This contact, therefore, marked the end of an often extensive period of interior deliberation, questioning, and change on his part, but it was just the beginning of an extensive process of assessment, evaluation, and approval on the part of the Catholic Church. After making the momentous decision to radically change his life, forego career and income, and physically relocate, the priest was met with polite but firm scrutiny and inexplicable delays. For some, though not most, of the priests, this was also a period of financial hardship, as they worked temporary jobs or drew down their savings to make ends meet.

The process was not quick. The theological certification process, which often included remedial study, took a minimum of one year. The concurrent Vatican review took even longer: the median time in transit, from submission of the credentials dossier to receipt of the rescript, was 17 months. A quarter of the dossiers were in process for more than two years. In addition to the time needed for proper deliberation, administrative delays were common. With a few exceptions, the experience of most converting priests was one of dealing with a slow, inefficient, and frequently forgetful bureaucracy in the Vatican, their local diocese, or the Pastoral Provision's national administrative office—and sometimes all three. Tales of dossiers that got buried under other paperwork for months, and were not jarred loose until a bishop or other advocate made a pointed inquiry, were not uncommon. In my interviews, three of the priest converts related that, at some point in the process, their dossier had been lost and had to be entirely re-created.

In part, this experience is due to the rarity of these conversions. In many ways, to call the Pastoral Provision a program or process is to overstate the level of formality and organization of the activities that a converting priest becomes involved in as he makes his way into the Catholic Church. Most Pastoral Provision ordinations were a first for the ordaining bishop and diocese, and few dioceses have received more than two or three married priests. The result has been that the diocese and bishop are usually discovering, often through trial and error, the complicated process of communication, decisions, and preparations necessary to receive Papal approval for the ordination.

In January 2009 the clarity and definition of the process improved greatly with the publication by the ED, then Archbishop Myers, through the work of his able assistant Monsignor James Sheehan, of a manual that outlines the process and requirements in detail.[31] The manual, titled *Into Full Communion*, lists 14 steps in the process from inquiry to ordination. All of the priests in this study were ordained prior to 2007, that is, before the 2009 manual was published; however, since it mostly codified existing practices, it offers a helpful framework to discuss the Pastoral Provision intake process both currently and as it existed prior to 2007.

Although the 2009 manual directs that the first step should be that "[the] candidate ... directs a request for consideration of his desire for priesthood and incardination to the Ordinary [bishop] of the diocese of his choice, who becomes his 'sponsoring bishop,'" the first step for most candidates prior to 2007 was to make contact with the Pope's ED to administer the Pastoral Provision in the United States.[32]

The Ecclesiastical Delegate

As noted above, from the beginning of the Pastoral Provision the CDF has appointed a US bishop to serve as its ED to manage and administer the process in the United States. In the three decades of the program there have been just three EDs: Bishop (later Cardinal) Law, Archbishop John Myers of Newark, and Bishop Vann of Houston, whose 2011 appointment was contemporaneous with the establishment of the Ordinariate.

The ED does not have a mandate to direct or promote the program, but, in an informal way, he does both of these things. For the potential priest converts who contact him, the ED has provided valuable assistance and encouragement. Since the ED generally has knowledge of priests who wish to convert and bishops amenable to receiving and ordaining them, his initial role in the process has often been to serve as a kind of match-maker. The ED is also the prime source of information about the process; he arranges and oversees the ministerial and theological evaluation of most candidates, and can advise candidates about particular conditions in Rome or their diocese that may affect the timing or prospects of their ordination.

Some Catholics, particularly participants in the Anglican Use, who see the Pastoral Provision as an evangelistic opportunity, have felt that the ED should promote the program more actively. But the reception of priest converts depends on the cooperation of bishops willing to ordain them, and many bishops have been reticent to do so, or to ordain more than one or two priest converts, due in part to ecumenical sensitivity toward the Episcopal Church (see Chapter 6). For similar concerns, the CDF has ruled more recently to limit the number of married priests in a diocese to two. Just as much as it is a goal of the Pastoral Provision to make sure the program is accessible and known to those who seek it, it is also a goal not to promote it among those who do not seek it. The ED, therefore, has tended to walk a fine line between information and promotion, or between management and advocacy, of the Pastoral Provision.

The Vatican Dossier

Once a bishop has agreed to sponsor him, each candidate assembles and submits a dossier of his credentials to the CDF for review and approval. The dossier presents the candidate's vital records, academic and ecclesiastical certificates, and other documents relating to his request for ordination, in a carefully prescribed format. The documents included may be photocopies, but must be certified as authentic by either a civil or an ecclesiastical notary, and sometimes by both. Once assembled, the dossier is submitted by the sponsoring bishop to the papal nuncio in Washington, D.C., who conveys it to the CDF in Rome in the diplomatic pouch.

Specifically, there are 14 documents (or sets of documents) that are presented in distinct sections in the dossier:

1. A letter from the sponsoring bishop indicating his willing-ness to ordain the priest. The letter should also "indicate the

assignment the bishop intends to give the candidate following the Congregation's norm that married priests may not have the ordinary care of souls."[33]

2. A letter from the candidate formally requesting ordination in the Catholic Church.

3. A record of the candidate's baptism, which must indicate that the candidate was not baptized in the Catholic Church.

4. A record of the candidate's marriage. If he was married in a Catholic Church or his wife was Catholic at the time of the marriage, a letter explaining these circumstances should accompany the marriage record.

5. Evidence of the stability and health of the marriage, to the satisfaction of the sponsoring bishop. This usually consists of one or more letters of attestation from a colleague or professional associate, as well as a letter from the sponsoring bishop stating that he is satisfied the marriage is stable.

6. A signed statement by the candidate's wife attesting to her agreement with and support of his petition for Catholic ordination. This is a canonical requirement for the ordination of a married priest or deacon in the Catholic Church.

7. A statement certifying the provision of Catholic religious education for any minor children the candidate may have.

8. A copy of the candidate's signed Profession of Faith. This consists of the Nicene Creed plus additional statements attesting to belief in Scripture and adherence "with religious submission of will and intellect to the teachings which either the Roman pontiff or the College of Bishops enunciate when they exercise their authentic Magisterium. . . ."[34]

9. Transcripts of the candidate's seminary education and any other graduate degrees.

10. Evidence of ordination in the Episcopal Church, normally a copy of the ordination certificate.

11. A full employment history, with a detailed resume of ministerial service in the Episcopal Church and any other churches.

12. The report of a confidential psychiatric evaluation of the candidate.

13. A biographical sketch, written by the candidate, which briefly recounts his life history and motives for seeking to become Catholic and to minister as a Catholic priest.

14. Any other pertinent documents the candidate or sponsoring bishop may wish to present.

Into Full Communion contains detailed instructions on the contents and format of the dossier. Prior to 2007, sponsoring bishops submitted dossiers in a variety of formats and varying degrees of completeness, which may have contributed to longer processing times in the Vatican bureaucracy.

The Assessment Process

The CDF, according to *Into Full Communion*, "will undertake an initial review of the dossier in a timely manner," after which, if there are no apparent problems, it will advise that the candidate can begin his canonical assessment, a program of assessment and study culminating in a written theological examination that takes, as noted, at least one year, while the candidate's petition for ordination is being considered more thoroughly.

Into Full Communion, with this interval in mind, calls for the sponsoring bishop to implement for the candidate a "program of spiritual, intellectual, human and pastoral formation." These four areas are the main headings for priestly formation presented in the 1992 papal document *Pastores Dabo Vobes* [I will give you pastors], which defined the goals of Catholic seminary formation worldwide.[35] The fourfold program of formation takes place within the context of both national and international processes of evaluation, and is itself also oriented to evaluation and screening. The concern for screening out unacceptable candidates, as well as couching the evaluation in the language of formation, mirrors the preparation processes of celibate Catholic priests.

In the course of seminary and preparatory training, celibate Catholic priests are exposed to a gauntlet of evaluations, both formal and informal, over a period of years. In addition to the fundamental goal of confirming the potential priest's genuineness and competence, and a pastoral concern for the good of the man himself, careful screening satisfies institutional concerns of the Church. These concerns are heightened, and thus motivate even stricter scrutiny, in the case of the married convert priests.

The harm to the Catholic Church's moral authority resulting from the well-known sex abuse scandals of recent decades obviously justifies strict screening of priest candidates. Similar or even greater rates of abuse by clergy in some Protestant denominations has not brought similar scandal, shock, or negative publicity, suggesting that, for better or worse, Catholic priests are held to a higher standard in the public consciousness, justifying even more thorough screening. The Pastoral Provision priests are not less likely to engage in scandalous sexual behavior just because they are married, but, due to the common perception that they *are* less likely, any misconduct among them is likely to be even more scandalous.

Although to non-Catholics sexual misconduct by married priests may be less scandalous than celibate misconduct, to Catholics it is potentially much more scandalous. For Catholics, sexual misbehavior by celibates violates chastity, but sexual misbehavior by married men constitutes adultery—a much more serious offense. Misconduct by celibate priests can bring embarrassment and criticism of the rule of celibacy, but misconduct by married priests can result in the much greater embarrassment of an offended spouse and divorce proceedings. In a Church that does not recognize civil divorce, and which bars remarried persons from its central sacrament, the prospect of a divorced priest is extremely problematic. Since misconduct or marital breakdown harms both the priest and the Church, Church authorities have a clear responsibility and motive to evaluate and assess the Pastoral Provision priests all the more diligently.

Catholic priests (though not bishops) are normally restricted for their entire career to the diocese in which they were ordained, a practice known as incardination. The essentially permanent mutual commitments between a priest and his bishop resulting from incardination provide another strong motive for the strict scrutiny of priests, particularly married priests. *Into Full Communion* explicitly acknowledges that "incardination imposes lifelong relationships and responsibilities" as a justification for careful evaluation of the Pastoral Provision priest candidates.[36] A bishop who sponsors a candidate for ordination who later compromises his ministry, or simply fails to thrive or be productive, will have to live with that problem for a long time.

Intellectual Formation and Assessment

As with celibate priests in the seminary system, the central focus of the assessment and preparation of married priests is on their theological and pastoral knowledge. Candidates for the Pastoral Provision are required to

have a Master of Divinity degree or its equivalent from an accredited seminary. In addition, as already noted, they undergo a process of formation
and preparation, culminating in a written assessment, prior to approval for
ordination. The written assessment consists of a full evaluation, administered by a theological faculty approved by the ED, to certify the candidate
to have the requisite knowledge for the priesthood—a canonical requirement for the ordination of any Catholic priest. As of 2007, the candidate
generally met twice with the examiners (with an interval of about a year).
Based on an initial oral assessment, he was usually recommended further reading, study, or formation in any area in which he was not already
clearly competent, before returning for the full canonical examination.

The subsequent canonical examination evaluated the candidate in
eight areas of knowledge, with oral and written examinations in the Bible,
Church history, canon law, doctrine, liturgy, sacraments, spirituality, and
moral theology. The eight subject areas are derived from the *Program of
Priestly Formation* developed by the US Conference of Catholic Bishops,
which governs the standard Catholic seminary curriculum in the United
States.[37] In most cases, the candidate sat for written exams over a period of
several days. His answers were evaluated by the Theological Faculty, who
scored them as "fail," "pass," or "pass with distinction." The examiners
then met with the candidate for the second round of oral examinations,
following which he was informed of his results. If the candidate failed in
one or more areas on the written examination, he was assigned further
study and subsequent re-examination in that area.

All but a handful of the priest converts interviewed in this study
passed all eight areas on the first attempt. Seven in ten (71%) of them
had received their Master of Divinity degree from an Episcopal or other
Anglican (e.g., Church of England) seminary. About half passed one or
more areas "with distinction"; two priests passed all eight areas with distinction. About a third of the candidates were judged, at the preliminary
oral assessment, not to need further study in any area, although in almost
every case the examiners made recommendations for voluntary further
reading for enrichment.[38] The area for which additional study was most
often assigned was Catholic canon law—which is not taught in Episcopal
seminaries. In general, this positive record attests to the strong seminary
education that most of the priest candidates received.

In the absence of diocesan resources for education and training, the
earlier Pastoral Provision priests developed a support system among
themselves to prepare for the canonical assessment. Father James Parker,

the first Pastoral Provision priest, who served as Bishop Law's assistant, operated a lending library of essential texts, circulated by mail. Much like cohorts of graduate students preparing for comprehensive exams, candidates informally passed on notes, papers, and outlines to successive ones. By 2007 this collection of materials comprised several hundred written pages.

The provision of a program and mentor to help the candidate prepare for his assessment and eventual priesthood codifies best practices prior to 2009. The priest converts in this study reported a wide disparity in the support and preparation for Catholic ministry provided by their sponsoring diocese. While some dioceses did pair the candidate with a priest mentor who took charge of his formation and preparation for the theological assessment, and one or two even supported him in taking formal courses as needed, prior to 2007 most dioceses essentially left the candidate to fend for himself.

Human Formation

The maturity of the candidate in what the Church calls "human formation" was determined primarily by an extensive clinical psychological evaluation. *Into Full Communion* also calls for the candidate priest to undergo a thorough physical examination. A confidential report of the psychological evaluation was presented to the sponsoring bishop and was included in the dossier sent to the CDF. It was normally the only item in the dossier that was never seen by the candidate. Elements in the psychological report may lead to a decision that the candidate should discontinue or delay his progress toward Catholic ordination, in which case he is normally apprised of this prior to beginning the theological assessment and formation process.[39]

The central part of the psychological evaluation was an interview of the candidate by a clinical psychologist or psychiatrist. The interview included a full life history, an assessment of the candidate's psychological functioning and maturity, and (explicitly since 2009) "an analysis of the stability of the petitioner's marriage and family life."[40]

In addition to the clinical interview assessment, the evaluation currently includes seven common measures of personality and psychological function: the Thematic Apperception Test (TAT); Sentence Completion Test; Rorschach Inkblot Test; Minnesota Multiphasic Personality Inventory-2 (MMPI-2); Michigan Alcohol Screening Test (MAST); Children of Alcoholics Screening Test (CAST); and Derogatis Sexual

Functioning Inventory (DSFI). The first four of these have been widely used, though not required in every instance, since the beginning of the Pastoral Provision; the final three have been increasingly used since the clergy sex abuse scandals of 2002 and are called for in the 2009 manual for every candidate's evaluation thenceforth.

Candidates for Catholic priesthood in the United States have generally been administered a thorough psychological evaluation at some point in the process leading to ordination since at least the early 1970s. While the main emphasis has been to better support the formation of the ordinand, a secondary function of the evaluation has been to help in screening candidates of questionable psychological stability from the priesthood. In the wake of successive clergy sex abuse scandals, more importance has been placed on the evaluation as a screening mechanism. In its discussion of "human formation," *Into Full Communion* clearly envisions that the process will have a substantial screening function. The manual calls for the evaluation to include "an analysis of the stability of the petitioner's marriage and family life," and "strongly advises" that "the sponsoring bishop conduct a criminal background check of the petitioner and his wife."[41] The manual observes that "problems or difficulties in the report . . . should be resolved for the good of the Church," meaning that the candidate would likely be rejected.

Discernment of Priestly Vocation

On applying to a diocese for ordination, married priest candidates were frequently referred to the diocesan Vocations Office, which oversees discernment and vocations processes designed for single men of college age. The interior formation and questioning featured in such programs were often not pertinent to this group of older men (aged 49 on average), who were married with families and with an average of 17 years already in pastoral ministry. Many of the priests or candidates expressed frustration over this disconnect. An older married priest commented on the treatment accorded a new candidate in his diocese, "The vocations director, God bless him, a young priest, doesn't have the faintest idea about what the pastoral provision is about, and so he's making the applicant jump through the same hoops as a young man trying to discern a vocation. He acts like he's a young man that's just discerning. It's very frustrating."

This problem is sometimes a serious barrier to ordination. Another married priest candidate, who fit the average profile of age and Episcopalian tenure exactly, but was turned down for Catholic ordination, explained, "A nun who was the head of the vocations office . . . came to our house and asked me if I felt I was called to the priesthood. And I didn't know what to say that would make me sound fresh and young and idealistic enough. I had no idea what to say. I said, 'I was a priest. I'm willing to serve in the Catholic Church.' And she felt there wasn't any enthusiasm."

At the same time, issues of adjustment from Episcopalian to Catholic ministry that are unique to the married priest candidates were often not addressed. *Into Full Communion* takes steps to correct this imbalance by identifying a series of unique issues for the Pastoral Provision priests to address as they consider entering the Catholic priesthood. However, it does not fully recognize or address the inappropriateness and confusion involved in treating a mature married convert priest like a young single man discerning a vocation for the first time.

In a section titled "Discernment of Priestly Vocation," *Into Full Communion* counsels that "the discernment process must include . . . serious discussion regarding issues specific to the life of a married priest in the Catholic Church in the United States," which is helpful, but also, unhelpfully, "an examination of the petitioner's readiness for ordination according to the standards required for ordination of celibate candidates."[42] Here the conflation of "discernment" with "examination" or screening leads to much confusion in the reception of the Pastoral Provision candidates. Certainly the Pastoral Provision candidates should undergo an examination that is at least as stringent as that of any priest aspirant regarding their competence and character for ordained Catholic ministry. But it should not be the same. The conditions and concerns of the vocational adjustment process of these married convert priests are quite different from those of celibate seminarians. *Into Full Communion* implicitly acknowledges this by listing a number of unique issues to be addressed in the married priests' "discernment" process.

Moreover, while ontologically equivalent in Catholic theology, the vocation of married priests is clearly not the same, in the functional senses addressed by diocesan discernment processes, as that of celibate priests. Two differences are obvious: married and celibate priests are called to different states of life regarding marriage; and married priests (of the Pastoral Provision) are restricted from serving, like most celibate priests do, as parish pastors. *Into Full Communion* calls for married priests to be scrutinized in areas that do not apply to celibate priests: their suitability for non-parochial ministry, the stability of their denominational affiliation, the stability of their marriage, their wife's adjustment to Catholic life, and provision for their children.

Examination of the married priest candidates in these areas no doubt helps the bishop to discern the candidate's vocation. No married priest voiced any objection to such scrutiny, even though it arguably applies a higher standard to the married priests than to celibate ones. What such scrutiny clearly does not do, however, is to try to apply to the married priest candidates the same standards required for ordination of celibate candidates. The two cases are simply very different. Confusion on this point, which looks likely to continue, has led to repeated misunderstanding and occasional delay for the married priest candidates. The process would likely function more smoothly if dioceses followed the simple advice of one such misunderstood priest: "Dioceses should understand and respect the distinction between a priest who is a convert and a young man who maybe is discerning a vocation."

Conclusion

The establishment of the Pastoral Provision opened a surprising and generous accommodation for married Anglican priests to become Catholic priests. Administering this generous institutional impulse, however, has not been a smooth process. The Catholic Church's desire to screen out unpromising ordination candidates and to thoroughly prepare promising ones is heightened by the unusual character of these priests as both converts and married men. When making their way into the Catholic Church, the deeply personal and spiritual aspirations of the married priests have often come up against a complex bureaucracy, multiple evaluations, and roles and expectations that do not fit them well. After three decades, many of the initial administrative problems have been overcome.

3
_____

Why Are Married Priests Becoming Catholic Now?

WHY DO MARRIED priests leave the Episcopal Church and become Catholic? This question is the focus of the next two chapters. We will first examine the context for these conversions before turning to the stories of the priests themselves.

People are likely to wonder why conversion is so important. They think of the Pastoral Provision as primarily (in the words of one observer) "a way married men could be ordained Catholic priests." But far more important than marriage to the Pastoral Provision arrangement—and in many ways more central to the experience of the priests themselves—is the fact of conversion. The Pastoral Provision, most fundamentally, is a set of understandings designed to facilitate entry into the Catholic Church of a particular class of potential converts. Most, though not all, of these converts have been married. The definitive characteristic of these men, then, is not that they are *married* priests, but that they are *convert* priests, who also, in most cases, happen to be married. While the fact that they are married may be the most interesting thing to Catholics, among Episcopalians it is the opposite. For them, there is nothing unusual about married priests, but for a priest to convert to Rome is rare. This will become clearer as we look more closely at the trends on conversion between Anglicans and Catholics in America.

To dramatize and illustrate what follows, it may help to consider the story of one priest's conversion in his own words.

FATHER JAMES WAS raised in a small town in the Midwest, with no connection to Catholicism.[1] Growing up, he writes, "[m]y mother's side of the family was Methodist; my father's side was Baptist. They compromised by

going to the Baptist Church." This didn't mean that their religious practice was superficial. "Our family was in church every Sunday, and often
attended Wednesday evening prayer meeting. When I was nine years old
I began attending Sunday evening youth group almost every week." Then
"[w]hen I was twelve, I walked forward at the end of a revival service to
publicly ask the Lord Jesus into my life as Lord and Savior. . . . I felt then,
as I feel still today, that God touched my life in a very special way that
evening." In high school he became the leader of an evangelical Protestant
student fellowship. All this time "I did not know any Catholics. . . . They
were just not in our social circles at all."

Then: "In my senior year of high school, when I was eighteen years old,
I attended an Episcopal Church for the first time. . . . There was a sense of
God's majesty, and the beauty and depth of his love, that was utterly new
to me. In the liturgy of the Mass, everything seemed to come together and
make sense. . . . It happened to be Palm Sunday, and I returned the next
week for the Easter Vigil and Easter Mass. These services made a deep and
lasting impression on me. I regard this experience as one of the turning
points of my life."

"From that time on I knew it was just a matter of time until I would join
the Episcopal Church. I kept up appearances among my Baptist family, but
I went to Mass at the Episcopal Church whenever I could." In college he
attended daily Mass at the Episcopal Chapel and encountered the Catholic
intellectual tradition (which is congruent with Anglicanism through the
sixteenth century) for the first time. "I became fascinated with Augustine,
Albert the Great, and Aquinas, and with the metaphysical dimensions of
Christian thought in general. My Protestant background had portrayed
religion more or less as an ethical or moral matter, and it was a stunning
surprise to discover religion's supernatural dimensions dealt with in such
a profound and intellectually respectable manner."

In his senior year of college he decided to become an Episcopal priest,
a decision his Baptist parents resisted. "They insisted that I talk with the
Baptist pastor about what they saw as a rash decision on my part. But the
Baptist pastor was very broad minded. After hearing my reasons and desire
to pursue the priesthood, he told my parents that God may truly be calling
me, and that they were lucky to have a son so interested in religion." James
went on to study at the Nashotah House Theological Seminary, founded
in 1842 during Anglicanism's Anglo-Catholic revival (more on this later),
where he "began to realize that how I understood myself as a priest was
more in line with the Catholic understanding than the Episcopal one."

Carol, an attractive young woman and member of the student fellowship James led in high school, came to the same college a year behind him. She was a Methodist, but at James's suggestion "she began to take spiritual direction from the nuns at an Episcopal convent not far from the college. . . . She began to come to daily Mass at the Episcopal Chapel, and we spent a good deal of time together." Carol converted to the Episcopal Church, and the summer after graduation she and James married. "Like Ruth with Naomi," he writes, "Carol willingly accepted my church which became her church, and vowed to support me in my seminary studies and life as a priest. . . . [S]he has been unstinting in her love for me and for the Lord, and always supported my vocation with grace and effort. No man has ever had a better wife."

At age 26, James was ordained an Episcopal priest, happily serving in a succession of increasingly significant pastoral positions. But he also began a process of frustration and discovery that would eventually lead to his leaving the Episcopal Church. Following from his Anglo-Catholic formation, he writes, "I tried to exercise a ministry in the Episcopal Church that contained many elements in common with the priesthood of the Catholic Church." But over time "[i]n my experience as a priest I found very little in the Episcopal Church as a whole that was relevant to the Catholic understanding of the faith which I had taken as my own. . . . It struck me that the Catholic Church seemed to be on the right side of all the issues. It had retained the faith, while all the other Christian churches had faltered, on divorce, contraception, abortion, and now homosexuality. All the great scholars seemed to be Catholic."

For many years James worked to move the Episcopal Church in a Catholic direction. "I became acquainted with the Oxford Movement of the nineteenth century, which attempted, with some success, to recall Anglicanism to its Catholic heritage. I admired intensely the men who formed the backbone of that movement: Keble, Pusey and Newman. . . . I [became] a member of the *Societas Sanctae Crucis*, the Society of the Holy Cross, which has the goal that its members work and pray for the reunion of Anglicanism with the Holy See."

But "[t]he decision by the Episcopal Church [in 1976], and later by the Church of England, to ordain women to its priesthood made it clear to me that corporate reunion is no longer possible. I felt quite shaken by this decision when it first occurred. My deepest objection was that in making such a decision on its own, the Episcopal Church had committed itself to a non-Catholic understanding of the Church and the priesthood.

It had abandoned with little concern or discussion the tradition of the Catholic faith, unchanged since the time of Christ himself. This action was repeated and confirmed in subsequent decisions to ordain homosexual priests and a woman bishop."

"At this point the writings and example of John Henry Newman spoke to me profoundly. He said that Anglicanism was a halfway house between skepticism and the Catholic Church. Sooner or later you have to choose one or the other, as he himself eventually chose to join the Catholic Church. I realized forcefully that the only way I could be a Catholic Christian was to become a Roman Catholic."

"I no longer trusted the teaching of the Episcopal Church. . . . I [came] to believe that [the Catholic Church] is the church founded by Jesus Christ, and that it alone contains and proclaims the whole Christian faith. . . . [T]he Episcopal Church had left any semblance of the Catholic faith, and in doing so had also left me, and that I now had no choice but to leave the Episcopal Church. I wanted to come home to the Catholic Church."

FATHER JAMES'S STORY illustrates many themes that are important to understanding priests who have converted under the Pastoral Provision:

- Growing up in an evangelical Protestant setting, highly religious but not strongly committed to a particular denomination. The combination of high family religiosity with weak or generic denominational bonds is common among the married priests, and seems to set the stage for leaving their religion of origin.
- Converting from another Protestant group to the Episcopal Church, before converting a second time, much later, to the Catholic Church. Such "double conversion," as we shall see, leads to a distinct kind of conversion journey among the married priests; only a minority of them grew up in the Anglican faith.
- Identification with the Anglo-Catholic wing of the Episcopal Church, as signified by attendance at Nashotah House seminary and membership in the Society of the Holy Cross (SSC). More married priests attended Nashotah House and affiliated with SSC than any other seminary or organization.
- The significance of the Episcopal Church's decision to ordain women. This decision had a particular effect on men who shared the same ordination but saw themselves as Catholic Anglicans. In many ways, the

Catholic Church created the Pastoral Provision in response to the 1976 decision by the Episcopal Church to ordain women. On the other hand, for most of the married priests, the main problem with the decision was not the ordination of women as such, but what it signified about the nature of authority in the Episcopal Church.

- The sense of being left behind by a church that has changed—the idea that "I didn't leave the Episcopal Church, the Episcopal Church left me." Many married priests speak, as Father James does, of "coming home" to the Catholic Church to recover what they had originally found, or sought to find, in the Episcopal Church.
- The importance, in the conversion decision, of interior awareness regarding matters of integrity and truth, rather than external conditions or social influences. Most of the married priests were driven to convert by a desire for inner peace and congruence, often with little regard for the external or social consequences of their decision. This sometimes led to uncomfortable financial or employment circumstances, often led to conflict in the extended family, and almost always led to the loss of most of their friends in the Episcopal Church.
- The influence of the Oxford Movement and John Henry Newman. Almost every Pastoral Provision convert, as discussed later in this chapter, has followed some version of Newman's road to Rome.
- Marriage to a supportive woman after making the decision to become a priest. Most of the Pastoral Provision wives, as we shall see in the next chapter, knew they were marrying a man who was planning to become a priest, and explicitly adopted the role and mission to support his ministry and co-minister with him. Most of them also became Episcopalian in the process of marrying their husbands, and all of them subsequently converted (or, in a few cases, came back) to the Catholic Church with their husbands.

History of American Anglican Catholic Conversion
Conversion in the United States

About a third of Americans have switched religions at some point in their lives, and the rate of switching is on the rise.[2] Almost all of this switching occurs at natural break points in life: at marriage, moving to a new city, or following the birth or entry into school of a child. Over two-thirds (69 percent) of switching involves movement among

Protestant denominations. Here are some typical scenarios: a Methodist woman marries a Baptist man, who decides to attend her church after they have the wedding there; a Lutheran family moves to a new state due to a job transfer and begins attending an Episcopal church that is close to their new home; a Presbyterian couple decides to join an Assemblies of God church after enrolling their child in the church's day school. A quarter of Protestants (25 percent) change denominations at least once in their lives. Half this amount (12.1 percent) convert to a non-Protestant religion, but only a relative handful (3.3 percent) convert to the Catholic faith.

Religious switching occurs most commonly between religious groups that are the most similar in terms of doctrine, liturgy, and church life, and becomes progressively rarer between groups that are more different from each other.[3] So, for example, it is much rarer for a member of one of the Assemblies of God, an evangelical Pentecostal denomination, to switch to the Presbyterian Church (PCUSA), a liberal denomination with a tradition of quiet, non-charismatic worship, than it is for a member of the United Church of Christ, which shares the PCUSA's theology and worship style, to do so. The Assemblies of God member, on the other hand, is much more likely to switch to another Pentecostal church or join the Southern Baptists, another evangelical denomination. It comes as no surprise, then, that the Protestants who are most likely to become Catholic are members of those churches that are most like the Catholic Church.

Protestant churches were formed, beginning in the sixteenth century, by rejecting (protesting) Catholicism. But some Protestants rejected more of Catholicism than others. Today the Lutheran, Episcopal, and to a lesser extent Methodist churches retain a form of worship and church government that is much closer to that of the Catholic Church than most other Protestant denominations. Like the Catholic Church, these denominations are all governed by bishops who rule a defined geographical area and ordain new clergy. They all have groups of traditionalists who affirm the value of church history and tradition for interpreting the Bible and reject recent innovations in doctrine. These churches also have a written order of worship that follows the basic outline of the Catholic Mass, and which, in the "high church" wing of all three churches, is celebrated with a ceremony and ritual that is similar to the worship of the Catholic Church. Most Lutherans or Episcopalians, and some Methodists, who visit a Catholic Mass find that there are far more similarities than differences in the worship experience. Many notice little difference at all, and report that they feel right at home.

These affinities are reflected in higher rates of conversion to Catholicism from these denominations. While 2.7 percent of those who began life as some other form of Protestant have converted to the Catholic Church, for Methodists, Lutherans, and Episcopalians, respectively, the proportion rises to 4.2 percent, 5.0 percent, and 5.8 percent.[4] The Episcopal Church, in particular, has seen itself as a "bridge church" spanning the Protestant-Catholic rift. This self-understanding stems from the nature of the Elizabethan settlement in the sixteenth century, which sought a workable compromise between the Protestant and Catholic impulses in English life. This sense is also fostered, particularly among High Church Anglicans, by the nineteenth-century Oxford Movement, which saw the Church of England as the *via media*, a "middle way" between Catholic rigidity and Protestant schism. As then, a relatively high number of Anglicans today both confirm and undermine the self-identity of a bridge church by traversing the bridge to Rome. The Episcopal Church has the highest rate of conversion to the Catholic Church of any Protestant denomination.

Despite the common perception to the contrary among Episcopalians, the bridge only goes one way. While nearly 6 percent of those raised Episcopalian have converted to Catholicism, only 0.7 percent of cradle Catholics have switched to the Episcopal Church in recent years—a rate almost 10 times smaller.[5] The Episcopal Church is not in any way a magnet for former Catholics: the rate of switching-in by Catholics is higher for most other Protestant denominations, including Methodists (1 percent), Lutherans (1.3 percent), and even Baptists (1.5 percent). The huge difference in Episcopalian-to-Catholic and Catholic-to-Episcopalian conversion rates reflects, in part, the huge difference in the size of their membership—which also explains the mistaken perception among Episcopalians that they receive a relatively large number of Catholics. The American Catholic Church has about 68 million members to the Episcopal Church's 2 million members. So while the rate of Catholics becoming Episcopalians is almost 10 times smaller, the relative effect of incoming Catholics on the Episcopal Church is about 3.5 times larger than the corresponding effect of incoming Episcopalians on the Catholic Church. In sum, the number of incoming Catholics may appear large relative to the size of the Episcopal Church, but it is minuscule relative to the size of the Catholic Church, and represents a much lower rate of defection from the Catholic Church to the Episcopal Church than the other way around.

On the other hand, the movement of clergy between the Episcopal Church and the Catholic Church is much more equal, with a small advantage to the Episcopalians. Stephen Fichter recently reported that the Episcopal Church identified 361 former Catholic priests currently serving as Episcopal priests.[6] This amount comprises 0.85 percent of the reported 42,307 currently serving Roman Catholic priests, who form the "pool" of potential priest converts. In the present study I have identified 84 former Episcopal priests, out of 15,051 total Episcopal priests, currently serving as Catholic priests, a rate of 0.56 percent.[7] These numbers, which are obviously imprecise and should be interpreted with caution, suggest in a general way that the rates of clergy transfer between these two religious groups are very small and much closer to being equal than are the rates of lay switching.[8] They also suggest a somewhat higher rate of Catholic priests becoming Episcopal priests than the other way around.

Catholic Converts

Each year in America about 130,000 adults join the Catholic Church; almost all of them switch in from a Protestant denomination.[9] This amount—equivalent to about two-tenths of 1 percent of the Catholic population—is trivial in terms of numerical increase: Catholic churches baptize over seven times as many infants, about 920,000 each year. Although Catholic conversions have increased since the low point in the 1960s and 1970s, they are still well below the levels of the "Golden Age of Catholic Conversions" from 1930 to 1960.[10] The inflow of adults, moreover, is offset by an estimated equal or greater number of persons who leave the Church each year.

But Catholic converts bring to the Church more than just numbers. They often come with vitality and commitment that exceed those of native or "cradle" Catholics. The stereotype of a fanatical new convert, intolerant of more moderate commitment on the part of older adherents, is clearly an exaggeration, but it expands on qualities that are generally found, in more moderate amounts, among American Catholic converts. Table 3.1 reports pertinent findings from a 1995 national survey that compared converts and cradle Catholics on a wide variety of measures. The survey shows clearly that Catholic converts are demonstrably more active in their religion than are cradle Catholics: more of them go to Mass weekly or more

Table 3.1 Selected Comparisons Between Catholic Converts and Cradle Catholics (in Percent)

Item	Catholic Convert	Cradle Catholic
"Is your spouse Catholic?"—*yes* (married persons only)	96	68
Persons in their thirties or forties with school-age children or younger living at home	82	58
"How religious are you now?"—*very religious*	43	22
"Are you registered as a member of a Catholic parish?"—*yes*	88	67
"How often do you go to Mass?"—*weekly or more often*	51	43
"One can be a good Catholic without going to Mass."—*disagree*	48	34
"Tell me how important it is to you: There are three persons in one God."—*very important*	62	52
"Tell me how important it is to you: Jesus was completely divine like God, and completely human like us in every way except sin."—*very important*	77	67
"Tell me how important it is to you: Jesus physically rose from the dead."—*very important*	82	71
"Tell me how important it is to you: In Mass, the bread and wine actually become the body and blood of Christ."—*very important*	71	62
"Helping needy people is an important part of my religious beliefs."—*agree strongly*	86	75
"It's important to obey Church teachings even if I don't understand them."—*agree strongly*	29	19
"There is something very special about being Catholic that you can't find in other religions."—*agree strongly*	53	38

Source: Catholic Pluralism Project Survey (1995).

often (51 percent of converts vs. 43 percent of cradle Catholics); more of them are registered members (88 percent vs. 67 percent); and converts are almost twice as likely (43 percent vs. 22 percent) to report that they are very religious.[11] This survey is one of the few surveys, and the most recent large one, to explicitly identify Catholic converts; other more recent surveys with less precise measures generally confirm these findings, albeit often with smaller differences.[12]

Converts are also more likely to believe doctrine and attach importance to Catholic teaching. In the survey, a higher proportion of converts than of cradle Catholics thought the core Christian doctrines of the trinity, incarnation, and bodily resurrection to be very important. Even distinctive Catholic emphases, such as transubstantiation and service to the needy, were more important to converts than to cradle Catholics. Converts were also more likely to affirm obedience to the magisterium about beliefs they did not understand, a key contrast to Protestant thinking, and to consider being Catholic unique and special among religions.

Those who switch religions for reasons of conviction, of course, might be expected to have higher levels of belief and practice. But the higher religiosity of Catholic converts is all the more striking because most of them have not switched for such reasons. In the United States, the vast majority of persons who change religions do so for "external" reasons, that is, not simply out of religious conviction. Most frequently, they switch to accommodate marriage, so the two partners will share the same religion. This appears to be a strong factor for the Catholic converts in the national survey: almost all (96 percent) of them are married to a Catholic spouse, compared to only two-thirds (68 percent) of cradle Catholics. The second most common reason for converting is to raise one's child in a particular religious tradition. The need to baptize or dedicate and religiously educate their child often stimulates a couple to resolve religious differences that they were previously able to tolerate. Perhaps they are attracted to the religious education program of a local church of a different religious tradition. Whatever the causes, this factor seems to be in evidence among Catholic converts as well. Twenty-five percent more of the converts than of the cradle Catholics were raising school-age children.

Even though they usually convert for reasons that are only secondarily religious, then, Catholic converts tend to be more religious in belief and practice than are lifelong Catholics. Quite possibly, the instruction that Catholic converts receive is more thorough, or more recent, or they are better disposed to receive it, than is the case for cradle Catholics. Perhaps greater conviction and commitment are discovered in the process of conversion, or are generated to justify conversion, even if they didn't motivate it to begin with. Whatever the cause, we can note that the higher rates of Catholic belief and practice of the Pastoral Provision priests express, albeit more intensely, qualities that are a general feature of Catholic converts.

There is yet a further trend in Catholic conversions that helps put the conversions of the Pastoral Provision priests into context. Hidden beneath the flood of 140,000 external converts each year is a small but steady number of persons who make the decision to become Catholic for vastly different reasons.

The Newly Catholic Faithful

Colleen Carroll, in *The New Faithful: Why Young Adults Are Embracing Christian Orthodoxy*, provides an introduction to the most recent edge of these unusual Catholic converts. According to Carroll, "a small but committed core of young Christians is intentionally embracing organized religion and traditional morality."[13] Rejecting empty materialism and relativism, the young people she chronicles are finding renewed personal meaning, not in a formless quest or privatized devotion, but in an intense engagement with classic Christian orthodoxy. While not all of the young new faithful are Catholic, the stories of Catholics and Catholic converts figure prominently in the movement. Significantly, there is no convert *from* Catholicism among the religiously revived young adults profiled. Among Catholics, Carroll notes, "[c]onverts and highly educated young Catholics are blazing a trail that leads back to Catholic tradition."[14] There is little hard data to back up the author's claims, but she argues that, while the numbers of such young traditionalists may be small, they form an elite group of religious virtuosi that has an outsized cultural and religious effect.

In the context of Catholic engagement with American culture, the "new faithful" are not new. They are the most recent expression of a small but distinguished stream of American (and British) converts who for at least 150 years have come to the faith out of deep interior conviction. Often their conversion puts them at odds with family and friends. Like the recent new faithful, in numbers such converts have been just a trickle, but their influence has been much greater than their numbers, both in the Church and outside it.

These converts of conviction have disproportionately come from the cultural elite. Although doubtless influenced by others, and not insensible to ritual and aesthetics, for the most part they have read their way into a place of interior consent with the claims of Catholic doctrine and moral teaching. Consequently, their numbers have been concentrated among the literary and intellectual professions, and those given to a certain independence of mind: artists, writers, jurists, academics, educators—and, more recently, ministers. Perhaps for this reason, the flow of converts has been extensively documented—Menendez's 1986 bibliography *The Road to Rome* lists more than 1,400 articles and books by and about English-speaking Catholic converts since the nineteenth century—and the more prominent ones of earlier generations have been well chronicled in recent years.[15] Of those who have been the subject of multiple biographies, Patrick Allitt, in the introduction to his excellent book *Catholic Converts*, lists John Henry Newman, G. K. Chesterton, Isaac Hecker, Orestes Brownson, Graham Greene, Evelyn Waugh, Thomas Merton, and Dorothy Day.[16] To this list could be added others of intellectual or cultural prominence on both sides of the Atlantic: Elizabeth Ann Seton, Gerard Manley Hopkins, Gabriel Marcel, Mortimer Adler, Ronald Knox, Dave Brubeck, Allen Tate, Edith Stein, Claire Boothe Luce, Marshall McLuhan, Rene Girard, Russell Kirk, Walker Percy, Graham Leonard, Malcolm Muggeridge, Robert Bork, Robert Novak, Bobby Jindal, and Tony Blair. In his 1987 book *The New Catholics*, Dan O'Neill presents the stories of 16 converts of conviction, a prior generation of the new faithful, who made decisions as adults to cross the Tiber. The names include "several best-selling authors, well-known university professors, a peace activist, a former Protestant missionary, an entertainer" and others—including one Pastoral Provision priest—all in what is today termed the "knowledge class."

Coming from the secular cultural and intellectual elite, Catholic intellectual converts have been at the forefront of the Catholic Church's engagement with elite culture. "When the church began to reassert itself in the nineteenth century, it used converts as its principal advocates," writes Allitt. The nineteenth-century Protestant converts Orestes Brownson, consulted by presidents, and Isaac Hecker, founder of the Paulist Fathers, initiated projects of engagement with American culture that were none the less far-reaching for having been often neglected by their contemporaries both inside and outside the Church.[17] Menendez assesses the Paulist Fathers, founded by Hecker with the accomplished converts Francis Baker, Augustine Hewit, George Deshon, and Clarence Walworth, to be "one of U.S. Catholicism's real success stories" for articulating the compatibility of Catholic faith with American values and ideals.[18] Many other converts of this era also left their mark. In addition to Seton, founder of the Sisters of Charity and many Catholic schools, and later named the first American saint, there were Rose Hawthorne

Lathrop, daughter of Nathaniel Hawthorne and founder of the Hawthorne Dominicans; the popular writers Anne Dorsey, Mary Agnes Tincker, and Joel Chandler Harris (whose pen name was Uncle Remus); the historian Carlton Hayes; James McMaster, Brownson's alter ego; John McLoughlin, head of the Hudson Bay Company; and a number of prominent members of the American episcopacy.

Nor did this trend diminish in the twentieth century. To the names in the previous paragraphs may be added the twentieth-century converts Dietrich von Hildebrand, an influential theologian and cultural critic; Christopher Dawson, a Harvard historian; Jacques Maritain, a mid-century philosopher and public intellectual; and Avery Dulles, a convert theologian who was named cardinal in 2001. John Tracy Ellis, in his famous 1955 essay bemoaning the dearth of intellectual accomplishment among American Catholics, remarked on a signal exception to his thesis: "the relatively high proportion of scholarly contributions that had marked the careers of many of the converts to the Church during the present century. . . . [O]ne wonders where the intellectual life of the Church of the United States would have been without them."[19]

Today the flow of highly committed converts from the knowledge class reflects in part the influence of the Second Vatican Council, which opened the Church to the modern age and in return opened the modern age to the Church. The charismatic globe-trotting of Pope John Paul II and the leadership of the Catholic Church in the American culture wars have also had their impact. Although it is not clear that the influx of intellectual converts, never more than a trickle, has increased, it certainly has not diminished. Today the list of prominent Catholic apologists largely overlaps that of Catholic intellectual or literary converts.

One feature that is particularly relevant to understanding the conversions of the Pastoral Provision priests is the fact that among the committed Protestants making their way to Rome are hundreds of clergy who have left their careers to join the Catholic Church. Since 1993 more than 1,200 ministers have contacted the Coming Home Network, a support ministry for Protestant clergy who are "coming home" to Rome. About two-thirds of these have already been received into the Church. Although these include Episcopalian clergy such as the Pastoral Provision priests, most of the converting clergy are Baptist, Lutheran, Presbyterian, and Methodist. As we shall see, most of the Pastoral Provision priests also began their conversion journey, not as Episcopalians, but as members of other Protestant denominations.

Newman and the Oxford Movement

Father James's conversion story illustrates the strong influence and example of John Henry Newman, a nineteenth-century convert, on future conversions from Anglicanism to Catholicism, including those of the Pastoral Provision priests. Unlike the continental Reformations of Luther and Calvin, religious change in England in the sixteenth century had come about not as the result of popular uprising but by the imposition of political will. In 1535 the Oath of Supremacy, naming the King as the supreme spiritual authority in England and denouncing the Pope, was required of clergy and religious on pain of death—hardly the sign of a popular movement—leading to about 50 martyrs in the following five years. For the next century, Catholic priests and laypersons publicly affirming the Catholic faith were subject to painful and humiliating public execution, often without benefit of trial. Two hundred eighty-four men and women, all remembered in honor by the English Catholic Church every May 4, are known to have perished for the Catholic faith between 1535 and 1670. These are only the ones who happened to be documented; the Church calendar notes that the full "number of those who died on the scaffold, perished in prison, or suffered harsh persecution for their faith in the course of a century and a half cannot now be reckoned."[20] The subjugation of Catholics (and other "dissenters" from Anglicanism) gradually diminished through the succeeding centuries, though Catholic worship continued to be illegal until 1791, and Catholics continued to suffer discrimination and reduced social standing, which continues to some extent to the present day.

In the 1830s the Oxford don and priest John Henry Newman led a Catholic restoration effort in the Church of England that became known as the Oxford Movement. Newman, like most of the Pastoral Provision priests 150 years later, was dismayed at the doctrinal weakness and vacillation of the Church of England in the face of social and cultural change. The Oxford Movement attempted to restore an interpretation of Anglican doctrine and practice that was in continuity with Catholic tradition. However, an intense study of Church history eventually led Newman to conclude that the English Reformation, when the authority of the Pope as head of the Church was rejected in favor of the English king, had been an error, and that the Roman Catholic Church, not the Church of England, preserved the true expression of the Christian faith. "To be deep in history," wrote Newman "is to cease to be Protestant." Once he came to this realization, conversion became imperative for his own salvation and personal integrity. Newman left a prominent parish and comfortable life in Oxford to be received and eventually re-ordained as a Catholic priest, spending much of the rest of his life arguing, in books and articles, for the truth of the Catholic faith relative to Anglicanism. Newman made substantial contributions to Catholic theology, was eventually named a cardinal, and was beatified, a major step toward being declared a Catholic saint, in 2010.

Through his writings and example, Newman's intellectual journey, sometimes known as the "Newman Road" or path, has inspired many subsequent Anglican converts. To attribute to his influence alone the flow of Anglicans to Catholicism since his time is probably an exaggeration, but not a large exaggeration. The Oxford Movement bore fruit in the Anglo-Catholic revival in both England and America, which in the 1830s disposed subsequent generations of Anglican clergy and committed laity to increasing affinity with Roman Catholicism. These people considered themselves to be Anglican Catholics, separated from Rome only by issues of jurisdiction, but in agreement on all important matters of doctrine and worship. In addition to baptismal regeneration and Eucharistic transubstantiation, which, though optional, had always been within the orbit of Anglican belief, Anglo-Catholics also tended to affirm such Roman Catholic beliefs as Mary's immaculate conception and assumption, and practices such as the rosary, sacramental confession, and Eucharistic adoration or benediction. Many also came to affirm Papal infallibility and that Anglicanism was in a renegade position, justifying their persistence in the Church of England or Episcopal Church by working for the eventual corporate reunion of Anglicanism with Roman Catholicism. It was from this Anglo-Catholic context that many of the married convert priests have come.

Due to America's less rigid class structure, the small size of the Episcopal Church, and the general tendency toward conversion among Americans, converts via the Newman Road in the United States have not generally been as prominent as in England. In both countries the absolute number of Catholic converts has been small, but in England the social effect was magnified by the concentration of such converts among the highly structured British elite. Gorman's 1910 record of "the more notable converts to the Catholic Church in the United Kingdom during the last sixty years" identifies, from among fewer than 5,000 converts, 586 Oxford graduates, 346 Cambridge graduates, 470 authors, poets, or playwrights, 370 Royal Navy and Army officers, 606 Anglican priests, 822 clergy wives and children, and 432 members of the nobility, not including 82 peers and peeresses of the British Realm.[21] The author comments that "there is hardly an English noble family that has not given one or more of its members to the Roman Catholic Church."[22]

The continuity of the Pastoral Provision priests with this former stream of Anglican converts should not be obscured by the fact that today's disputed moral or ecclesiastical issues are quite different than they were a century ago. As we shall see, the particular issues of concern do not lead directly to conversion. They only do so when they precipitate reflection that leads to Newman's conclusion—that Anglican authority is fundamentally flawed. Today's precipitating issues, such as the ordination of women and/ or practicing homosexuals, may be very different than in the past, but their effect on Catholic Anglican conversion is much the same. Anglican clergy converts, in fact, have tended to come in waves in the wake of successive changes. Allitt notes that in response to Pope Leo XIII's 1896 bull *Apostolicae Curae*, which concluded that Anglican orders were invalid, "a cluster of [Anglo-Catholic] clergymen ... resigned from their livings and converted to Catholicism." Experimentation with an "open pulpits" policy in the Episcopal Church in 1908 similarly led to a brief spike in Anglo-Catholic conversions to Rome.[23]

Evangelicals Coming to Rome

A significant portion of the nineteenth-century English converts to Rome came not, or not only, from the Anglo-Catholic wing, but from the evangelical side of Anglican piety and worship. Newsome's *The Parting of Friends* relates the impact and difficulties created by the unexpected conversion of prominent nineteenth-century English evangelicals, including many members of the Wilberforce and Manning families, to the Catholic faith. In a statement that anticipates the experience of many of the Pastoral Provision priests, Newsome notes: "It has long been observed that many of the most active supporters of the Oxford Movement were those who had been brought up in the Evangelical tradition; and that those who underwent one conversion were liable to undergo another and to end their spiritual wanderings in the Church of Rome."[24]

Likewise, a surprising proportion of recent intellectual converts to Catholicism have come from the evangelical end of the Protestant spectrum. As we shall see, this is also true of the Pastoral Provision priests. Marcus Grodi, the founder of Coming Home Network, is a converted conservative Presbyterian minister, as is Scott Hahn, the most well-known recent clergy convert. A series of popular books have attested to conversions from fundamentalism to Catholicism.[25] Though not numerically huge, the trend is deep enough to worry evangelical leaders: "I have been concerned about the growing exodus from evangelicalism of some of its brightest and best, for, variously, Canterbury, Rome, or Mt. Athos," writes Larry Eskridge of the Institute for the Study of American Evangelicals.[26] One might add that, like all the Pastoral Provision priests who converted to the Episcopal Church, those leaving for Canterbury often find it a way-station to Rome.

Religion scholar Scot McKnight, studying 28 prominent evangelicals who became Roman Catholic, describes the typical features of their conversion journeys. Many elements of their stories are strikingly similar to those of the Pastoral Provision priests. Like the Pastoral Provision priests, a large portion (half) of his sample were prior converts, having converted to another Protestant church before converting again to the Catholic Church. The issues of authority and truth are as important for the evangelical converts as they are for the Pastoral Provision priests, and for similar reasons. Generally speaking, the process of intellectual discovery and change is about the same for both groups. In a passage that echoes Newman's assertion that Church history undermines Protestant belief, McKnight notes: "The crisis created in some [evangelical converts] about the *temporality of modern evangelicalism* cannot be denied or even minimized. It is no trivial matter that evangelicals have quartered Church history and excluded the first three quarters." Furthermore, "it is both the Church fathers' articulations as well as the *liturgy* that play equal and convincing roles for many [evangelical converts]."[27] Carroll also attests to the attraction of the young new faithful to sacraments and objective liturgical expressions of faith. Most importantly, as with the Pastoral Provision priests, McKnight notes that none of the conversions involved a fundamental awakening or reorientation of belief, but that "in each case, it was not a conversion to faith in Christ but a *conversion to (what is perceived to be) the fullness of the Christian faith*"[28] (emphasis in original) by persons who were already active and committed Christians.

McKnight's reference to the "temporality of modern evangelicalism" obscures the point that what is disturbing to the awakened historical consciousness of evangelical (and Anglican) converts is not that Protestantism is discontinuous with the history of the Church, but that its evident precursors in the early Church are anathema to modern Protestantism. To critique post-Apostolic Christianity is to align oneself with heretics. The same point was pivotal for Newman:

> It was difficult to make out how the Eutychians or Monophysites were heretics, unless Protestants and Anglicans were heretics also; difficult to find arguments against the Tridentine Fathers which did not tell against the Fathers of Chalcedon; difficult to condemn the Popes of the sixteenth century, without condemning the Popes of the fifth. ... The principles and proceedings of the Church now were those of the Church then; the principles and proceedings of heretics then were those of Protestants now. ... What was the use of continuing the controversy, or defending my position, if, after all, I was but forging arguments for Arius or Eutyches, and turning devil's advocate against the much-enduring Athanasius and the majestic Leo?[29]

The Pastoral Provision priests followed a similar logic to its conclusion in the decision to become Catholic. For the married priests, the attempt to join evangelical vitality with a Catholic sense of sacrament and tradition eventually led, not to Anglo-Catholic compromise, but to the security and stability of Catholicism itself. In the next chapter we will examine the structural or psychosocial elements involved in their conversion decisions.

4

Why Did the Married Priests Convert?

A *Typology of Religious Conversion*

Current Sociological Understandings of Conversion

The question at hand—why did married priests convert?—is best understood within the context of a larger question: Why does anyone convert?

Religious conversion, as a psychosocial phenomenon, has long been of interest to scholars of religion. The New Testament recounts that Saul, soon to be renamed Paul, while traveling to Damascus to persecute Christians, was confronted with a powerful vision of Jesus that knocked him to the ground and convinced him of the truth of Christianity. This dramatic, life-changing event was replicated en masse in religious revival gatherings throughout the United States around the turn of the twentieth century, in which participants became "born again" through a "conversion experience." During the same period, the new disciplines of social science were coming into their own, resulting in a spate of scholarly interest in this widespread and powerful religious phenomenon. One of the most well-known expressions of this interest was *The Varieties of Religious Experience* by the psychologist/philosopher William James, which focused on the "twice-born" souls who were relieved from troubled guilt by a sudden joyful experience of personal integration. This paradigm of conversion as an individual, interior event resulting in profound personal change has dominated psychological studies of conversion ever since. Though scholars in the field appropriately critique and qualify the idea, the root perception of conversion has been that of "a radical reorganization of identity, meaning, and life."[1]

Such a radical orientation, however, is not necessarily or even usually associated with religious realignment. Many people come, through sudden event or gradual process, to a radically heightened intensity of religious devotion or relationship with God without changing churches. Far from leading to a change of affiliation, such a conversion typically cements one's full participation in the church with which he or she is already affiliated. In some denominations, such a conversion experience is a scripted rite of passage expected of all or most serious young members. On the other hand, very little religious reaffiliation involves a radical reorientation of life. As noted above, most changes of affiliation occur among the most compatible religious groups; very few people who switch denominations attribute the move to a profound religious change.

The word "conversion" can have a number of other meanings, depending on the context and who is using it. In Christian theological terms, it refers to the transformation of one's character to become like Christ or like God. In this sense, St. Paul's "conversion" did not happen on the Damascus Road, but probably during the subsequent time, possibly years, that he spent in the desert after he had accepted Christianity. Psychologists also sometimes speak of conversion as a reorientation of personality. These senses have little association with the popular use of "conversion" to refer to the act or process of coming to adhere to a new religion. Sociologically, conversion has a much more modest usage: it simply means switching religious affiliation from one group to another. Without excluding the possibility of internal transformations or personality change, this is the basic sense in which I will use the word in this chapter.

Empirically, the causes of religious conversion have been so diverse as to resist classification. In a review of studies of conversion, Snow and Machalek (1984) identified no fewer than six groups of causes of religious conversion that had been advanced by social scientists: "(a) psychophysiological responses to coercion and induced stress; (b) predisposing personality traits and cognitive orientations; (c) situational factors that induce stress; (d) predisposing social attributes; (e) a variety of social influences; and (f) causal process explanations involving the confluence of a range of elements."[2] Lofland and Skonovd, in a classic statement in the field, identified six types of religious conversion, which they call "motifs": intellectual, mystical, experimental, affectional, revivalist, and coercive.[3] Gooren's review of the more recent conversion research identified a nearly identical and similarly diverse typology of causal factors: personality, institutional, social, cultural, and contingency factors.[4] These are not mutually exclusive factors; all of them may be at work, more or less, in bringing about a particular conversion. Conversions themselves, as a comprehensible process over and above the types of individual influences, also express, as we have seen, a "variety of experience." It is evident that the types of conversion are similar to, though not identical with, the classes of causal factors.

Conversion as Religious Migration

David O'Rourke's thoughtful reflection on Catholic conversion points out that, at its most basic level, religious conversion involves simply turning from one path to another.[5] The shift, even when it is experienced in a significant moment or encounter, involves a process of turning away from one direction in life and toward another. In this understanding, the turning may be a complete turnabout or a small deflection from the original direction; either way, it is a new direction. This turning can be conceived, I suggest, as a kind of religious migration, a double turning away from one religious identity and toward another religious identity. The precipitating characteristics can be pictured as the factors that attract or repel from the poles. Such factors are referred to by social scientists as the "push" and "pull" factors of a migration decision. Any turning in life—from one political party to another, one career to another, or one country to another—involves such factors.

O'Rourke also emphasizes that, notwithstanding any elements of supernatural mystery or divine grace that may be involved, the turning is also a human process, rooted in the dynamics of human life.[6] As with any human behavior, those dynamics are generally recognized as psychosocial, consisting of ideas, dispositions, and desires that arise from the interior self as well as physical and social conditions.[7] Conversion, then, involves a combination, or possible combination, of both internal motivations and external pressures. Although there is no necessary connection between religion and spirituality or belief, in practice the two often overlap, and ideally they overlap a lot. Religion, moreover, always takes place in the context of social and psychological factors that are not themselves religious. It thus is plausible to distinguish internal dispositions (beliefs) from external conditions (circumstances) among the factors precipitating a religious conversion.

The four types of factors entailed in these two distinctions—push and pull, internal and external—provide a helpful analytical framework for thinking about the conversions of the Pastoral Provision priests and their wives. This framework attempts simply to identify the structure of the possible causes for any religious reaffiliation. I am not suggesting that all conversions consist of all four elements—quite the contrary. It is best to think of these concepts as what Max Weber proposed as an "ideal type." Weber, an early sociologist, proposed that social reality could be best understood by posing extreme, ideal concepts or patterns of behavior, in relation to which the flux and variation observed in social life could be meaningfully ordered.[8] Perhaps no religious conversion consists purely of a change in belief or a change in friends or affiliation without the other also occurring, at least to a minimal extent. But the idea of such extremes gives us fixed points, as it were, in relation to which we can range and compare the elements of actual observed conversions.

The four quadrants (see Figure 4.1) produced by cross-classifying the two ranges of factors—push to pull, internal to external—represent four identifiable types of conversions. As an empty structure, this might be called a migration model of conversion, since it conceives of a religion transition as analogous to a physical or political one. But the particular kind of migration/conversion involved may be very different, depending on which of the four factor types are emphasized. To the extent that a single factor type predominates in a particular conversion process, these also then represent four distinct types of conversions.

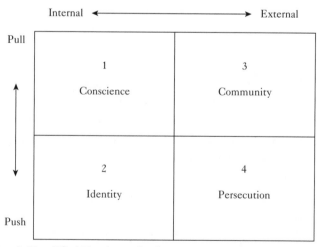

FIGURE 4.1 A Simplified Typology of Religious Conversion

Quadrant 1 refers to internal factors that attract or move the potential convert to the religion to which he or she eventually converts. Becoming convinced of the doctrine and appreciating the ethos of the destination religion are perhaps the most common forms of Type 1 factors. But Type 1 factors could also include adopting attitudes or discovering aesthetic sensibilities that are compatible with the new religion. Social science typologies sometimes refer to "intellectual conversions," in which one changes beliefs from the old religion to the new; in the classic literary understanding and in common parlance, this is, in large part, what conversion means. I have called conversions of this type "conscience" conversions, as the influence of internal attraction often results in a crisis of conscience when the convert finds himself or herself formally committed to one religion while believing and approving the teachings of another religion. A Type 1 conversion typically occurs in order to resolve such a crisis of conscience. Empirical studies show that changing religions for reasons of belief in this way accounts for only a small fraction of religious conversions. This was, however, the most common type of conversion among the Pastoral Provision priests.

Quadrant 2 defines internal push factors, that is, beliefs or attitudes that make the potential convert uncomfortable or inauthentic if he or she remains in his original religion. If Type 1 factors explain why he is attracted to the religion he eventually adopts, Type 2 factors explain why he needs or wants to leave the religion in which he began. Type 1 factors are necessary and may be sufficient to bring about conversion. But, since a conversion must have a specific destination, no conversion could be based on Type 1 factors alone. It is not enough to want to be elsewhere; one must also have a specific place one wants to be.

One of the most consistent findings of social science research on conversions is that the process of conversion often begins in Quadrant 2, with a vague sense of unease with the beliefs, attitudes, or dispositions of one's current religion. Exploring this inchoate unease may lead to a realization that one's authentic self is out of place in one's current religion. The potential convert defines himself or herself at this point as a seeker, and the impulse toward conversion proceeds from the process of self-definition. The convert realizes that his identity is no longer compatible with continued identification with the religion he is in.

Sociological accounts of religious conversion often point out, naturally enough, that a convert generally adopts not only a new set of beliefs but also a new circle of friends. The external, non-conscientious factors that draw one to a new religion, expressed in Quadrant 3, may consist of other things: increased employment prospects, lower taxes, or citizenship. Religious conversion can often bestow non-religious, material advantages. But repeated sociological research has confirmed that the bulk of external attractions in all conversions have to do with relationships. The most common occasion of religious conversion of any kind is marriage, when one of the partners converts to the religion of the other. The factors in this quadrant thus have for the most part to do with community.

Just as incentives to adopt a religion may be a factor in conversion, disincentives to continue in one's current religion may exist. The policy of "conversion or death" adopted in some warlike contexts has resulted in some celebrated martyrdoms, but it probably also spurred many conversions. Acts or policies of violent persecution or social intolerance against a religious group may be the clearest examples of the factors collected in Quadrant 4, though we could also include here the loss of any of the Type 3 external incentive factors. Restrictive moral codes or rules of behavior also influence some to exit the group, often with a sense of escape, as has been the experience of many raised in a strict fundamentalist sect or involved in a totalitarian religious cult.

This theoretical model can encompass a wide range of conversion issues and types. To see how it may apply to the Pastoral Provision priests will require identifying and organizing the elements that brought about their particular conversions.

Pastoral Provision Conversion Themes
Rationale

Each priest was invited to explain in his own words why he had converted. The resulting conversations often involved lengthy, complex accounts of the circumstances and thinking of these Episcopal priests that resulted in the decision to "swim the Tiber." From these stories I was able to discern certain main themes (see Table 4.1).

Although the external factors of the conversion journey—such as circumstance, timing, background, and job situation—varied widely, the internal factors—the precipitating beliefs, issues, and dispositions—were remarkably similar for the bulk of the convert priests. Just a few themes were expressed repeatedly. Two-thirds (68 percent) of the respondents considered their conversion a response to discovered truth. Six in 10

Table 4.1 Summary Themes of Reasons Given for Becoming Catholic
(in Percent; *n* = 53)

I discovered or affirmed that Catholic claims and teaching are true.	68
The Episcopal Church has lost and/or the Catholic Church preserves authority to teach Christian doctrine.	59
I grew more Catholic and/or the Episcopal Church grew less Catholic.	42
I have always been Catholic, even as an Anglican.	32

(59 percent) described the issue of religious authority as the root factor in their conversion. Four in 10 (42 percent) noted, looking back, that for a long time they had been moving toward the Catholic Church and/or that the Episcopal Church had been simultaneously moving further away from the Catholic Church. A third (32 percent) also described themselves as already effectively Catholic when they were Episcopalians. These are by no means all of the themes expressed, and they are not mutually exclusive—some of the priests expressed more than one of these ideas—but together they are remarkably comprehensive. Ninety-six percent of responding Pastoral Provision priests mentioned some combination of these four themes in describing their conversion journey from the Episcopal Church to the Catholic Church. Let us look at each of them more closely.

Already Catholic

Almost one-third (32 percent) of the responding priests recalled having a Catholic self-understanding when they were Anglican. "I never thought of myself as not being Catholic, as an Anglican," one said. Or in the words of another, "[A]s an Anglican I always believed myself to be a Catholic anyway."

For many of these priests, joining the Catholic Church simply clarified institutionally what they understood, or came to understand, about themselves. One priest, trained in a Lutheran seminary, explained, "People kept saying to me, you're too Catholic, you're too Catholic. So it was a gradual understanding that I'm not too Catholic, I just am Catholic. So to be true to myself, I left." Another related, "Some of my friends, when I left the Episcopal Church, said, 'You never really were an Episcopalian. You just called yourself one.'"

For this reason, and those noted above, some denied—a few vociferously—that the word "convert" applied to them at all. All they had done, they objected, was to transfer jurisdiction or come into communion with the Catholic Church. One particularly vehement priest told me, "I hate that word 'convert.' That's what you say to Jews and Muslims and Buddhists and whatever. But if you're baptized, you come into full communion, to the Catholic Church. You're back to the rock whence you were hewn. I didn't convert. I was baptized a Christian, a child of God. ... But I was not in communion, and [then] I came into full communion with the Church. I went home."

Almost all the married priests, in fact, referred to their conversion as "coming home." While the subjective sense of homecoming may be a psychological feature of completed conversions of all types, it appears to be particularly strong among converts to Catholicism. A national support group for Protestant pastors who converted, or are in the process of converting, to the Catholic faith is named the Coming Home Network. In his study of evangelicals who became Catholic, McKnight reported that "in nearly every case, the convert believes that he or she has 'come home' or 'entered the fullness of the faith' or has experienced conversion to the 'truth of the Catholic faith.' "[9] This sense of homecoming fits with the Catholic Church's understanding, since Vatican II, of Protestantism as a privation, but not a complete rejection, of what the Catholic Church expresses fully. And just as Protestant groups following the Reformation left the original Church, so Protestants now returning to that Church may understandably have a heightened sense of rediscovering their origins. Since in many ways conversion accounts reflect a present state more than a past process, the phrase "coming home" thus expresses a Catholic evaluation of the result of conversion.

Moving Apart

Forty-two percent of responding priests spoke of themselves and the Episcopal Church as moving, at some point, in opposite directions. Half (50 percent) of these described the Episcopal Church as moving away from its own former moral or doctrinal positions, which they still held, leaving them marooned. As one priest, one of the earliest converts, put it, "By the time I left the Episcopal Church, or they left me, so to speak, the Catholic tradition of the Episcopal Church was dying out, if not completely nonexistent." A large majority (82 percent) recognized that, when they were Episcopalians, they had gradually moved toward positions and attitudes that were more Catholic. A third (32 percent) expressed both of these perceptions. The remainder overlapped with another distinct thematic group of respondents, who asserted that they had always been Catholic.

As noted earlier, the four themes summarized in this section were by no means mutually exclusive; many of the respondents expressed several of them. The themes were combined in many diverse ways, with a variety of emphasis and qualification, and were augmented by dozens of other comments that addressed less prominent or common issues of the convert priests' transitions to Catholicism.

Truth

The themes of truth and authority are closely related in almost all of the conversion accounts, though they interacted in different ways. Most (about 60 percent) of the priests began their journey to the Catholic Church with beliefs that were contrary to those of the Catholic faith. A third (32 percent) of the respondents reported that they had always agreed with the Catholic Church; another third (36 percent) described their discovery of Catholic truth as a central factor in their conversion journey. Most of this last group also mentioned "truth" as the first and most important factor in their conversion. When I asked, "What do you usually say to people who ask you why you became Catholic?" one priest responded, "I say this is where the truth is." Another expressed the same sentiment, "Truth. That's it. People ask me that all the time, and I say, truth. We decided the Catholic Church was true and right."

As this last comment makes explicit, the truth in question in these responses involves both true stances on morals and doctrine and an affirmation that the Catholic Church is the true church. What is not in view in these comments is fundamental religious truth, such as the existence or character of God or any core Christian doctrine. All of the Pastoral Provision priests were highly committed adherents of the Christian faith before they became Catholic. All of them had been baptized earlier in life, prior to becoming Catholic, and all of their baptisms were accepted and ratified by the Catholic Church upon entry. None of the converts describes his coming to Catholicism as a turn from unbelief to faith, or a discovery of God de novo. These conversions, in fact, were not conversions *to* Christianity but *within* Christianity. Although many involved spiritual experiences and existential searching, the transitions of these men into the Catholic Church were primarily religious, as distinct from spiritual, transitions.

For many of these men, as for generations of Anglican converts before them, leaving Anglicanism turned not on a new understanding of God but on a new understanding of Anglicanism. In the words of a recent literary convert, "The real question for me (as for Newman) was not whether Catholicism was right but whether I as an Anglican *was* a Catholic."[10] The factors motivating a departure from the Episcopal Church focused, therefore, on a process of self-definition or self-realization. This realization came both, or variously, as the priest's growing awareness that as an Anglican he was outside true Catholicism and that, albeit Anglican, his true identity was already Catholic.

Authority

If the truth of Catholic teaching was their primary attraction to the Catholic Church, the failed authority in the Episcopal Church was the primary push factor. Most (59 percent) of the converts cited the issue of religious authority as the underlying or implicit factor that impelled them to join the Catholic Church. This finding complicates and somewhat contradicts the popular notion that Anglican priests or lay intellectuals who become Catholic are primarily rejecting liberal trends in the Episcopal Church. There was an element of such rejection, but, with only one or two exceptions, it was not the major feature of any of the conversion accounts that I collected. A quarter (25 percent) of the respondents stated that the problem of authority was central to their decision to become Catholic, without mentioning any particular disputed moral issue. A minority of the priests did mention a particular moral stance of the Episcopal Church that had troubled them: ordaining women priests, openly homosexual priests, support for abortion, or laxity in permitting divorce. But only 10 to 22 percent mentioned each of these issues—women priests was the most frequent—and only a third (34 percent) mentioned any one of them.[11] Like Father James, almost all the priests who did mention one or more of these issues added that the real problem for them was not the particular issue involved, but that the debate and consideration of the issue in the Episcopal Church made clear to them fundamental deficiencies in the ability of Anglicanism to clarify or resolve disputed doctrinal issues. As one priest put it, "The primary issue was the issue of authority. The women's issue was an issue, but not because they were women. My issue . . . was how they handled it, and how they came to that place where they were being ordained. The house of bishops just sort of folded, and there was no discipline." Another observed, "The first thing that started me thinking about becoming Catholic were the moral issues, particularly the pro-life issue. . . . I felt that . . . there's no real authority. There's no one here to say, this is right and this is wrong. .... I began to look around and said, 'Where can I find that kind of authority that comes directly from Christ?' Well, there was only one place: the Catholic Church."

In addition to authority, about half of the priests who mentioned particular issues also cited ongoing institutional turmoil and controversy as a motivation to consider leaving the Episcopal Church; the cradle Episcopalians were three times as likely to cite this factor as were those who had converted to the Episcopal Church.

Truth Converts

While the issues of truth and authority were mentioned by virtually all the convert priests, about a third (36 percent) of them said that truth was central to their conversion. When asked, "What do you usually say to people who ask you why you became Catholic?" these priests expressed an exclusive and primary, even coercive, understanding of the demands of religious truth in their response. For example, one said, "[I answer:] The truth that the Catholic Church affirms. I'll compromise anything but truth." Another responded, "Because I became persuaded that the Catholic Church is the church. It was either that or give up my faith."

These "truth converts" exhibited a common set of characteristics, more in line with a classic intellectual conversion, than was the case for the remaining priest respondents. A fifth (21 percent) of them, compared to only 3 percent of the remaining priests, first became interested in the Catholic faith as a result of their seminary studies. Almost two-thirds (63 percent) of the truth converts, compared to less than half (47 percent) of the remaining priests, felt that Catholics had to agree with all Church teaching in order to be considered faithful. When asked about eight controversial behaviors, such as abortion, homosexual activity, or suicide, that the Catholic Church teaches are sinful, a higher proportion of truth converts than of the remaining priests responded "always a sin" on all eight items. For them, the attainment of truth, which they believed to be resident only in the Catholic Church, trumped all other considerations. Becoming Catholic may or may not have been practical or attractive, but for them it was not optional.

The truth converts joined the Catholic Church with fewer reservations or conditions, and have somewhat lower status today. None of the truth converts, but over half (56 percent) of the remaining respondents, thought that their Anglican orders were valid. A fifth (21 percent) of the truth converts, but only 7 percent of the remaining priests, reported that their interim transition was long, uncertain, or involved a difficult move. The truth converts were more likely (29 percent vs. 21 percent) to have faced financial struggles during the interim period, and less likely (47 percent vs. 59 percent) to say that they feel personally comfortable or at home in the Catholic Church. When asked "Would you have become Catholic if you knew you could not function as a priest?" none of the truth converts, but 38 percent of the remaining respondent priests, answered "No."

Many of the truth converts (and their wives), in fact, expressed concern that the generosity of the Pastoral Provision might encourage conversions that were not fully authentic. "At what point," one asked, "does the removal of a barrier to conversion become an incentive for conversion?" Another elaborated: "I think it is a very dangerous thing to be encouraging men to come into the Catholic Church with conditions. I will become a Catholic if you will ordain me. I will become a Catholic if you will set me up in an Anglican Use congregation. I think the only reason for becoming a Catholic is because it's Christ's Church. And you've come to realize that, and you know you need to be Catholic for your soul's health."

Only a third (33 percent) of the truth converts are serving as de facto pastors, compared to almost half (47 percent) of the remaining priests. On the other hand, the truth converts reported a greater sense of internal satisfaction. They were only about half as likely as were the remaining priests (28 percent vs. 54 percent) to regret the loss of friends as a result of their conversion. They reported slightly higher happiness and internal peace or relief in becoming Catholic. Seventy percent of the truth converts, but only 50 percent of the remaining priests, reported feeling closer to God today than a year ago. Nine in 10 (93 percent) of them, compared to only six in 10 (61 percent) of the remaining respondents, saw the Catholic Church as the fulfillment or completion of issues that arose during their Anglican sojourn.

Assessing the Factors Influencing Conversion

As suggestive as these themes are individually, in order to understand the resulting conversions in the aggregate it was necessary to map them onto the simplified religious migration schema described earlier. To accomplish this, I and two independent coders took each of the unique thematic comments identified in the conversion accounts and assigned them a position within one of the four quadrants (see Figure 4.1). Most of the comments were clearly interpretable in this way. To be as definitive as possible, we followed a conservative method in classifying comments that were not clear. In cases where we could not decide or did not agree which of the two alternate emphases of one of the two dimensions was stronger, we coded the comment neutral on the dimension in question. If we could not reach a conclusion with regard to both dimensions, we dropped the comment from the analysis. We were able to clearly classify 221 (76 percent) of 291 total comments, or thematic traces, representing 39 distinct themes. The distribution of themes on the conversion typology is shown in Figure 4.2.

Two clear trends are apparent in Figure 4.2. First, internal factors predominate over external ones in the conversion accounts. Two-thirds (68 percent) of the comments reference internal factors; less than a fifth (18 percent) refer to external factors. These were self-described internal journeys of conscience and identity, often taken with little regard to circumstances or even in the face of opposing conditions. The facilitating effect of social networks or community (Type 3 factors), which figures prominently in sociological accounts of conversion, is in little evidence here. Indeed, as we shall see, the most frequently mentioned difficulty in their conversion by these priests is the loss of the friends and community they enjoyed in the Episcopal Church.

Likewise, external conditions inducing the priests to leave the Episcopal Church (Type 4) are rarely mentioned (comprising only 6 percent of mentions) in the conversion accounts. On the contrary, many of the priests noted that financial (41 percent) and career/status (29 percent) conditions were better for them in the Episcopal Church. This probably does not mean that external financial or career conditions are not influential in these conversions, but rather that this group of clergy is self-selecting with regard

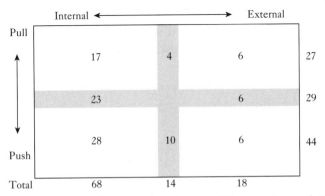

FIGURE 4.2 Distribution of Conversion Account Themes: Pastoral Provision Priests (in Percent)

to them. Given positive external reasons of higher income and career opportunity to prefer staying in the Episcopal Church, clergy who may otherwise have converted to the Catholic Church have doubtless chosen not to do so. Since all the Episcopal priests who could be deterred in this way were deterred, the Pastoral Provision priests consist, by self-selection, entirely of priests for whom such favorable external conditions in the Episcopal Church were not a sufficient deterrent to conversion.

The interior experience of conversion for these priests consisted of somewhat more push than pull. Of the 45 comments that could be allocated, 28 (62 percent) expressed a push. In accord with previous research, almost all the priests described their internal conversion journey as originating in push factors. At some point in the past, every Pastoral Provision priest was a committed Anglican priest; for almost all of them, factors in the Episcopal Church, rather than the attractiveness of the Catholic Church, initially changed that. Almost all of them began to feel some discomfort or incongruence with their role as Episcopal priests before they seriously considered the Catholic Church. This process is consistent with the fact that three-fourths of them were converts to Anglicanism; clearly these men had had an attraction to Anglicanism at some point. The personal process for the priests also reflects the fact that the Episcopal Church underwent major changes, while the Catholic Church changed very little, during their time as Episcopal priests. As noted earlier, many priests felt they were moving away from the Episcopal Church, or the Church was moving away from them, or both.

Although some married priests expressed a negative evaluation of some trends and stances, what stands out is the relative lack of sustained criticism of the Episcopal Church. The tone of the priests' comments is more sad and wistful than judgmental. They are quick to express appreciation of many of the qualities of Anglicanism and gratitude for their time in the Episcopal Church. Walker Percy makes a similar observation regarding former Anglican Catholic converts: "[T]here is a lasting affection for the lovely Anglican things, for the Book of Common Prayer, for dear England herself—and a sadness at her cutting off from the magisterium."[12]

Intellectual Conversions of Conscience

So far we have been discussing the themes in the priests' conversion accounts as if each comment was independent and of equal weight. In fact, most of the priests expressed multiple themes—the average was 4.2, ranging from 1 to 9 comments. I "connected the dots" between comments for each priest by converting them into a single scale value that reflected the four categories of our typology, then combined these values into a single point on the typology grid. To make these points comparable among all the priests, I then standardized them by weighting them by each priest's total number of comments. I excluded priests who did not have enough comments reflecting the four main themes to make this process meaningful, reducing the priests in this analysis to 36. This produced a single point on the typology grid that expressed the summary effect of all the factors influencing each priest's conversion. In essence, this point tells us what type of conversion, on balance, each priest experienced. These points are shown in Figure 4.3.

Figure 4.3 accentuates the strong interiority expressed of priests' conversion journeys. Even when external factors are mentioned, they are almost always offset or contextualized by more frequent mentions of internal factors. All but four (88 percent) of the resultant conversion accounts are on the internal side of the fence. Furthermore, nine of the responding priests, or a quarter of all those shown in Figure 4.3, fall at the most extreme (far left) value for internal factors. As with the individual comments, the conversion types fall in a broad range on the push-pull dimension, with the push conversions slightly more frequent than the pull conversions. All in all, the internal sense of no longer being able to remain in the Episcopal Church was a stronger factor for more of the priests than was the sense of attraction to the Catholic Church.

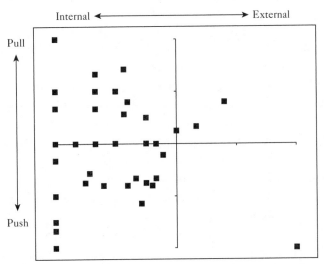

FIGURE 4.3 Distribution of Conversion Types: Pastoral Provision Priests

These findings demonstrate clearly that the conversions of the Pastoral Provision priests are highly interior, focused almost exclusively on internal beliefs and dispositions. In most ways, they conform rather closely to what sociologists identify as an "intellectual" or "activist" conversion. Lofland and Skonovd describe an intellectual conversion as one in which "individuals convert themselves in isolation from any actual interaction with devotees of the respective religion" by means of "individual, private investigation ... by reading books, watching television, attending lectures, or other impersonal or 'disembodied' ways." Most important, "a reasonably high level of belief occurs prior to actual participation in the religion's ritual and organizational activities."[13] All of these features are true of the Pastoral Provision priests. Lofland and Skonovd, focusing on young converts to deviant religions, note that this type of conversion is rare. Writing in 1981, they expected it to be more common in the future, since such conversions are fostered by the privatization of religion and by the ready availability of impersonal sources of information. They might also be more common, we might add, for older converts or for conversions among more established or mainstream religious groups.

By way of contrast, the typical Catholic priest who has converted to the Episcopal Church, and is now serving as an Episcopal priest, would conform most closely to Lofland and Skonovd's "affectional" conversion motif. In affectional conversions, personal attachments are central to the conversion process.[14] Fichter found that eight in 10 (81 percent) former Catholic priests who are now Episcopal priests married during their transition into the Episcopal Church.[15] Over half of them offered what Fichter called "reasons of the heart" (as opposed to "reasons of the head") to explain why they resigned their Catholic priesthood. In this case it would be the affectional bond with their wife, not necessarily with a group of Episcopalians, that functions as the pull factor into the Episcopal Church. The chief distinguishing element of affectional conversion is participation in the new religion before fully believing in it. This is hard to assess for this group. However, the fact that 61 percent of them married before joining the Episcopal Church suggests that participation, in this case in marriage, preceded Protestant belief. Fichter also reports that as many as a third of them were "[n]ot necessarily persuaded by the theology of the denomination they joined (although they found that it was "close enough")."[16] This suggests, consistent with an affectional conversion, that belief was not paramount in their conversion motives.[17] Similarly, previous research has found that theologically liberal clergy are more likely to leave the ministry, which is consistent with the experience of Catholic priests who left to become Episcopalian, but not with that of the Pastoral Provision priests, who are more theologically conservative than most Episcopalian (indeed, than most Catholic) clergy.[18]

Like the Pastoral Provision priests, the formerly Catholic Episcopal priests tended to minimize the boundary crossed in their conversion by maintaining that they were still Catholics in the Episcopal Church. The two groups of convert priests are also alike in that they separated their priestly identity from their denominational identity, working to retain the former while changing the latter. Priests in both groups could affirm the succinct statement of one Pastoral Provision priest: "I tell people, I never had any doubts about my vocation, I just didn't know what church it was in."

While almost exclusively interior, most of the married convert Catholic priests expressed their motivations as either predominantly push or predominantly pull. As Figure 4.3 shows, 42 percent of the conversions were dominated by internal push factors and 31 percent by internal pull factors. These emphases are not wholly distinct, and there is a lot of overlap in them, as indicated by the fact that one in six priests (17 percent) are equally weighted between push and pull factors in their conversion. Both the push and pull groups of priests broadly agreed on the themes of authority and truth, but they evaluated their institutional implications somewhat differently. The larger (push factors) group emphasizes the implications for identity of the Episcopal Church's loss of authority and departure from traditional doctrinal truth. For example, one priest from this group expressed, "I said, I've finally had enough. This is ridiculous. I was embarrassed to be an Episcopalian. . . . You might as well just forget trying to defend and know orthodox belief."

For these priests, the pressing concern was for maintaining their own identity in the context of a church that had collectively adopted an identity that they judged incompatible with theirs. This was expressed most often as a concern for the authenticity or effectiveness of their ministry. They were not denying that the Catholic Church is true, but their focus was on the problem presented by the fact that the Episcopal Church is not true. Their leaving the Episcopal Church was primarily an act of self-definition.

For the pull group, the focus was not on the perceived absence of truth in the Episcopal Church, but on the presence of truth in, or authenticity of, the Catholic Church. At issue was not so much their ability to minister to others, but their own salvation. And the context of concern was not so much personal identity as it was conscience. As one priest in this group said, "Where I'd come down [was] that given the opportunity to know the truth, then one at that point has a moral obligation to live that truth. And I would say, along with Lumen Gentium, that that's going to compel you to move into the fullness of the Catholic faith." The reference here is to the Second Vatican Council's Dogmatic Constitution on the Church (*Lumen Gentium*) 14: "Whosoever, therefore, knowing that the Catholic Church was made necessary by Christ, would refuse to enter or to remain in it, could not be saved." Another priest in this group said simply, "Through my own prayer and study and reflection, I reached an understanding that our Lord Jesus had founded one only Church. And having reached that understanding, I had no choice. I had to become a Roman Catholic."

Leap, Then Look

Consistent with the above, the married priests typically converted intellectually, in the abstract, before they actually encountered the Catholic Church concretely. This sometimes led to difficult practical struggles, as they adjusted and worked to bring their social, professional, family, and liturgical lives in line with their new internal state. One married priest observed, "As converts, we're Catholics by conviction and not by convenience. For a lot of us, it wasn't convenient. But it was conviction." Their attraction, moreover, was to the Catholic idea, and the ideal Catholicism they have subscribed to is often far removed from the actual, concrete Catholic community they join. The irony of this is not lost on many of them. One said, "People ask me what's the difference between the Catholic Church and the church I grew up in, and I say, 'Well, the Catholic Church is a little too Protestant for me.' And it is."

For many married priests, becoming Catholic was a kind of double conversion, first to Catholic conviction, then to Catholic culture or ethos. As one married priest articulated this double dynamic, "I underwent an intellectual conversion, ... [but] when I became Catholic, there was at least a part of me that also wanted to become Catholic culturally ... it's not just the ideas of being Catholic, I want to embrace the whole thing, warts and all, whatever it is." For some, this sense of having to adjust other areas of one's life to an intellectual conviction extended even to spiritual or theological matters. One married priest commented, "My journey was first intellectual, and then spiritual. In many ways, I became a Catholic reluctantly." Another observed, "I made my decision to become a Catholic, before I fully understood every single nuance of Catholic theology. I'm still learning it."

The extent of struggle and displacement indicates the unusual importance to these men of religious truth or sincerity. As clergy, they can be expected to have been more committed to their former beliefs than lay converts may be. Nearly all profess to be highly religious in their childhood and adolescent development. But the importance of aligning with religious truth, or of operating on a secure religious basis, takes an overriding, perhaps obsessive, place in their lives relative to other practical, professional, and relational matters. One priest acknowledged this focus by relating it to the Gospel image of the pearl of great price, in which Jesus said, "Again, the kingdom of heaven is like unto a merchant man, seeking goodly pearls: who, when he had found one pearl of great price, went and sold all that he had, and bought it."[19] The priest told me, "It is kind of a Gospel thing, a pearl of great price, this deep interior call of God. . . . You've got the pearl of great price, you know, but all his friends and neighbors are probably saying, what an idiot. All he has is this silly pearl. They don't understand, and it messes everything up. His wife was probably saying, don't sell that, it's not worth it for a stupid pearl."

Single, Double, and Serial Converts

Three-quarters (75 percent) of the married priests were not raised in the Episcopal Church, but, like Father James in the previous chapter, had already converted to the Episcopal Church from another Protestant denomination before eventually converting again to the Catholic Church. Most Pastoral Provision priests, in other words, were not just converts, but double converts. One in eight (13 percent) were serial converts who had changed religions three or more times. The remaining quarter (25 percent) were cradle Episcopalians who had been ordained Episcopal priests before converting, only once, to the Catholic Church. The single converts were noticeably different from the double converts in many ways, some of which were accentuated among the serial converts.

The married Catholic priests who had been raised in the Episcopal Church had higher levels of stability, devotion, and agreement with Catholic teaching than did the double converts (See Table 4.2.).[20] The double converts were a little more likely to have been raised in a household of mixed religious identities, in which the mother and father were of different faiths, or of no religious affiliation at all. This was even more likely to be the case among the serial converts. Among the priests who had switched three or more times before becoming Catholic, almost half (46 percent) had been

Table 4.2 Selected Comparisons Between Single and Double Converts (in Percent)

Item	Single Convert (Cradle Episcopalian) $n = 21$	Double Convert (includes Serial Converts) $n = 64$
Mother and father of different religions	29	38
Raised with no religious affiliation	0	10
Had a "born again" experience	14	56
Has spoken in tongues	0	25
Never married	0	16
Married more than once	0	13
Age at joining the Episcopal Church (median)	0	20
Age at Episcopalian ordination (median)	27	29
Tenure as Episcopal priest (median)	20	18
Self-described "High Church" Episcopal priest	100	69
Was a member of the Society of the Holy Cross	86	32
Years considering Catholic conversion (mean)	1.0	2.3
Age at joining the Catholic Church (median)	47	47
Length of interim period in years (mean)	2.6	4.0
Received by Catholic bishop "very well"	86	74
Has a "great deal of confidence" in the church	27	49
Conversion loss: Beauty of Anglican liturgy	39	62
Conversion gain: Internal peace, relief from conflicts	31	8
Conversion gain: New friends and support	31	23
"Closer to God" than this time last year	79	53
Never practices Eucharistic adoration	8	25
Makes confession at least once a month	57	42
Makes an annual retreat	83	66
Practices a devotion to one or more saints	83	50
Celebrates Mass daily	71	50

(continued)

Table 4.2 (Continued)

Item	Single Convert (Cradle Episcopalian) $n = 21$	Double Convert (includes Serial Converts) $n = 64$
Sex outside marriage is always a sin	100	78
Abortion is always a sin	100	89
Using condoms as AIDS defense is always a sin	83	61
Opposes ordaining married men as a rule	64	44
Opposes readmitting resigned married ex-priests	83	38
Social reform is of "great" or "some" importance for satisfaction	82	61

raised in a mixed religious household, and a quarter (27 percent) had been raised with no religious affiliation. The double converts also had a greater variety of religious experience. Over half (56 percent) of them, compared to only 14 percent of the cradle Episcopalians, had had an evangelical experience of being "born again." A quarter (25 percent) of them, but none of the cradle Episcopalians, had had a Pentecostal experience of speaking in tongues. The double converts were also more varied in their participation in the institution of marriage. Thirteen percent of the double converts, but none of the cradle Episcopalians, had been married more than once; 16 percent, but none of the cradle Episcopalians, had never married.

All of the cradle Episcopalians were of the High Church or Anglo-Catholic variety; this was true of only two-thirds (69 percent) of the double converts. Almost nine in 10 (86 percent) of the cradle Episcopalians, but less than a third (32 percent) of the double converts, had been members of the Episcopalian Society of the Holy Cross, the Anglo-Catholic group whose petition, in part, prompted the Pastoral Provisions. Compared to the double converts, the cradle Episcopalians were also more likely (22 percent vs. 9 percent) to have attended Nashotah House, the most Anglo-Catholic Episcopal seminary, and to have avoided Virginia Theological Seminary, the most "low church" seminary (6 percent vs. 11 percent).

Overall, though, there was no relationship between conversion and having attended any particular Episcopal seminary. The seminaries or theological schools most commonly attended by the Pastoral Provision priests were Nashotah House (12 percent), Virginia Theological Seminary (10 percent), Berkeley Divinity School at Yale (8 percent), General Theological Seminary, New York (7 percent), and Oxford University (7 percent). One in 10 priests was involved in military chaplaincy as an Episcopalian; this is over 10 times the rate of military chaplaincy among Episcopal priests in general. Service as a military chaplain exposed priests to frequent contact with Catholic priests serving as chaplains, and provided financial stability for some of the converts as they prepared for Catholic ordination.

The double converts typically joined the Episcopal Church during college or seminary training. The median age at joining was 20; three-fourths (75 percent) of them became Episcopalian by age 24. On average, they became ordained by age 29, two years older than the single converts, but spent two fewer years in the Episcopal priesthood, with the result that both single and double converts joined the Catholic Church at the same age (47).

The double converts appear to be somewhat more idealistic than the cradle Episcopalians, who are more practical. The cradle Episcopalians tended to spend substantially less time (2.6 years vs. 4 years for the double converts) in the interim period between churches. They were also more likely (86 percent vs. 74 percent) to report that their Catholic bishop had received them "very well." Yet the double converts were much more likely (49 percent vs. 27 percent) to say they had a great deal of confidence in the Church. The cradle Episcopalians were much less likely (39 percent vs. 62 percent) to miss the beauty of Anglican liturgy, and more likely (31 percent vs. 8 percent) to acknowledge a sense of peace and relief from conflict following their Catholic conversion. They were also somewhat more likely (31 percent vs. 23 percent) to report gaining new friends and support in becoming Catholic.

The cradle Episcopalians also reported a higher level of devotional practice and assent to the Catholic faith than did the double converts. The single converts are more active than the double converts in going to confession, making an annual retreat, Eucharistic adoration, and practicing devotion to a Catholic saint. Seven in 10 (71 percent) of the single converts, compared to half (50 percent) of the double converts, celebrate Mass every day. Perhaps as a result, the single converts were more likely (79 percent vs. 53 percent) to report that they feel they have grown closer to God in the past year.

Although all the Pastoral Provision priests expressed strong assent to Catholic doctrines, the single converts expressed notably stronger assent than did the double converts. All of the single converts, but 10–20 percent fewer of the double converts, affirmed the official Catholic teachings that extramarital sex and having an abortion are always sinful. Eight in 10 (82 percent) of the single converts, compared to only six in 10 (61 percent) of the double converts, said that using condoms as a defense against AIDS is always sinful. The difference between the two groups was even larger for current Catholic positions on non-doctrinal questions. On these questions the single converts agreed with current Catholic practice much more strongly than did the double converts. Sixty-four percent of the single converts, but only 44 percent of the double converts, agreed with current Catholic practice in opposing the regular ordination of married men; and over twice as many single converts as double converts (83 percent vs. 38 percent) opposed the idea of considering some way to readmit ex-priests to some level of priestly ministry. The single converts were also more likely to affirm the Catholic emphasis on social reform as a source of personal satisfaction.

The serial converts, who switched religions even more frequently than did the double converts, were even more likely to have had a weak or unstable childhood religious home environment (see Table 4.3). Almost half of the serial converts did not have a mother and father of the same religion (46 percent) and/or did not attend church at least once a week as a child (45 percent). Over a quarter (27 percent) were raised with no religious affiliation. The serial converts were even less likely than were those who converted exactly twice to have been High Church Episcopalians and to feel closer to God than they did a year ago.[21]

Truth and Authority

The narrative context and associations of the themes of truth and authority were somewhat different for the cradle Episcopalians than for the double converts. While those who had converted to the Episcopal Church often described a process of becoming increasingly Catholic while in the Episcopal Church, those born Episcopalian were likely to describe themselves as having always been Catholic in their self-understanding. While the issue of truth was important for both groups, it was evaluated in subtly different ways. For the double converts, the primary problem resulting from the failure of Episcopalian authority was the loss of the ability to preserve and know traditional doctrinal truth, which they regained

Table 4.3 Selected Effects by Number of Switches
to the Catholic Church (in Percent)

Item	One (Cradle Episcopalian) $n = 21$	Two (Double Convert) $n = 42$	Three or more (Serial Convert) $n = 11$
Mother and father of different religions	29	36	46
Raised with no religious affiliation	0	5	27
Weekly church attendance growing up	80	91	55
Born again experience	14	53	64
Age at joining the Episcopal Church	0	18	25
"High Church" Episcopal priest	100	71	60
Number of children	2.9	2.9	3.8
"Closer to God" than this time last year	79	61	27

by converting to the Catholic faith. In most cases, these men joined the Episcopal Church because they believed the historic teachings and affirmations of Anglicanism; ironically, they often left the Episcopal Church for the same reason. Many agreed with the sentiment put cogently by one priest, speaking of himself and his wife: "We didn't leave the Episcopal Church; the Episcopal Church left us."

For the cradle Episcopalians, the primary problem that followed from the failure of Episcopalian authority was the loss of Anglican catholicity, with an attendant loss of confidence in the validity of the sacraments and their own orders. The former group was more disturbed that the Episcopal Church was heterodox or in error; the latter was more disturbed that it had become schismatic and thus no longer legitimate. This difference is seen most clearly in the different evaluations that each group gave, on average, of the significance of the ordination of women. Almost all (93 percent or more) of the priests in both groups opposed the ordination of women. The double converts, however, tended to speak of the ordination of women as one of a number of issues, such as abortion, homosexuality, and divorce, on which the Church had failed to preserve revealed truth. The cradle

Episcopalians, on the other hand, uniformly lamented the ordination of women primarily as a step that irrevocably halted any possibility of reunion with the Catholic Church.[22]

Where Do the Converts Come From?

The double converts, who by definition were not born into an Episcopalian family, were raised in a wide variety of other Protestant denominations (see Table 4.4). After Episcopalian, the Pastoral Provision priests were raised, in descending order of frequency, as Methodists, Baptists, Generic Protestants (such as a community church), Lutherans, another form of Anglican, and a variety of other groups. The percent raised in each of these groups more or less corresponds to the size of each group in the US population. Three percent were raised with no religion.

Only four of the priests were raised in another Anglican denomination. All of these were raised outside the United States—three in the Church of England and one in an Anglican church in Australia—and did not convert to the Episcopal Church so much as transfer into it. Thus, although most Pastoral Provision priests converted to the Episcopal Church, and became committed Anglicans to the point of ordination to the priesthood, none of them actually converted from another Anglican church or denomination. This point dramatizes an unusual characteristic of the range of denominations in Table 4.4. As noted above, Protestant religious switchers typically tend strongly to switch "close to home," that is, between the most similar groups. We would thus expect converts to the Episcopal Church to be most likely to come from other liberal Protestant denominations, and least likely to come from conservative or independent groups. But this is clearly not the pattern for the group of converts who have become the Pastoral Provision priests. Compared to the typical religious convert, the Pastoral Provision priests appear to have come from all over.

Figure 4.4 illustrates this point. For this figure, Protestant denominations have been arranged into Liberal, Moderate, and Conservative.[23] The numbers report the proportion of converts to the Episcopal Church coming from each of these categories compared to their proportion in the US population. They can be interpreted simply as the odds, or probability, that an Episcopalian convert would come from each category. A figure of 1.0 expresses the absence of any particular tendency for members of the religious category to have converted to the Episcopal Church; an amount

Table 4.4 Origin Religious Affiliation of the Pastoral Provision Priests (n = 84)

Denomination	n	Percent
Episcopal Church	18	21
Methodist	14	17
Baptist	11	13
General Protestant	5	6
Lutheran	4	5
Other Anglican	4	5
Presbyterian	3	4
United Church of Christ	3	4
Disciples of Christ	3	4
Dutch Reformed	2	2
No Religion	3	4
Other**	5	6
Unknown (No information)	9	11

**Includes* one Assemblies of God, two Independent Fundamental Church of America (IFCA), one Catholic (but never baptized), and one Zen Buddhist.

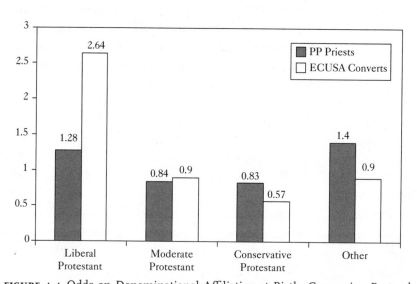

FIGURE 4.4 Odds on Denominational Affiliation at Birth, Comparing Pastoral Provision Priest "Double Converts" and All US Episcopalian Converts

Source for comparison: General Social Survey (NORC) 1972–2008 (n= 53,043). Data are a probability sample of all US adults. Non-Protestants, Black Protestants, and Episcopalians are excluded.

greater or less than 1.0 means that they are respectively more or less likely be Episcopal converts (than their initial proportion in the population would indicate). As expected, US Episcopalian converts are over twice (2.6 times) as likely to come from another liberal Protestant denomination. These odds drop sharply to 0.9 for a moderate Protestant origin, and decline further to 0.57 for conservative Protestants. The Episcopalian converts who later were ordained Pastoral Provision priests, by contrast, are only a little more likely (at 1.3) to have come from a liberal Protestant denomination. They are less than half as likely (2.6 vs. 1.3) to have done so than the typical Episcopal convert, and are half again more likely (.83 vs. .57) to have come from a conservative Protestant origin or from some other denomination (1.4 vs. .9).

This finding suggests that, just as Anglicanism does theologically, for many of the double convert priests the Episcopal Church serves as a kind of sociological bridge to Catholicism. Unlike other Catholic converts, Anglicanism is not a bridge for them because they already have an affinity with the Catholic Church, but precisely because they do not. The Episcopal Church, which classically has encompassed a broad range of perspectives from Low Church evangelical to High Church Catholic, offers an accessible point of entry for these disproportionately conservative converts. Even though it has moved in a decidedly liberal direction in past decades, the formal expressions of Anglican theology are readily accessible to an evangelical Protestant. The affirmation of Scripture and conscience against the constraints of tradition and authority that characterize the Thirty-Nine Articles of Religion and the Anglican divines are quite compatible with a Baptist perspective. At the same time, congregations and rectors in the Episcopal Church enjoy a large degree of autonomy, which promotes the institutionalization of the varying perspectives in the Church on a local level. Although a conservative or Catholic-leaning Protestant is not likely to find the average Episcopal congregation in line with those perspectives, if such a potential convert intentionally seeks out such a congregation, he or she is likely to find one. The social status constraints, further, that may have dampened conservative-to-Episcopalian switching in the past, and are perhaps still stronger in England, are no longer prominent factors in the United States; these men, moreover, all of whom have since become Catholic, are probably less affected by status considerations than most.

Conclusion: Protesting Protestantism

As we have seen, the issue of the teaching authority of the Church was crucial for almost all the convert priests. Yet the intellectual journey traveled by most of them contains a kind of paradox, or, more harshly, a contradiction, with regard to the issue of authority. To some extent, this paradox is present in any religious conversion, or for that matter any change of allegiance; but it is particularly acute for religious professionals or priests, and has a particularly poignant history with regard to Anglican-Catholic conversions. The claim of the Catholic faith is that religious truth does not reliably derive from personal judgment but from the collective teaching of the Church. A faithful Catholic receives the teaching of the Church as superior to his or her own personal opinion. But in order to submit to the teaching authority of a new church, these ordained priests had to reject the teaching authority of the church in which they were already serving. In essence, each of them took a stance toward the Episcopal Church that they were to reject as impermissible toward the Catholic Church.

In this regard, their movement to the Catholic faith first involved a rethinking of their Protestant beliefs and orientation. The fact that three-fourths of them first converted from a "more" Protestant denomination to Anglicanism, the most Catholic of Protestant churches, makes this clear. The rethinking involved may be more comprehensive for those of a more evangelical orientation, but even among the Anglo-Catholic cradle Episcopalians, becoming Catholic entailed a definite change of mind about the validity of the Episcopal Church order under which these priests were ordained and had ministered.

Although for most it did not occur in a social or relational vacuum, the process of rethinking was primarily an internal one, involving not only frequently difficult external disruptions, but even more important, in the experience of the priests themselves, wrestling and struggling with former deeply held convictions. This was stimulated for some, and exacerbated for all, by the contrasting process of change in the Episcopal Church, which on many issues was moving in the opposite direction from the convert priests. Having lost the argument with their Church added tension and urgency to the argument within themselves. Ironically, in order to defend positions that were faithful to the Anglican tradition they had inculcated, they had to critically re-evaluate the Anglican hierarchy to which they owed loyalty.

In such a situation, it is possible to conclude that the problem is unfaithful leadership. Most dissenting Episcopal priests, including those studied here, have adopted or assumed such a view. The Anglican structure is sound, they believe, but the current leaders have abused or subverted their responsibilities to such an extent that the Church under their jurisdiction has become corrupted. In the Biblical image, they are false shepherds leading the flock astray. Such a conclusion leads to "diocese shopping" among Episcopal priests, or, more severely, to defection to an Anglican splinter group. Such breakaway groups often adopt, with minor adjustments or additions, the Church structures and liturgical forms of the Episcopal Church of a former era, attempting to replicate what the Episcopal Church would have been if it had not been "led astray." These groups, which prefer to call themselves "Continuing Anglican Churches," argue that they are maintaining the true, historic Anglican faith and order, in contrast to the Episcopal Church, which has subverted both.

The Pastoral Provision priests, by and large, have gone a step further, in concluding that the problem is not merely political but systemic. They perceive that the possibility, and perhaps the inevitability, of unfaithful leaders is not a peripheral aberration, but a core component of Anglicanism. The problem is not merely on the surface of current conditions, but goes all the way down. This recognition, of course, mirrors and is no doubt influenced by the similar conviction to which John Henry Newman eventually came. Despite its traditional forms of worship and socially conservative tendencies, at the root of Episcopalian governance is adherence to the Protestant principle of private belief. If each person can accurately perceive or interpret Christian truth on his or her own, then a democratic process that amalgamates individual views can establish collective policy regarding truth, or its best approximation. The Episcopal Church, not incidentally, prides itself on having one of the largest and most representative forms of democratic governance of any institution in the world. Such a structure of authority enables openness to distinctly new understandings of Christian truth. But if Christian truth does not originate with individuals, but is rather received by them, then democratic Church structures will not reliably reflect that truth. Indeed, if Christian tradition has an objective content that must be transmitted to successive generations, then only central hierarchical structures like those of the Catholic Church, which cannot easily be influenced by political forces from below, can be assured fidelity to the received truth. Something like this realization developed, some more and some less, in the thinking of the priests who chose to avail themselves of the Pastoral Provision.

Many of the convert priests expressed some sense of this argument by noting, as we have seen, that although they were troubled with the Episcopal Church's changing mores on one or more particular issues, such as divorce, abortion, or ordaining women or homosexuals, what led to their leaving the Church was not that issue in itself, but the way the issue was addressed, that is, by the use of democratic procedures that overturned long-standing tradition. In the eyes of the convert priests, by departing from Catholic order, the Episcopal Church effectively undermined its own legitimacy. This realization reversed the polarity of the authority question: fidelity now became a motive, not to obey, but to leave, the Church.

5

What Are Married Priests' Wives Like?

Introduction

"What kind of woman would marry a priest!?" Speaking in the church foyer after the service, the speaker abruptly let go of my hand as her voice rose in disapproval. The friend she was visiting had just informed her, with a broad smile, that the priest she was meeting was married. "A truly wonderful woman," I replied, explaining to her that we had the Pope's permission for our exceptional arrangement. Her stern visage slowly began to soften, and when, a few minutes later, she met my wife, she was all smiles.

Yet it's a good question: What kind of woman *would* marry a priest? What personal qualities and marital arrangements are necessary for a healthy marriage to coexist with priestly ministry? How does the wife of a Catholic priest understand her place in the Church? What struggles does she face, and what gifts does she bring to the lived experience of pastoral ministry?

Such issues are the focus of this chapter. They are important for a number of reasons.

As the Catholic Church opens the door to more married Anglican clergy, an understanding of their wives and the components of a successful and happy clergy marriage takes on greater practical importance. Our knowledge of clergy marriages in other religious settings can be enhanced by considering, as a new point of comparison, the particular character of Catholic priests' marriages. Not least, a look at the characteristics of priests' wives also breaks new ground in our understanding of priests and marriage that has implications for the rule of celibacy.

Ministry and Ministers' Wives
Wife as Liability or Asset?

In Catholic clerical discourse and culture, the possession of a wife is widely assumed to be a liability for priestly ministry—hence the rule of celibacy. Married priests, it is believed, experience competition between Church and family concerns that limit their availability for ministry when compared to their celibate counterparts. In Chapter 7 we will discuss this claim more at length, as an argument for clergy celibacy. Here I only note that, in order to properly understand the implications of how the married priest couples handle these possible tensions and the other mutual influences of ministry and marriage, we need to consider them in the context of an important but often overlooked element in priestly marriages: the expectations of clergy wives.

In direct contrast to Catholic thinking, in Protestant ministerial culture and experience having a wife is a career benefit. As more clergy than not came to marry in Protestant churches following the Reformation, the clergy wife developed a distinctive role and presence in parish life. Most Protestant churches did not have anything approaching religious orders for women, and would not begin ordaining women until the mid-twentieth century. The role of the minister's wife served as one of the few outlets for women with skills or desires for religious leadership. Becoming a minister's wife allowed her to serve the Church through her husband, and put her at the center of parish life, with a certain prominence among the women. By the mid-nineteenth century, the expectation that the minister's wife served as a kind of adjunct to support and augment the work of the pastor had become generally established in most Protestant settings. By the mid-twentieth century, researchers were able to identify a set of distinct traits or functions that comprised a well-defined role of the pastor's wife.

Wallace Denton, writing in 1962, identified two main role expectations for minister's wives. First, he affirmed the expectation of co-ministry or support for the work of the parish: "Ministers' wives expect and are expected to participate, to a greater or lesser degree, in their husbands' work. . . . One of the primary aspects for the role of the wife of a minister is her participation in her husband's work."[1] Second, the wife is expected to foster a supportive and positive home environment to replenish the spiritual strength of her husband for service to the Church. On this point,

Oates quotes Oswald Dykes, writing at the turn of the twentieth century, who explains clearly the justification for this expectation:

> In no other calling is a man so dependent on home influences for keeping him day by day in the fittest condition for doing his public duty in the holy ministry; simply because in no other calling does the quality of work depend so absolutely on the moral and religious state of the workman. . . . To be able to go forth from home to one's work in a self-collected and reverent mood, and to return to it as an arbor of refreshment where one is sure of sympathy—all this means a great deal to the busy pastor, and it is precisely this which a suitable partner and a carefully ordered household ought to furnish.[2]

Douglas (1965) found that a minister's wife was expected to be a godly wife and mother; exemplary in service and participation in the Church; a teacher or trainer of other women in spiritual matters; and to visit the sick and grieving. She "was to uphold a mood of friendliness, graciousness, sincerity, flexibility and tact while maintaining a sense of humor, wisdom and humility."[3] In 1955 the prominent Methodist minister and Yale professor Halford Luccock, writing in *The Christian Century*, summarized these various roles in terms of three traits sought after in a minister's wife. First, the minister's wife is expected to be a "professional saint." Like the minister, she must be aware that her behavior is subject to special scrutiny to see that she sets a good example of Christian character. So she must be "a living example, meek, humble and a woman of prayer." Second, she is the "wifely pastor's assistant," helping with the work of the Church wherever needed, whether teaching Sunday School or producing the weekly bulletin or cleaning the altar linen. A special skill in music is an advantage for meeting this expectation. Third, she must be utterly devoted to supporting her husband in his exertions, sheltering him from undue demands and distractions so he can be more fully available to the congregation.[4]

By the mid-twentieth century, the co-pastoring support of a wife had become not only helpful to a minister but also essential. In the late 1920s, McAfee had underlined domestic support as the most fundamental requirement of a minister's wife. Whether the minister's wife "genuinely enters into the spirit of their joint task" or "is indifferent to the work of her minister-husband," he observed, can make or break his ministry.

"He was called to throw his life into the work and he cannot do it to the full unless he is sustained in the effort at his home."[5] By the 1960s, the additional traits described by Luccock above were no longer optional; they had become rigid and circumscribed. With respect to these expectations, Denton depicts the pastor's wife as a slave "forced to follow a predetermined path of action as a train does [without] even the freedom of being an automobile."[6]

These roles are still in force today, though, like many marital roles, they may have been stronger and more fixed prior to the 1960s. One of the best indications of their current persistence is found in the job market for Protestant pastors. Most Protestant congregations hire pastors directly, following a competitive interview and evaluation process that mirrors the process for secular corporate employment. In the competition for parish placement, single candidates are clearly at a disadvantage. They are often perceived in less positive personal terms, as less mature or a potential source of trouble. Zikmund notes that search committees may view single clergy as "potential homosexuals, or almost as bad, swinging heterosexuals."[7] On the other hand, a wife who fulfills the traditional roles provides valuable support for her husband's ministry. In addition, there is also often a sense that the congregation is pleased to gain a wife who will be active in the work of the Church as an additional, unpaid, bonus for hiring the minister.

The advantage of marriage for a pastor is stronger in the evangelical wing of Protestantism, where the cultural and practical pressures noted above are buttressed by a reading of Scripture that favors married Church leaders and a desire to reassert a model of family values in the face of cultural threats to the traditional family. Evangelical pastoral job announcements often explicitly note that they are looking for a "family man" (or, increasingly, woman). Only one in seven (14 percent) of liberal Protestant pastors are unmarried, about half of the corresponding proportion in the general US population. Among evangelical pastors, the proportion unmarried drops to only one in 20 (5 percent). R. Albert Mohler, president of Southern Baptist Theological Seminary in Louisville, Kentucky, tells seminary students that "if they remain single, they need to understand that there's going to be a significant limitation on their ability to serve as a pastor."[8]

Recent research has found that the traditional role of the minister's wife has not disappeared, but has been complicated by the overlay of additional expectations, such as work outside the home, that add struggles with role confusion and role ambiguity into the mix.[9] The pastors' wives whom Douglas studied in the 1960s struggled, predictably, with loneliness due to lack of friendships, stress due to a lack of time and money, and the feeling of being on guard because of a lack of privacy. Brunette-Hill's recent review of the literature identified a similar list of "four primary areas of concern for the pastor's wife: a relatively low standard of living; limited or no choice in housing type, size, style or location; a diminished sense of personal identity, and an agonizing loneliness."[10] Subsequent research has confirmed that clergy wives still lack privacy, or "live in a fishbowl."[11] They also experience stress due to demands made by the ministry environment on their personal and family life.[12] Recent studies of Southern Baptist clergy wives concluded that "[t]he struggles of the pastor's wife in the 21st century have not changed much from those struggles in the 20th century and before."[13]

Corporate and Clergy Wives

Many of the characteristics of the clergy wife role are not unique to a religious context, but tend to occur in any marriage where one partner is in a highly demanding or absorbing career role. It is probably not a coincidence that the Protestant "clergy wife" role, which was first studied at any length just after World War II, bears many similarities to role of the "corporate wife," which was first identified during the same period. Both can be seen as reflecting the more general cultural trend since the mid-twentieth century toward conforming marriage to the needs and norms of the workplace. William Whyte, in his studies of corporate conformity that led to the publication of *The Organization Man*, identified the importance of the characteristics of the corporate executive's wife to his career.[14] Rosabeth Kanter's seminal 1970s study of gender roles in a large industrial corporation presented a detailed account of formal and informal ways that corporate wives subordinated both their own goals and the needs of the family to their husbands' careers.[15] Clergy wives who exemplify the role, including the married Catholic priests' wives, have exhibited many of the same qualities.

Like corporate wives, a clergy wife is technically not an employee of the Church her husband serves, but her life is bound up in the parish life and culture. She is often called on, as are corporate wives, to support his work in social ways, to greet parishioners and host dinners, and to be ready to adjust to the demands of his schedule. Only rarely was a priest's wife formally employed by the Church to do any of these things. Nonetheless, her relationship to the parish is sociologically similar to that of an employee. On this point regarding corporate wives, Kanter cites Levinson, an industrial psychiatrist: "when a man has a responsible leadership post, *for all practical purposes both he and his wife are employed.*"[16] We might paraphrase, when a man is a parish pastor, for all practical purposes both he and his wife serve the parish.

Clergy wives who protest any involvement in the Church on the ground that the Church did not hire them, but only their husband, misunderstand the social reality of their situation, though they may be technically or legally correct. Because the pastor, like the corporation executive, is in an iconic leadership role, the contribution of the pastor's wife to a parish has a symbolic worth far above the instrumental value of the specific work that she does. It is impossible for her to reject all parish involvement without the parish feeling slighted and having it reflect poorly on her husband's relationship with the parish. The question is not whether the pastor's wife will be involved in the parish, but whether she will be involved well.

Not only do the roles and dynamics of marriage and the workplace overlap for clergy marriages for much the same reasons as they do for corporate marriages, but the conflation of marriage and ministry is even stronger, since marriage itself is central to most churches' social vision and since part of the "business" of the Church is to promote loving and happy marriages. Although clergy wives are, theoretically and ideally, individuals with their own relationship to God and the Church, in lived reality their marriage to a priest makes it practically impossible for clergy wives to disentangle their relationship with God or the Church from their relationship with their husband. The priests' wives often carried support for their husband's work to a higher level than a corporate wife, becoming actively involved in the substantive work of the Church in ways traditional for clergy wives, such as in music, child care, teaching women, or the altar guild.

Even the clergy wives who were not as actively involved made sacrifices for the Church, in terms of both real and opportunity costs, that were comparable to those of corporate wives. As with corporations, clergy career progression, which typically involves pastoring successively larger congregations, required frequent relocation. Just as the corporate wives, the "husband absence" induced by a parish's time demands on their pastor left the wife to be the full-time caregiver for their children, and often precluded or delayed her pursuit of further education or her own career.

Kanter reported that the ideal corporate wife provided technical, social, and symbolic support in succession as her husband's career progressed.[17] The engineer's wife who helped with research and making business contacts progressed to hosting social events when her husband became manager, then to helping him project the friendly, familiar (literally) face of the corporation when he rose to senior executive. By contrast, since a pastorate includes, and conflates, the technical, social, and symbolic roles of the minister from the first day he is on the job, clergy wives tended to provide the same types of support, not in succession, but all at once, from the beginning of their husband's career.

Both Whyte and Kanter observed that corporate culture often informally evaluated the executive's wife on behavior that was properly private and domestic. Kanter quotes Wilbert Moore on this point: "The man, and his wife, simply cannot divest themselves of corporate identification. Their every activity outside the immediate family is likely to be tinged with a recognition of the man's position. He represents the company willy-nilly. His area of privacy, and that of his wife, is very narrowly restricted."[18] Substituting "parish" for "company," this statement would apply equally well to clergy wives. As noted above, even when not directly involved in parish functions, a clergy wife is expected to represent the faith in every aspect of her life—and people are actively inspecting her for evidence of this. What type of clothes she wears, how she manages her children, the clubs and civic activities she takes part in, are, for both the corporate and the clergy wife, subject to intense scrutiny.

Like clergy wives, corporate wives struggle with the tension or contradiction between inclusion and exclusion in their husband's workplace, sentimentality or instrumentality in friendships, and the limits on their privacy. The dominating context of the corporation, or parish, both encourages breadth and limits the depth of friendships. The stresses of executive life on friendships that Kanter describes would be recognizable to any pastor's wife:

[F]riendships were no longer a personal matter but had business implications. . . . Awareness of the operation of the social network meant that a degree of calculated choice had to enter into fully sentimental ties. . . . The public consequence of relationships made it

difficult for some wives to have anything but a superficial friendship with anyone in the corporate social network.[19]

Clergy wives report similar stresses and limits on their friendships,
and both clergy and corporate wives, predictably, complain of loneliness.
The priests' wives also acknowledged such limiting elements on their
friendships, made even stronger due to their husband's priestly status in
the parish. One wife, whose husband is the pastor of the only Catholic
Church in a small Midwestern town, explained: "I would say a bigger
liability even than time perhaps is friendship. Who do you have as your
friend? Who can you talk to, freely and openly? Nobody. You can't be
friends with people in the parish. You can be acquaintances with them,
you can go out to dinner with them, enjoy their company, but you can't
sit down and say, 'if my husband doesn't quit snoring or whatever, I'm
gonna—because that's *Father.*'"

The loss of friendships due to conversion was the most commonly
noted regret of the priests' wives, who were also less likely than their husbands to feel that they had been very well received by laypersons in the
Catholic Church.

Like the corporate wife, moreover, a pastor's wife must be constantly
aware of the secondary effect her actions have on her husband. "The
importance of a wife," observes Kanter, "stems not only from her own
skills and activities . . . but also from the testimony her behavior provides,
its clue to the character and personal side of her husband." The practical effect of this power is to reinforce the subordination of the wife. The
clergy wife as well as the corporate wife "must often hide her own opinions in order to preserve a united front, play down her own abilities in
order to keep him looking like the winner and the star."[20]

In sum, both the corporation and, even more strongly, the Church
co-opt the resources of marriage to serve the institution. Kanter points
out that the tendency of an organization to implicate wives in their husbands' careers is greater in total institutions, like the military or a board-
ing school, where there is less work-life separation generally, noting such
an "organization's tendency to swallow up its members and consume
them and their families."[21] As both Catholic theology and Protestant experience recognizes, churches also tend to be such organizations, demanding a particularly single-minded commitment from their leaders that
tends to overwhelm their marriages. Sociologically, the rule of celibacy
or the co-opting of clergy wives can be viewed as divergent institutional

strategies to the same end: to claim all the personal resources of the pastor for the work of the Church.

A Vocation to Marry a Vocation

Encroachment by the workplace is hardly unique to corporate or clergy marriages, of course. Despite the ideology of a fundamental separation between the sphere of work and that of family, any modern two-earner marriage, which is most marriages today, already cedes large areas of family autonomy to the workplace. The distinguishing feature of corporate/clergy marriages is not the subordination of family life to the workplace, but the interpenetration of corporate identity, whether executive or priestly, into the otherwise intimate realms of family roles and relationships. It is not just the executive, but also his marriage, and by extension his wife, children, and even network of friends, who (as we have seen) are overshadowed by his corporate identity, and thus become, as it were, creatures of the corporation or parish.

Whether such intrusion by the workplace is acceptable to corporate wives (and the research suggests that their responses vary widely), among clergy wives, and even more strongly among the married priests' wives, it is a permissible, even welcome, aspect of their marital situation. A successful clergy marriage involves not only traditional wifely subordination in the marriage economy, as with corporate wives, but also a commitment to the shared goal of ministry to God's people on the part of both husband and wife that to some extent overrides or subordinates otherwise usual marital expectations. The role of the clergy wife thus presumes but also expands upon a traditional family economy in which the wife supports her husband's career, rather than seeking an independent career of her own. In addition, clergy wives have traditionally served as a kind of adjunct minister to augment the work of their husband in the Church.

Denton wrote of clergy wives that "[i]n marrying, they marry more than a man. They also become part of a role with a long tradition—the ministry."[22] Key to understanding the lives and marriages of the priests' wives is the recognition that, for them especially, as Greeley puts it (as a point in favor of clergy celibacy), "to be a clergyman's wife is at least as much a religious vocation as to be a clergyman."[23] The ideal of a vocation may be stronger for some wives than for others, but it is nearly universal among them, and centers on subordination and support of their husband's vocation.

One older clergy widow, looking back on her lifetime of ministry with her priest husband, reflected, "I feel that the priest's wife has a vocation. I don't think her vocation is to teach Sunday School or sing in the choir or run the women's guild, I think her vocation is to provide a home of peace and contentment and tranquility for her husband and family. And to be there for her husband, for him." Many of the wives emphasized the necessity for a vocation to clergy marriage in cautionary terms: "Most women can't be married to a clergyman," one said, "That role is a vocation. . . . Young women who are being dated by somebody who is ordained or wishes to be really better have their minds right about what they're getting into." These views were not a product of age or an earlier era, however. A young priest's wife with five children, married to the pastor of an active parish, expressed the need for or call to vocation and subordination in even stronger terms: "Any vocation where the man's wife is not completely supportive of what he's doing will bring scandal to the Church, not advantage. In the Episcopal Church you hear this all the time, well he has his career and I have mine. And that can't be. The woman has to be wholly invested in the husband's priesthood."

Women who married their husbands after he had already committed to becoming a priest very likely made a more intentional choice to accept the role and vocation of clergy wife. More than two-thirds (68 percent) of the married priests' wives had married their husbands after he had received or while he was studying for his professional ministerial degree. By contrast, John and Linda Morgan found this to be true for only a third (31 percent) of Episcopalian clergy marriages overall.[24]

Much more than clergy wives in other settings, the married priests' wives appear to have been attracted to their husband's priesthood as well as his person, and entered a marriage committed to their husband's vocation. As one wife told me, "I wanted to marry a priest as a way of serving Christ." Another confessed, "Ever since I was in high school I've always wanted to either be a minister or marry one, because I knew I had some sort of a vocation in that regard." In Catholic parlance, these women had discerned a vocation to marry a vocation.

Quietly Co-ministering

The clergy wife's vocation is thus a kind of secondary vocation, a vocation to be involved in the vocation of another. In what is still the most extensive study of clergy wives, in 1965 Douglas identified three types of clergy wife, which he labeled teamworker, background supporter, and detached.[25] Teamworker wives had a visible role in Church leadership, serving as active co-ministers alongside their husbands; background supporters did substantial work in the parish behind the scenes; detached wives had little involvement in the parish or their husband's ministry. Kanter noted a similar pattern of levels of involvement among corporate wives: "They are sometimes involved directly with the corporation, sometimes only with and through their husbands, and sometimes completely uninvolved."[26]

Douglas found that detached wives comprised only a small proportion of clergy wives generally. Among the married priests' wives, who have all cooperated with change and loss to support their husband's ministry identity, none could be described as "detached" from their husband's ministry. On the contrary, almost all of them express a strong and vital interest in the work of the Church and their husband's ministry in particular. Many were active teamworkers with their husband before Catholic ordination, but in their current situations almost all the priest wives fit the category of background or indirect supporter. Their unique status—or lack thereof—in Catholic life constrained direct involvement in their husband's ministry. Others preferred to work in the background in the Episcopal Church and continued that in their new setting in the Catholic Church. Thus, either by choice or by default, in their Catholic life the priest wives have supported their husbands and the Church by working in the background.

At least until recently, clergy wives have had relatively low career aspirations, with fewer working outside the home than in other types of marriages. This is still very much the case with the priests' wives. The Morgans found that 60 percent of Episcopal clergy wives had careers or career ambitions.[27] In their current situation, just over half of the priest wives (53 percent) worked outside the home. About 15 percent of the priests' wives began working after their Catholic conversion to help make ends meet, meaning that less than four in 10 (38 percent) of them worked before then. Considering that the proportion found by the Morgans has certainly increased in the intervening decades, it is clear that the priest wives were much less career-oriented, as a group, than are Episcopalian wives or women in general. As we will see, most of those who did work, moreover, did so with the support of the family in mind, not an independent career.

Whether they worked or not, being able to help in their husband's parish or otherwise serve the Church was fundamental to their well-being. The Catholic priest wives who were employed full-time (53 percent of them) volunteered an average of two hours per week in their husband's parish; those who were not employed devoted an average of six hours a week to the work of the parish. The latter group reported fewer losses (1.9) in becoming Catholic than did the former (2.6). The number of hours volunteering in her husband's parish was positively correlated both with how well the wife felt she had been received in the Church (.43) and her overall reported happiness (.55).[28] Being able to volunteer in the parish, it appears, allowed at least a partial expression of the co-ministering role they had adopted in the Episcopal Church. Many of the employed wives, moreover, expressed satisfaction in indirectly supporting their husband's ministry in light of his diminished earning power due to conversion. A quarter of the employed wives had jobs in a Catholic parish or parish-related institution such as a school.

At the same time, consistent with traditional marriage roles, the wives had a much higher commitment to children and family than is the norm for American marriages. On average, the Catholic priest marriages produced just under three children each (2.95), one child more than the US average (1.9). Eleven percent had five or more children. Only 3 percent were childless, compared to about 10 percent naturally childless among all marriages.[29] Both the priests and the wives, but especially the wives, tended to come from large families themselves. The priests reported an average of 2.6 children in their family of origin; the wives came from families with an average of 3.7 children.

Converting Together

Striking evidence of the unusual devotion and subordination of the priests' wives to their husband's vocation is the fact that each has accompanied her husband on his personal and professional journey from one religious group to another. In a minimal sense, this is true of them by definition; since the Pastoral Provision process requires that an applicant's wife communicate in writing her support of his ordination, a wife who resisted her husband's ordination would preclude his conversion. But these wives went much further. Although there is no requirement or even expectation that the priest's wife also converts, in every case these former Episcopalians not only tolerated but seconded the decision of their husband to convert.

Most (63.1 percent) were received into the Catholic Church at the same time as were their husbands. One in five (18.2 percent) of the wives were born Catholic; three-quarters of these (13.7 percent overall) had become Episcopalian following marriage or their husband's Episcopal ordination, and one-quarter (4.6 percent overall) had never left the Catholic Church. An additional tenth (9.1 percent) converted to Catholicism shortly before their husbands did, and another fifth (18.2 percent) within three years following his reception into the Catholic Church.

Moreover, with one or two possible exceptions, in every case the impetus to convert came from the husband and was received by the wife, who had to respond or adjust to his initiative. In their combined religious journey, the husband led and the wife followed. When asked, more than 90 percent of the wives agreed that, if their husband had not decided to become Catholic, they would very probably not have become Catholic themselves. In the following two interview samples, note how the wife's decision to convert follows directly from her marriage commitment:

PS: If he hadn't become Catholic, do you think you would have become Catholic?

PRIEST'S WIFE: No. My becoming Catholic is very much related to our marriage. Since the time we met, Church has been central to our lives. So I couldn't imagine being a different religion than him. We've known people for whom that works; but not for us. It's just central to who we are as a couple.

PS: Why did you become Catholic?

PRIEST'S WIFE: For me, I can almost just easily say, "Because he did." 'Whither thou goest, I shall go.' In a very real sense, I think that's true. And I actually converted to Episcopalianism in the first place for the same reason.

The exceptionally high degree of sympathetic conversion found in these responses reflects the wives' strong senses both of vocation and of subordination to their husbands' ministry.

Not only did priests' wives follow their husbands' lead in conversion, most of them did so more than once. In no case among these clergy couples did the husband switch to his wife's faith in joining the Episcopal Church. By contrast, in every case, both in becoming Episcopalian and in later becoming Catholic, the wives' switched to the religion in which their husband was called to minister. Like their husbands, four-fifths

(80 percent) of them were not raised Anglican, and most (60 percent) had converted to the Episcopal Church at some time before they converted to the Catholic Church. A fifth (20 percent) of the wives were baptized and raised in the Catholic Church. The remaining three-fifths of the wives came to the Episcopal Church from a variety of Protestant denominations, in proportions that are very similar to those of the priests themselves.

Most (75 percent) of the fifth of the wives who had been raised Catholic never converted to the Episcopal Church; these were the only priest wives who resisted becoming Episcopalian. Understandably, these women reported no struggle in their husband's conversion, but a sense of joy and satisfaction that their family had become religiously unified. For the few women who had left the Catholic Church to become Episcopalian, return- ing to the Catholic faith with their husbands involved feelings of chagrin that amplified their personal struggle. One such wife shared, "Part of my struggle in coming back into the Catholic Church was that I had to admit to myself that I had erred in leaving the Catholic Church. So it was very, very difficult." Like all the wives in her situation, however, this wife did not regret converting to the Episcopal Church. She left the Catholic Church to become Episcopalian, she explained, for the same reason that she later left the Episcopal Church to return to Catholicism: she decided that "it would not be wise or healthy for our family to be divided."

Like this wife, maintaining family unity was the most frequently expressed motive for conversion, both for their Catholic and their ear- lier Episcopalian conversions, by the priests' wives. One wife, who had strongly considered joining an Eastern Orthodox Church when her hus- band became Catholic, explained that she decided to become Catholic also because "I felt that if we were going to do this, we would pretty much have to do it as a family, or else it would cause problems within the fam- ily over time. So it wasn't an easy decision to make, but I think it was the right decision." Another wife used a very similar justification to explain her decision to join the Episcopal Church when her husband did: "I've always felt it was very important for our family to worship together. Not that it's like we have to share a brain or anything, but I know in raising our children, I could have chosen to stay Southern Baptist. I didn't have to become Episcopalian. But . . . I didn't want to go to one church, and my kids and my husband to go to another church. So that's why I pretty much became an Episcopalian." Since Catholic conversion followed marriage for all the priest wives, their choice to maintain family unity by converting was made in the context of their prior decision to marry out of a sense of vocation. A religiously divided family not only disadvantaged their children and strained their marital relationship, but it would also have made any vocational support of their husband's ministry very problematic.

As I noted earlier, almost none of the converting priests discussed the changes in their own religious convictions with their wives until they had already decided or were very close to deciding to convert to the Catholic Church. This was often initially unsettling to the wife, who resisted converting, as the following wife expressed in her interview:

> [W]hen he started talking about it I just looked at him and said, "I'm not going to make those kind of changes. I've made enough changes for you, and this is it. Forget it. You're asking too much of me, to make another big huge change. I like the Episcopal Church, I'm in it and I believe what the Episcopal Church believes" ... suddenly here I am with two children, 9 and 6 at that time, and suddenly he's wanting to change everything again. So I was not at all interested at first.

In most cases the husband, after the crystallization of his own convictions on conversion, worked to convince and catechize his wife. One priest explained, "When it was time to become Catholic, I told her, 'This is where I want to go, but not until you're standing right next to me and ready to go.'" This process took various forms. Many of the wives, like their husbands, already had beliefs that were very close to those of the Catholic Church. Others struggled with the challenge; some sought further instruction from a Catholic priest or attended the course of preparations for the Rite of Christian Initiation of Adults (RCIA), a year-long process designed to introduce adults to the Catholic faith. In one or two cases, it took years before the wife was ready; in one or two others, the wife formally joined the Catholic Church before her husband did.

For the priests' wives, the pattern of subordination exemplified in their conversion decisions is consistent with, and in many respects constitutive of, their self-understanding as clergy wives and their original decision to marry. The process they followed, with the husband taking the initiative and the wife following in a matter of personal religious conviction, exemplifies a model of male domination that is generally thought to be inconsistent with wifely fulfillment in marriage. The wives, while often aware of this irony, consistently reiterated that they did not feel compelled or restricted in their choice to follow their husband's lead; indeed, just the opposite. Many of them expressed simply that they were not a "loner" or "independent." One said, "I'm not one to go out on my own." The following interview exchange clarified this typical quality of the wives particularly well:

PRIEST'S WIFE: I would have to say that the pattern has been, he has led and I have followed. Into the Episcopal Church, and into the Catholic Church. I've never regretted it, but probably of my own volition I would not have done it. Only because I'm not that adventuresome as he is.

PS: Some people, when they hear you say that, will say, "Gee, she's done just what feminists have been trying to get women away from doing. She's just completely subordinated her person to that of this man, and has missed out on so many things . . ." What would you say in response to that?

PRIEST'S WIFE: I have thought of that. Look at my cousin. She leads the life I would have led had I not gone the path that I did. She's still living in the town we grew up in. Still mired in the limitations of the Protestant Church we grew up in. She's happy with her life, and I love her dearly. And I am so blessed to not be her.

If I hadn't been led to become an Episcopalian, to become a Catholic, I don't know that I would have done it, and my life would have been much poorer for it. So I'm sure some women's libbers would look at me and say, "Huh." Because I'm well educated and I'm not a dumb person. But I am not an innovator. But once I'm led to something, by and large I'm very glad I was.

PS: So what I'm hearing you say is that following, and sort of subordinating yourself in that way to your husband, has, you feel, contributed to your fulfillment in life and not stifled it.

PRIEST'S WIFE: Exactly. It turned out to have been a blessing.

In stark contrast to prevailing norms of marriage, for these women identity was not a matter of self-assertion; rather, fulfillment was found by following their husbands' innovations.

Preferring Church over Family

Despite—or perhaps because of—their devotion to the priority of the parish, the mingling of marriage and ministry in these clergy-wife relationships inevitably channels stress from the parish to the family. When one asks celibate priests about their struggles in parish life, they often talk about loneliness; priests' wives, when asked the same question, usually talked about family stress. They reported two main types of such family stress, both of them typical of clergy families: their husband's lack of time for family; and restrictions on parish friendships imposed by their husband's clerical role.

In their marriage relationship, the priest wives illustrated many of the same struggles that research has consistently found characterize the lives of minister's wives generally. The biggest struggles, for most, are over the conflicting demands of Church and family for their husband's time, attention, and devotion. Many priests' wives said that they felt they were in competition with the Church for a man they both admire. They expressed, in other words, precisely the sense of ambivalence expressed by Douglas's ministers' wives in the 1960s: "My husband is one of those wonderful, humble, lovable, understanding people that almost everyone likes, and I feel flattered daily that he loves me ... sometimes it's hard to share him with the rest of the world ... and at times I literally hate the church for taking so much of his time."[30]

The root complaint of the priest wives is simply that the husband is too often gone, leaving them to tend to family needs by themselves. For some, the stress turns into anger at their husband for being so busy. One priest wife complained, "It's hard for my husband because he's pulled in two directions. It's very demanding. Constant meetings, constant calls, constant everything. I resent it at times, when I have to take care of the kids all by myself. It gets tiring." This priest's family has two children in college and two at home; the wife works a half-time job in order to make ends meet.

The priests' wives often see themselves as similar to wives of men in other high-demand professions. One wife of a retired priest recalled, "It is true, as a [married priest] who had teenagers and little children and stuff, he was gone all the time. But it's the same as with doctors and lawyers and CEOs and all that kind of stuff ... it's really hard on a family." We have already seen that corporate wives suffer similar encroachment on family time. However, the time pressures facing a clergy family are different and more intense than for other professional families. First, priests work longer hours, on average, than most other professionals. According to the Bureau of Labor Statistics, 33 percent of attorneys and 43 percent of physicians worked more than 50 hours per week; but over 53 percent of the married priests do so. Clergy wives have husbands who are less accessible, in fact, than is true for other hard-working professions. Second, it is not just a matter of the hours away from family. Douglas found, in fact, that "MWs [minister's wives] have *more time* with their husbands than do most wives ... but the distribution of this time is different from that of most families."[31] Time at home is often not leisure time or family time, but is devoted to Church life in one form or another. This is particularly true if they have a study or Church office at home, or live on Church property, as is usually the case in a Catholic rectory.

The implication of having a vocation to marry a vocation is that commitment to the marriage is not equally balanced. Notwithstanding their acknowledgment of the stresses involved, for the priests' wives, the competition between the parish and the marriage for limited family resources like their husband's time almost always had a single resolution. With only one or two exceptions, when the dual vocations of priesthood and marriage conflicted, the demands of the Church took precedence. The wife of an older priest recalled, "When I met [my husband], he said of course you must understand that the parish comes first, last and always. And it always has."

Many wives clearly link their sense of vocation to this imbalance, but do not see it as being unequal:

PS: Now, you've said that you see your vocation as being first to him. Do you also think that his vocation is first to you?

PRIEST'S WIFE: No, I see his vocation as being to the Church.

PS: So for you the commitments of your marriage are not entirely reciprocal. I mean, you have a call to be devoted to him in a way that he doesn't have a call to be devoted to you. Is that true?

PRIEST'S WIFE: Different, but not unequal. But yeah, I see a difference . . . in terms of a religious vocation, our ministries that God gives us, my primary one is to minister to him. Because he's ministering to others. That's what God called me to do.

That sense of call, so clearly expressed, leads almost all priests' wives to support their husbands' ministry in the Church, even when that detracts from their marriage. The younger wife of the busy pastor of a large parish related her acceptance and support of this subordination of affection in clear terms: "My husband is more devoted to the Church than marriage. If I know he's got to do work in the Church, I don't have any hesitation for him to do that. On the contrary, I say God bless you, and go do something good. And I pray for him, I do the Rosary for that situation. So I support him in prayer, for his ministry."

Far from competing with the Church, then, the typical priest's wife is eager to support and encourage her husband's ministry in and to the Church as much as possible. This attitude, of course, provides further evidence of their strong commitment to the ministry of the Church. In this attitude may also lay an answer to the problem of the divided vocation of a married Catholic priest. While structural conflicts may still exist, in his personal commitment and anxiety the dilemma of a married man between pleasing the Lord or pleasing his wife is resolved if the wife in question makes it clear that she is most pleased when the man is pleasing the Lord. Indeed, it is possible that in such a marriage a priest may be encouraged to exercise even greater devotion and sacrifice for Christ and the Church than he may otherwise have done.

Other Features of Priests' Wives
Less Conservative

The different motivations for conversion of the wives is also reflected in their views on Catholic moral teachings, which were somewhat less orthodox or extreme than those of their husbands. Figure 5.1 compares the views of the priests and the wives on eight moral issues. These issues represent those on which there is the most disagreement with official Church teaching among American Catholics. The responses are scored so that the bars in the figure report the percent who agree with Catholic teaching on each item.

The data in Figure 5.1 show clearly that the wives are less conservative than the husband priests. For every moral issue queried, a lower proportion of the wives responded that the behavior was always sinful. Forty-four percent of the wives, compared to 52 percent of the priests, held morally rigorous views, responding that all of the moral behaviors listed in Figure 5.1 were always sinful. No wife gave a more conservative response than her own husband on abortion, stem cell research, human cloning, or (with one exception) the use of condoms to prevent AIDS. A minority of the wives more often said masturbation (22 percent) or birth control (14 percent) were sinful than did their own husbands, and a large minority (40 percent) said the same for suicide; these responses are consistent with general gender differences on these issues. Even on these items, however,

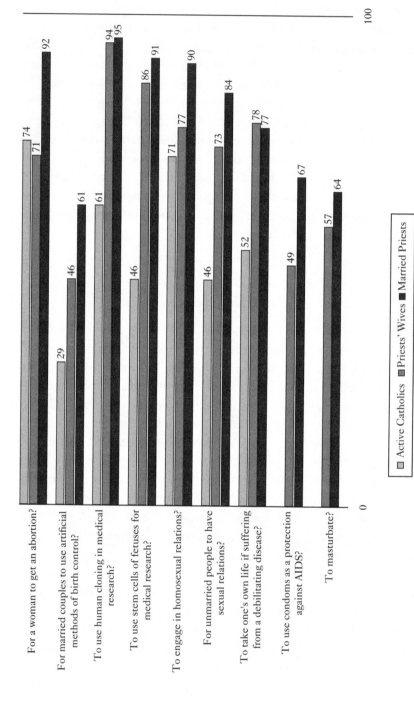

FIGURE 5.1 "Do You Think It Is Always, Often, Seldom, or Never a Sin" (Percent Responding "Always")

Legend: ■ Active Catholics ■ Priests' Wives ■ Married Priests

For a woman to get an abortion? — 74, 71, 92

For married couples to use artificial methods of birth control? — 29, 46, 61

To use human cloning in medical research? — 61, 94, 95

To use stem cells of fetuses for medical research? — 46, 86, 91

To engage in homosexual relations? — 71, 77, 90

For unmarried people to have sexual relations? — 46, 73, 84

To take one's own life if suffering from a debilitating disease? — 52, 78, 77

To use condoms as a protection against AIDS? — 49, 67

To masturbate? — 57, 64

0 100

a majority of the wives offered the same or a more liberal response than did their own husbands.

Consistent with this picture, only 77 percent of the wives, compared to 92 percent of the priests, described their own views on religious and moral doctrines as conservative. Fifteen percent of the wives, compared to only 6 percent of the priests, moreover, thought that the Pope's views were too conservative. The relative liberalism of the priests' wives should not be overstated; though slightly more liberal than their husbands, the views of the wives are still significantly more conservative than those of most Catholics, clergy or lay (as Figure 5.1 shows), and much more conservative than most Episcopalians. The relative moderation of the wives' views, however, is consistent with the suggestion that their conversions were not, like their husbands', primarily intellectual conversions of conscience.

Supporting Celibacy

Their experience with marriage has also shaped the views of the priests' wives on questions of celibacy and ministry. Ironically, married priests and their wives are about twice as likely to oppose the ordination of married priests as are celibate Catholic priests. Like their husbands, the wives are about evenly divided on this issue: half (50 percent) of them oppose any changes in the rule of celibacy, a position held by only a quarter (28 percent) of celibate Catholic priests.

Few hold a position that is adamant or ideological on the topic, and almost none reports having experienced scandal or rejection by Church members as a result of being married. Rather, their views reflect the practical and structural difficulties that come with ministry as a priest family. Family stress, lack of income, high demands on scarce family time, and the absence of any role for wives and children figure largely in their assessment of the merits or demerits of a married priesthood. On this issue, the married priests and their wives largely see themselves as exceptions that prove the rule.

For similar reasons, a number of the priests and their wives believe that the restriction of married priests from parish ministry is a wise one. The following comments attest to this:

> I definitely see the wisdom of the pastoral provision saying that a priest should not have the care of souls or a parish assignment. And I've told him that and I believe that. It's not good for the marriage.

The marriage came first. It's not good for a marriage, and I can't even imagine what it would be like to have children and be in a [parish] situation.... I don't think that bishops should be accepting men with young children.... I think there is a wisdom in the Church [for priests] being celibate, first of all. And also in the pastoral provision, that a priest should not be a pastor.

I think having a family makes it more difficult. There's certainly more potential for conflict.

If you're married and you still have children in the home, I don't think you should be a senior pastor. Because I don't think you do have the time that the Church demands of you. I believe if you are mature, though, and you're settled—in your late forties/early fifties, and your children are out of college, you know, you're stable—then I don't believe there's any reason why you couldn't handle a parish.

The Morgans found similar, unexpected opposition to the ordination of women in their sample of Episcopal priest's wives. Forty percent opposed it overall, and among the women most committed to supporting their husband's ministry, three-fourths (74 percent) opposed ordaining women. At a loss to explain this view for theological reasons ("we have not been able to discover any particularly strong feelings about orthodoxy and tradition among the women"), they concluded:

What we may assume from this study is that these women have had such a negative experience in their roles as priests' wives ... that they would not encourage, but rather discourage, women from pursuing the same field which they have found to be so unhappy and unfulfilling for the spouse.[32]

Staying Together

An extreme indicator of marital dissatisfaction is, of course, divorce; lower rates of divorce suggest higher marital functioning or commitment. Although just a generation ago divorce was rare among clergy, and would often mean the end of a ministerial career, today, as Zikmund observes, "[c]lergy seem to divorce at much the same rate as laity, and probably for about the same reasons."[33] Since most divorced persons remarry, the most reliable measure of the incidence of divorce is not those who are currently divorced but the proportion of persons who have ever been involved in a divorce, regardless of their current marital status. By this measure, the US Census reports that 22 percent of American men have been divorced at some point in their lives. A 1995 survey by Hartford Seminary found that the corresponding rate among male clergy was 20 percent.[34]

Although some observers lament that the rate of clergy divorce is not much lower, what is more striking is that it is not much higher than it is.[35] Given the intense stress confronting clergy families, it is remarkable that so many of them are happy and healthy. That the clergy divorce rate is not higher than those of laypersons, therefore, suggests that clergy marriages are somewhat more stable or functional than marriages in general. McMinn and his collaborators chose clergy families for research on family coping precisely "because they face a good deal of stress on a daily basis, yet most function in a relatively healthy manner."[36]

The Hartford Seminary survey also found that a quarter (25 percent) of male Episcopal priests have been divorced at some point in their lives. By comparison, the marriages of the Catholic married priest couples are unusually stable: only 11 percent of them have ever been divorced. As noted in Chapter 1, only 3.4 percent of the married priest families have divorced or separated since converting to the Catholic faith. As we have seen, the healthy functioning of the clergy family is due in large part to the work and commitment of the minister's wife.

Clergy wives are undaunted by hardship, but uncertainty or ambiguity about their role creates distress. In a recent study of Southern Baptist clergy wives, Brooks found that their role expectation was a highly significant ($p < .001$) predictor of marriage satisfaction, while lack of privacy, lack of time, loneliness, and financial strain were not. The low divorce rate, even for clergy, of the Pastoral Provision families suggests that the convert priests' wives are especially committed to this supportive role.

Another reason for the low divorce rate among the convert priest families may be their doctrinal conservatism or the high proportion of those from an evangelical background. The Hartford Seminary survey found that the rate of divorce varied greatly by denomination, with much less divorce occurring among clergy in the more conservative or evangelical denominations. A fifth (20 percent) of ministers in all denominations had ever been divorced. The highest rate was found among Unitarian/Universalists, where 44 percent of male ministers had ever been divorced; the lowest was among the Southern Baptists, where only 4 percent of male ministers had ever been divorced.

Struggle with Loss of Role

The crucial importance of role definition for a clergy wife was confirmed by the reports of the Pastoral Provision wives. More than their husbands, the wives experienced the lack of a defined role for a clergy wife in their new situation as a great loss. Role expectations for clergy wives may be diminishing, ambiguous, or undergoing change and challenge in the Episcopal Church—but they are nonexistent in the Catholic Church. Almost all the wives acknowledged the loss of role or identity at some point in their interview. Several of them expressed this in words almost identical to those of one wife: "People in the Catholic Church don't know what to do with you as the wife of a priest." Many of the wives compared their experiences in the two churches: "there was of course some loss of identity. As an Episcopal clergy wife you have a certain identity, which is just graciously bestowed upon you and you don't have it when you leave. You become a non-entity in many ways." Others also clarified their loss as that of a co-ministerial role: "Being the wife of an Episcopal priest, you always feel part of the ministry. And I'm not part of this. I'm totally separate."

The effect of conversion on role identity was much more profound and negative for the Pastoral Provision wives than for the priests. About a third of both priests (29 percent) and wives (32 percent) mentioned the loss of role or identity in their conversion as a disappointment, but the wives were more likely to identify this as their most important loss, while for the priests the loss of liturgy and of friends was more important. Ironically, the support that clergy wives provided led, for many of them, to the loss of that very role.

For the priests, moreover, the loss of the priestly role was only temporary, during the period after they had left the Episcopal Church and before they were ordained as Catholic priests. Even as Catholic laypersons, however, the priests sought and expected to return to a priestly role and status. The same proportion of married priests that mentioned the temporary loss of their priestly role as a difficulty (29 percent) noted the contrary experience of greater fulfillment in their priestly role as one of the things they gained in becoming Catholic (30 percent). But the role and status that most of the wives had adopted at their marriage, the role of a clergy wife, was lost permanently, with no expectation that it would be restored, even when their husbands were ordained once again. Consequently, while the greatest satisfaction reported by the priests was the sense of belonging, or coming home, that they gained in the Catholic Church, for the wives the sense of belonging was a distant second, as a source of satisfaction, to the development of new friends and support networks in the Catholic Church. As already noted, the support of friends for their conversion was positively correlated ($r = .45$) with the wives' reported happiness. Taken together, these findings strongly suggest that the wives experienced a greater sense of displacement and disappointment in not finding or having an identifiable place or role in the Catholic Church.

Conclusion: Assertively Submissive

The lives and devotion of the priests' wives, as evidenced in this chapter, challenge prevailing views of marital fulfillment, and therefore also many common assumptions about Catholic clergy marriage.

According to family scholars, since the 1960s Americans have increasingly pursued an ideal of marriage "in which the spouses are free to grow and change and in which each feels personally fulfilled."[37] This ideal of "individualistic marriage," as Cherlin terms it, extends and augments the ideal of "companionate marriage," which holds that married partners should be intimate loving companions. With the growth of individualistic marriage, marital role expectations of all sorts have declined in favor of a diverse set of arrangements that serve the unique interests of the marital partners. To the extent that roles exist in a marriage, they should be open-ended and temporary. The underlying goal of marriage is for each partner to better find maximum personal fulfillment.

From this perspective, marriages that impose a strong role, such as that of the corporation or clergy wife, inevitably limit their personal growth. A marriage role that permanently subordinates the interests of one partner to that of the other, as in the vocational ideal of the clergy spouse, cannot fail to be regressive, even oppressive. Even worse, women, such as the priests' wives, who choose to suppress their own individual initiative and even marital companionship in order to increase their husbands' workplace effectiveness fail to achieve either of the important ideals of marriage. If those ideals are valid, such marriages must be much less fulfilling for the wife. But we have found just the opposite: the priests' wives are happier and their marriages far more stable than the American average. In their ability to externalize their religious commitments to their marriages, to enter marriage as a vocation of service, priests' wives embody an ideal of marriage that both contradicts and compares favorably with prevailing American ideals of marriage.

The commitment to marriage and family was also the primary factor impelling these wives, without exception, to venture forth on a risky and costly journey of faith from one religious communion to another. Although they share this distinction with their husbands, the wives' conversions are more remarkable in several respects. While the husbands faced the intellectual contradiction of affirming authority by rejecting authority, the wives confronted the practical contradiction of stabilizing the family by uprooting the family. Less troubled by theological differences and possessed of a clearer perception of the costs involved, their courage in converting is greater than that of their husbands, who generally leaped before looking in their conversion decisions. While the husbands faced the likely prospect of restoration of their priestly role, in whole or part, with even greater authenticity, the wives faced the distressing loss of a distinct role as clergy wife.

Unlike their husbands, these women converted, not as independent thinkers or as intellectuals, but as wives and mothers with care of a marriage and family; their Catholicism might be said to be the religious expression of their sense of family devotion. If (to overstate for emphasis) their husbands are devoted first to truth, they are devoted first to husband and family. In stark contrast to the ethic of self-expression, their lives are devoted to the subordination of self, to their husband and family certainly, but more importantly, to Christ and the mission of the Church through service to their husband and family.

Though largely unacknowledged, the character of the wives is of central importance to the story of the Pastoral Provision. As remarkable as it is that all the wives converted to the Catholic faith, it is equally remarkable that no husband converted without his wife. Had his wife not subordinated her interests as she did, suffering the loss of friends, security, and a role that defined her marriage, it is doubtful any man could have negotiated the difficult transition from Episcopal to Catholic priesthood with his marriage (or sanity) intact. No doubt other Episcopal priests, whose wives were less supportive, have been inclined but practically unable to complete the journey. Ironically, it was only with the support of such wives that many of the married priests could have made their journey to enter a priesthood that excludes wives.

The vocation of the priests' wives to support their husband's vocation challenges the idea that marriage must always or usually be detrimental to the devotion, effectiveness, or ministry of a priest. Such a conclusion takes into account only the person of the priest, as if a married priest were simply a man in another state of life than a celibate priest. But marriage, by definition, introduces another person into the equation. As we have seen throughout this chapter, the presence of a wife does not just subtract from a priest's potential to serve the Church, it can also add to it in important ways. A married priest may be less single-minded about serving the Church, but he also brings another mind and heart that may aid and join him in serving the Church. A wife may distract from ministry, but she may also encourage a man's focus on ministry. In practice, as we have seen, the dilemma of conflicting vocations for the married priests—whether to serve the Church or the family—is largely resolved by the unifying commitment of the clergy wives, who see their vocation as serving the Church through the family, and are fundamentally devoted to supporting and encouraging their husbands' ability to serve the Church. In short, a wife brings not only liabilities, but also assets, that may enhance and augment her husband's ministry.

Ironically, the challenge they present is due entirely to their strong faithfulness and support for the Church, and emphatically not to any wayward or dissident impulse. They are unlikely revolutionaries, and will no doubt meet the suggestion that they challenge the status quo with bemusement and denial. They are more likely to voice an opinion in favor of priestly celibacy than are most celibates. Precisely because their personalities are so submissive and not given to challenge, they emphasize the lost opportunities of the celibacy rule. If it is women such as these who are likely to marry priests, the Church is far poorer for not having them in it than it may have formerly conceived.

6

Why Aren't There More Married Priests?

Introduction

"Why aren't there more of you?" The surprised woman in front of me had just said that she had never met a married priest before, though she had been an active Catholic all her life. Like a lot of thoughtful Catholics, she was concerned about a pending shortage of priests and had believed that allowing married men to become priests would lead to an influx of applicants. Yet she had just discovered that the Catholic Church already permitted married priests, albeit in a limited way, but only a very small number of men had applied. Why?

The numbers have indeed been small, both in real terms and compared to initial projections. As of January 1, 2008, there were just 77 married Roman Catholic priests in the United States.[1] Since 1981, a total of 84 married former Episcopal priests had been ordained under the Pastoral Provision, but by 2008, 12 of these men were deceased. Twelve celibate former Episcopalian priests had also been ordained during this time (three of these are now deceased), with varying levels of participation in the Pastoral Provision process. Seventy-two of the active married priests were former Episcopal priests who were ordained via the Pastoral Provision; five married clergymen from other Christian religious groups were also serving as Catholic priests, not by means of the Pastoral Provision but by individual petition for exception from the rule of celibacy.[2]

Not only has the overall number of ordinations been small, it has gradually decreased (see Figure 6.1). In the first decade following the declaration of the Pastoral Provision, 39 men, almost half the eventual total, were

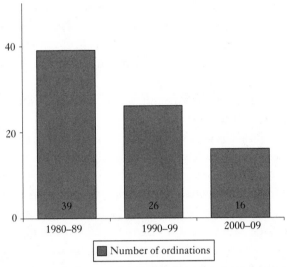

FIGURE 6.1 Distribution of Married Priest Ordinations by Decade

ordained. Much of this was pent-up demand; 22 men were ordained in the first three years after ordinations began, 16 of them in 1984 alone. During the 1990s, ordinations averaged fewer than three per year, and dropped to less than two per year during the 2000s. As already noted in Chapter 3, this trend is the opposite of what was predicted in the initial years of the program, when it was expected that, once the program became well established, the number of ordinations would increase.

The Bishops: Many Support, But Few Ordain

There are several reasons that there have been so few married priest ordinations, but underlying them all is a single critical factor: jurisdiction. Whether married Pastoral Provision priests are ordained depends crucially on the voluntary participation and support of the US bishops for something that, for most of them, is not central to their diocesan mission.

No bishop has an obligation to ordain a married priest; and, unlike the newer Ordinariate, there is no bishop or ecclesiastical authority devoted primarily to married or Anglican convert priests. They are ordained as secular priests for service to a particular Latin Rite diocese. Nine in 10 of them serve in parishes at least part-time, and all of them, even the few who minister to a group of converts using the Anglican Use liturgy, must be supported and eventually ordained by a diocesan bishop. The

US Ecclesiastical Delegate for the Pastoral Provision does not ordain the priest converts (except, on rare occasion, as a priest for his own diocese, like any other bishop would) or normally provide any oversight or support for them beyond administrative assistance and advice to the bishops who do choose to ordain them.

While in collective decisions and public statements the bishops have repeatedly expressed support and appreciation for married priests, and no bishop has publicly objected to the Pastoral Provision in principle, only a small minority of bishops have actually ordained a married priest in their own diocese. Married priest ordinations have taken place in only a quarter (26 percent) of US dioceses, concentrated in the South and particularly in Texas. This concentration is not due entirely to different dispositions of the bishops involved—Chapter 1 discusses the skew in ordinations more fully—but the willingness of a bishop to ordain and accept a married priest in his diocese is a crucial factor.

If the bishops support the Pastoral Provision, why don't more of them choose to ordain married priests in their diocese? What are their reservations? In order to answer these questions and get a better understanding of the bishops' views generally, I sent them a survey asking about their views on the Pastoral Provision and experience ordaining married priests.

Mixed and Cautious Support

Like their record of ordinations, the survey revealed that the bishops' attitudes toward the Pastoral Provision are decidedly mixed. The bishops were presented with 14 statements gleaned from preliminary interviews with a small number of bishops, and asked for their level of agreement. The results are shown in Table 6.1. In the table the items are listed in descending order of agreement.

The bishops were evenly split on the statement "I personally feel a strong sense of support for the Pastoral Provision." Half (51 percent) agreed with the statement, while half (49 percent) were either neutral or disagreed with it. Likewise, about half the bishops (54 percent) agreed, and half did not agree, that "the success of the Pastoral Provision would not call into question the rule of celibacy"; that they admired the Pastoral Provision priests they had known (55 percent); and that they would welcome the opportunity to ordain a Pastoral Provision priest (55 percent).

Not more than four in five bishops agreed about any issue presented in the survey. The greatest number (80 percent) agreed that they had a good

Table 6.1 Views of the US Bishops on the Pastoral Provision

Evaluative Statements	"Agree" or "Strongly Agree"	"Neutral/No Opinion"	"Disagree" or "Strongly Disagree"
I have a good general understanding of the Pastoral Provision.	80	6	14
The conditions that led to creating the Pastoral Provision are still valid today.	72	22	7
All else equal, I would rather ordain an older man whose children are grown than a younger man with young children.	58	27	15
I would welcome the opportunity to ordain a (or an additional) Pastoral Provision priest in my (arch)diocese at this time.	55	22	23
I generally admire the Pastoral Provision priests I have known.	55	40	5
The success of the Pastoral Provision would not call into question the rule of celibacy for priests in any way.	54	8	38
I personally feel a strong sense of support for the Pastoral Provision.	51	31	18
I have heard few objections to the Pastoral Provision from my priests.	52	21	28
While awaiting the Holy See's approval for the ordination, a diocese has no responsibility for financial support of the convert priest who has resigned his Anglican ministry.	45	27	28
In light of the irregularity of such ordinations and the importance of the rule of celibacy, it would be prudent to ordain only a very few married Anglican converts.	42	21	37
I am kept up to date on recent developments regarding the Pastoral Provision.	37	22	41

(continued)

Table 6.1 (Continued)

Evaluative Statements	"Agree" or "Strongly Agree"	"Neutral/No Opinion"	"Disagree" or "Strongly Disagree"
The Church should expand the Pastoral Provision, e.g., to other countries.	31	50	18
In light of the shortage of priests, it would be prudent to ordain as many suitable married Anglican priest converts as possible.	20	21	59
The Church should discontinue the Pastoral Provision.	12	17	71

Note: Percentages may not sum to 100 due to rounding. Items in the table are presented in descending order of agreement.

general understanding of the Pastoral Provision, but they were almost evenly split on the question of whether they were up to date on recent developments in the program (37 percent thought they were; 41 percent disagreed). Almost three-quarters of the bishops (72 percent) also agreed that the conditions that led to the Pastoral Provision are still valid today. A small majority of bishops (58 percent) agreed that they would rather ordain an older man whose children are grown, and they were split on the issue of a diocese's financial responsibility for a convert priest prior to ordination. Almost half (45 percent) thought that a diocese has no responsibility for financial support during this time, but substantial minorities disagreed (28 percent) or were neutral (27 percent) on this question.

This ambivalence among the bishops reflects, in part, the fact that the impetus for the Pastoral Provision came from the Vatican, and with particular urgency from Cardinal Ratzinger, and not from the United States. Although the Catholic Church is popularly viewed as steeply hierarchical, the ability of the Vatican to impose practices on diocesan bishops is often quite limited. While not disagreeing with the policy in principle, some bishops clearly differ with the Vatican in their view of the wisdom or prudence of the program.

Caution among them is largely prompted by two sets of issues: celibacy—both theologically and in terms of the stress of incorporating married priests into a celibate diocesan presbyterate—and financial concerns. Concern for celibacy also leads many bishops who otherwise support the program to advocate limiting the number of married priests, and contributes to financial constraints on ordination by prohibiting married men from serving as parish pastors.

Celibacy Concerns

A desire to avoid undermining the discipline of celibacy pervades the norms of the Pastoral Provision. Bishops are advised that "special care must be taken on the pastoral level to avoid any misunderstanding regarding the Church's discipline of celibacy."[3] Priests and dioceses are asked to avoid undue publicity. Like Catholic deacons, married Pastoral Provision priests must promise not to remarry if they are widowed. Pastoral Provision priests may not become bishops or serve as parish pastors, thus ensuring that celibate men will continue to dominate diocesan and parish leadership. And any men who are presented for ordination from a Catholic Anglican Use parish formed under the Pastoral Provision must be celibate.

The views and comments of the US bishops on the survey reflected a similar concern for the sensitive issue of celibacy. Just over five in 10 (54 percent) agreed, but just under four in 10 (38 percent) disagreed, with the statement "the success of the Pastoral Provision would not call into question the rule of celibacy for priests in any way." Seeking to avoid scandal to the faithful or dissension among the celibate Latin Rite presbyterate, Eastern Catholic immigrants with a tradition of married priests in their homeland have, for the past century, been prohibited from ordaining married priests in the United States. The introduction of married priests, even as rare exceptions, into the Latin Rite itself, therefore, touches on an issue that is sensitive for both Latin Rite and Eastern Catholic clergy. The bishops affirm most, but not all, of the Vatican's directives designed to safeguard celibacy, and also add a few strategies of their own.

Acceptance by Other Priests

The US bishops expressed strong concern about potential tension between celibate clergy and married priests. Church policy anticipates that if some priests can be married, others who are required to be celibate may feel they are being unfairly treated, encouraging dissatisfaction and defection.

Quite apart from personal feelings, moreover, the practical and relational complications of incorporating men who are in a different state of life into a closely knit brotherhood of celibate priests is challenge enough.

A sizable minority of the bishops reported that there was substantial objection to the Pastoral Provision among the priests in their own diocese. Over a quarter of the bishops (28 percent) disagreed with the statement "I have heard few objections to the Pastoral Provision from my priests." Another fifth (20 percent) of the bishops were neutral on this item, meaning that only just over half (52 percent) of them agreed that their priests had expressed few objections to the Pastoral Provision. When considering a Pastoral Provision ordination (Table 6.2), three-quarters (75 percent) of the bishops rated the issue of the married priest's reception by the presbyterate as "very important"; 60 percent rated it as one of their top two concerns. It is not unusual for a bishop to consult with his presbyteral council to gauge their receptivity before agreeing to consider a Pastoral Provision candidate.

The issue is particularly sensitive because older Catholic priests today—and half of priests are over the age of 60—are survivors of an era when many of their colleagues left the priesthood in order to marry. In the two decades prior to 1985, that is, immediately following the Second Vatican Council (1962–1965), almost 7,000 US priests resigned from the ministry—over half as many men as were ordained to the priesthood during that period. When resignations since that time and men who dropped out of seminary in order to marry are included, the number reaches 25,000.

When we consider that there are fewer than 40,000 active Catholic priests in the United States, we can estimate, roughly but conservatively, that for every two celibate Catholic priests today there is one resigned priest who has married. Almost all of them remain Catholic and are active in parishes. Many Catholic priests retain relationships with their former colleagues and classmates, and nearly all Catholic pastors maintain a pastoral relationship with former priests who are in their parishes. The result is that for most Catholic priests today, the conflict between marriage and clerical ministry is not simply one of abstract theology or even personal devotion, but a very sensitive and personal issue that has deeply affected them.

The bishops raised all of these issues directly in response to the survey. Over a third (34 percent) of the bishops listed what one bishop called "the perception of a double standard on celibacy" as their most serious concern about ordaining a married priest. This was, by a wide margin, the most frequent concern mentioned. Such an ordination, another bishop explained, "creates tension among our priests who are celibate but would like the option to marry." Another observed, "There ought to be a similar process [for] Eastern Catholic Priests."

Another, typifying a common concern, wrote, "We have any number of ordained men who have left the active priesthood to marry and who would love to return to active ministry, but may not do so. It is very hard to explain to them why they may not serve and at the same time use the Pastoral Provision."

Maybe Only a Few

Whether or not bishops feel that ordaining Pastoral Provision priests challenges clergy celibacy, they tend to favor caution in ordaining only a limited number of such priests. Married priests are ordained as exceptions to the rule of celibacy, the reasoning goes, and if they become too common the exceptional nature of their ordinations will erode. The Vatican has recently acted on this concern by adopting a policy that "in order to give due regard to the value of clerical celibacy, it is ordinarily the practice ... that the number of married priests in any particular diocese under the Pastoral Provision be limited to two."[4]

Three-fifths (59 percent) of the bishops disagreed with the goal of "ordaining as many Pastoral Provision priests as possible," and two-fifths (42 percent) agreed that "it would be prudent to ordain only a very few married Anglican converts." As would be expected, respondents who agreed with one of these last items tended to disagree with the other, and their answers were related to their opinion on how the Pastoral Provision might affect the celibacy rule.[5] But even among bishops who expressed a strong sense of support for married priests, one-third (33 percent) advocated ordaining only a few. Likewise, among bishops who felt that ordaining married priests does not call clergy celibacy into question, one-third (35 percent) supported ordaining only a few Pastoral Provision priests, and 45 percent disagreed with ordaining as many as possible. In open-ended feedback, only five of the 80 bishops (6 percent) who commented thought that the small number of Pastoral Provision ordinations was unfortunate. More than five times this many (33 percent) thought that the limited number was "appropriate" and "should be minimal," reflecting "prudence and discretion" in admitting married men to the priesthood.

The views of the bishops were similarly diverse on questions about restricting or increasing the Pastoral Provision program. On the question of expanding the Pastoral Provision, for example to other countries, almost twice as many bishops (31 percent) agreed with this idea than opposed it (18 percent), though half (50 percent) were neutral. Likewise, one in eight bishops (12 percent) believed that the Church should discontinue the Pastoral Provision, but over five times this proportion (71 percent) disagreed with this idea.

One indicator of restrictiveness is the extent to which bishops are unwilling to ordain additional married priests once they already have ordained one or two. On this point also, the bishops' views and behavior were widely diverse. Overall, having already ordained a married priest in the past, or the presence of one or more already in the diocese, appears to have no effect on a bishop's willingness to ordain another married priest; about 70 percent of bishops report that they would welcome the opportunity to ordain a married priest or an additional married priest, regardless of how many are already in their dioceses. The apparent lack of relationship is misleading, however. As Figure 6.2 shows, bishops who had already ordained one to three married priests were less than half as likely

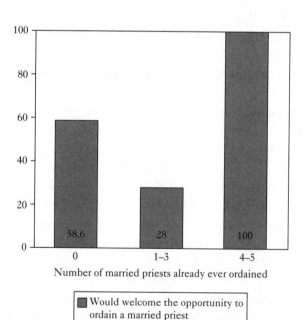

Number of married priests already ever ordained

Would welcome the opportunity to ordain a married priest

FIGURE 6.2 Effect of Married Priests Already Ordained on the Bishop's Willingness to Ordain a Married Priest

to say that they would welcome an opportunity to ordain another married priest as were bishops who had never yet ordained one. However, bishops who had already ordained four or more married priests were unanimously in favor of ordaining another one. Only one bishop in 20 (5 percent) is in this latter group, however; as we have already noted, married priest ordinations have been concentrated in a handful of dioceses, while over two-thirds of dioceses have not ordained any. Since Pastoral Provision applicants are rarely local to the Catholic diocese that eventually ordains them, and bishops who have never ordained one are more willing to do so than those who have ordained one to three of them, the new Vatican restriction limiting the number ordained in each diocese to two will likely have the effect, probably intended, of spreading ordinations out to involve more dioceses or bishops.

Practical Concerns

The survey asked the bishops to rate the importance to them of five practical concerns related to ordaining a married priest: the stability of his marriage, financial support for him and his family, his reception by the presbyterate, finding him proper employment or placement, and the reception and role of his wife in the diocese. We then asked them to circle their two most important concerns. We found that *none* of these concerns was unimportant; more than nine in 10 bishops rated each of them as important. Detailed results are shown in Table 6.2. The bishops' concern about the difficulties involved in ordaining a married priest is so universal among them that, while it may help us understand why ordinations have not been more widespread, it cannot suggest which difficulties are more important than others in affecting the bishops' ordination decisions.

Although it would be inaccurate to say that the bishops consider the wife's reception and role unimportant, it is clearly, in their minds, the least important of the concerns shown in Table 6.2. Less than half (37 percent) of the bishops rated this concern "very important," a far lower proportion than for any other item; and no bishop circled this item as among his two most important concerns. Given this relatively low rating for the importance of the wife's reception, it is telling that the highest rated concern was the stability of the priest's marriage. Apparently, the bishops have a very strong concern over the priest's marriage but much less concern for his wife in her own right. This irony mirrors the struggle of the wives, discussed in Chapter 5, to receive the support and validation of their bishop.

Table 6.2 When Considering the Possibility of Receiving a Married Priest, How Important Are Each of the Following Practical Concerns? (in Percent)

	Very Important	Somewhat Important	Somewhat Unimportant	Very Unimportant	Circled (%)	Mean
E. The stability of his marriage	93.0	6.3	0	0.7	55.5	3.92
G. Financial support for him and his family	77.9	21.4	0.7	0	32.2	3.77
B. His reception by the presbyterate	75.0	23.0	1.4	0.7	60.0	3.72
F. Finding proper employment or placement	70.8	27.8	0.7	0.7	16.9	3.69
C. His reception by parishioners	66.9	29.7	3.4	0	28.6	3.63
D. The reception and role of his wife in the parish or diocese	37.1	53.8	7.7	1.4	0.0	3.27

We have already discussed the priest's reception by the presbyterate and parishioners. The remaining concerns involve the related issues of financial support and employment placement. Both of these impediments to the ordination of married priests are strongly affected by the fact that married priests cannot normally serve as parish pastors.

Compensation and Deployment
The Pastorate Problem

Just as married priests were shoehorned into diocesan vocations processes that were formed for other purposes, they often did not easily fit into diocesan deployment processes. The fact that the married priests cannot serve as parish pastors makes it much harder for a bishop to employ and compensate them.

Pastoring a parish is by far the most common role of a Catholic priest. In a certain sense, Catholics think of all priests as pastors, a perception expressed in the practice of addressing priests as "Father." In fact, eight in 10 diocesan priests are, at any given time, either pastors or pastoral associates; the rest, who serve in schools, chaplaincies, or diocesan offices, will almost all serve as pastors at some point in their careers.[6] For many priests, since the celebration of the Mass is the central activity of the priesthood, the parish, a local community gathered and defined by their common worship in the Mass, is where the action is.

It was not until early 1981, six months after the Pastoral Provision norms had been published, that Vatican officials clarified that as a general rule married priests would not be permitted to serve "in cura ordinaria animarum" [in the ordinary cure of souls] but should work in an administrative, social, or scholastic function. In practical terms, this meant that married priests could not serve as pastors of parishes or as chaplains outside any Pastoral Provision parishes. This greatly changed the anticipated profile of the married priests, and imposed real practical difficulties on aspiring candidates, most of whom were already parish pastors.

Bishop Law and others of the American hierarchy objected, unsuccessfully, to this restriction when it was first articulated. In responses to our 2009 survey, most bishops still disagreed with it. In response to an open-ended question on this point, two-thirds (65 percent) of the bishops who expressed an opinion did not feel this restriction was necessary or effective. A few felt that it was unjust. The policy was "artificial," said one bishop; others wrote that it "treated them as second-class citizens" or was "prejudicial." "Exclusion from parish ministry is misguided when we have lay pastoral administrators in parishes," noted another.

The overwhelming majority of dissenting bishops, however, argued that restriction from the pastorate for married priests was simply pastorally unnecessary: "People would have no difficulty." "Our people do not question married priests serving as pastors." "People accept their ministry well." "I see no problem with [Pastoral Provision priests] serving as pastors." More than 50 bishops expressed thoughts similar to these. As noted in Chapter 1, about a third of the Pastoral Provision priests currently serve as de facto parish pastors, usually by means of an assignment as parish administrator. To the laypersons in these parishes, the lack of the canonical title of "pastor" is a distinction without a difference; sociologically, and in their experience, these married priests are their pastors.

Since the greatest personnel concern of bishops today is to find pastors, and a married priest is normally restricted from serving as a pastor, he is much more difficult to place than an ordinary celibate priest. Moreover, by restricting married priests from serving as pastors, the Church precludes the most common source of priestly income: the material support of a parish. For the bishop who must assign him, then, the Pastoral Provision priest presents both a deployment and a financial challenge. The financial challenge is real, but it is not as great as most bishops think.

The Myth of Higher Cost

From their survey responses it is clear that most bishops believed that the cost of supporting a married priest is substantially higher than for a celibate priest. A few bishops noted that they opposed implementing the Pastoral Provision in principle on grounds of introducing pay disparities among the clergy. More commonly their concern was practical. A recent article in a popular Catholic magazine lays out the typical case: "The average salary of a diocesan priest is $20,000, and living arrangements in a parish rectory allow for many economies. Married priests would most likely want to live outside the rectory, would need much higher salaries to support a family, and there would be an exponential increase in insurance costs. Where would the money come from?"[7] However, based on an examination of actual costs, every factual claim in this argument is untrue.

It is true that summary reports of salary data do seem to support the perception that a married priest costs more. Average overall taxable compensation for married Catholic priests is half again higher than that of celibate priests. This is misleading, however: when all the included allowances and benefits are taken into account, the difference in total compensation between a married and a celibate priest is far smaller. And when all the costs of maintaining a priest in a parish are considered, the difference in the average expense involved is very small to negligible. In some situations, a married priest can cost much less than a celibate one.

The comparison is complicated by the unique history and character of the ways that parishes provide material support to their clergy. Until recently, most of the material needs of priests were supplied by a system of benefices and customary gifts. Priests often received regular stocks of food, eating off the "larder of the parish," or the right to crops or rental income produced by parish-owned land or "glebe." In virtually all such arrangements, clergy were provided a house at parish expense, and parishes supplied other goods and services that varied greatly according to their means and ability. In the past 60 years, many of the customary benefice arrangements have begun to be displaced by cash compensation, but many in-kind provisions, particularly those related to rectory housing, still remain. Today, Catholic clergy are supported by a complex patchwork of in-kind provisions, allowances, and stipends.

Generally speaking, married Catholic clergy receive more of their compensation in cash, and much less in kind, than do celibate priests. I was able to compare the 2007 average compensation of celibate priests, including the estimated value of goods and services, with the corresponding amounts for married priests.[8] In addition to their salary, celibate priests also received cash allowances to cover social security tax, auto insurance, and other expenses, which were $5,844 more, on average, than corresponding allowances received by the married priests. Excess costs related to housing—utilities, maintenance, furniture, liability insurance, and housekeeping supplies—provided by the parish for a celibate priest amounted to another $5,227. Parishes also paid an average of $6,266 per celibate priest to provide personnel to care for the rectory, doing maintenance and repair, yard work, snow removal, and in many cases cleaning and cooking, which married priests or their wives performed at no charge to the parish. When these differences are taken into account, it costs a parish only $4,961 more to maintain a married priest, or less than 10 percent of their overall compensation. This difference is less than 2 percent of the average 2007 Catholic parish budget, conservatively estimated at about $300,000.[9] In sum, the common wisdom—that married priests must cost substantially more than celibate priests to maintain—appears to be highly overstated.

Married priests also often come with financial advantages that substantially reduce their costs to a parish. Health insurance would usually be expected to cost more for a married priest and his dependents, but about a third (30 percent) of the time it can cost the parish nothing: this proportion of married priests reported that they received health insurance through their wife's employer. Likewise, a diocese's pension liability may be higher for a married priest, since it would usually want to make provision for his wife as well. On the other hand, most of the Pastoral Provision priests were eligible for at least a minimal pension—and some received a full pension—through the Church Pension Fund of the Episcopal Church, and most of their wives will contribute Social Security benefits in addition to those of the priest to the household economy in retirement. About a third of the married priests' wives also have their own pension or 401k retirement savings, in addition to that of the priest. When all is said and done, the cost and liability of a married priest to the parish and the diocese is only slightly higher than, and may sometimes be lower than, that of a celibate priest.

Compensation and Deployment Strategies

Even if they do not cost more, or much more, married priests still present a bishop or diocese with significant challenges relating to compensation and deployment. A married priest necessarily complicates financial protocols that were established on the assumption that all priests would be unmarried. *Into Full Communion* (the manual for administering the Pastoral Provision) recognizes this difficulty when it advises: "It is very important that the sponsoring bishop realize that the financial needs of a married priest are completely different from those of a celibate priest. The sponsoring bishop and the petitioner should have an open and frank discussion regarding finances in the context of the foreseen pastoral ministry determined by the sponsoring bishop."[10] In practice, as noted above, the petitioner was often already in a job that became his pastoral ministry by the time the petitioner and bishop might have had such a discussion; and neither of them was aware of the extent of the differences and complications involved in supporting a married priest. In most cases, particularly for the first married priest ordained in a diocese, the differences were only discovered as a result of problems that developed.

As noted above, many married priests do not need health coverage from the diocese, since they are covered by their wife's employer. For those that do, however, a problem is presented by the fact that diocesan health insurance plans for priests typically do not provide an option for family coverage. Many dioceses have put their married priests who need it on the corresponding plans that they maintain for their lay employees. Others have contracted individualized plans for the married priests and their families.

Likewise, diocesan retirement plans typically do not provide for spousal benefits or care. In the case of two of the earlier Pastoral Provision ordinations, the diocese failed to take this responsibility into account, which led to trouble when the husband predeceased the wife and she was left in difficult financial straits. Catholic canons require a bishop to provide for his priests in their old age, but say nothing about his obligation to a priest's wife, much less his surviving wife. In both cases just mentioned, the bishop acknowledged a moral obligation to provide care for the surviving wife, but was unable to do so to the extent or in a manner that fully satisfied the wife (or himself).

These cautionary tales underscore the importance of preparing for retirement and spousal/survivor support for the married priest in a deliberate manner. The burden of doing so is mitigated by the fact that most of the Pastoral Provision priests are vested in the Church Pension Fund of the Episcopal Church, a well-capitalized defined-benefit pension plan, from which they are eligible to receive a minimum pension, and which does provide a small income to the surviving wife. As with health insurance, many dioceses also have retirement plans for lay employees that are appropriate for married priests. It is in the interest of both the priest and the diocese to engage in an explicit review of retirement provisions to make sure that his wife is adequately provided for in the event of his untimely death.

Another frequently overlooked concern is for the education of the priest's children. Since he has a particular obligation, as well as a strong interest, in raising his children in the Catholic faith, it is appropriate to provide assistance to cover the usually high cost of Catholic schooling. Scholarship assistance for the children of clergy is common in Protestant settings, including the Episcopal Church, but is understandably absent in the Catholic Church. Parishes with schools sometimes waived and almost always discounted tuition for the children of a married priest who served in that parish. However, no assistance was usually provided for the children of married priests based outside parishes. Some dioceses considered their married priests eligible for the same discounts that were commonly provided to teachers in the diocesan schools.

As already noted, the biggest difference in married priest compensation has to do with housing, specifically that, unlike celibate priests, married priests tend to live in their own homes. This difference also complicated deployment considerations. Although a minority of the married priests did live in a house (21 percent) or an apartment (7 percent) supplied by their diocese or other institution, as might a celibate priest, most (68 percent) of them, as noted above, owned their own home. Almost all of the non-parish-based priests owned their own home, and only one in five of those who served a parish full-time (11 percent of the total) lived in a church rectory.

A married priest also undergoes an interim period, often several years, between leaving his Anglican ministry and being ordained as a Catholic priest, which complicates compensation and deployment considerations. A quarter (24 percent) of the married priests reported that they experienced financial struggles during the interim period. On the bishops survey, only a quarter (28 percent) of the bishops felt that they have some responsibility for the candidate's financial support during this period. A plurality (45 percent) of the bishops disagreed, and another quarter (27 percent) were neutral on this question. The hesitancy of most bishops to commit to supporting a candidate during this period, much as they would a seminarian, certainly inhibits some married priest prospects from seeking ordination in those dioceses. But even for the majority of married priest candidates who were financially self-sustaining during this period, the diocese's delay in initiating financial arrangements made subsequent deployment and compensation arrangements more difficult.

Almost all the married priests who owned their own home purchased it during the interim period before ordination, subsequent to their conversion and relocation into the diocese where they were serving. Thus, upon ordination, the diocese was sometimes presented with a fait accompli that led to frustration either on the part of the bishop, who felt limited in his freedom to place the priest or constrained to support housing expenses that he had no part in choosing, or on the part of the priest and his family, who felt abruptly uprooted if he asked them to move.

Anticipating these problems, some bishops placed married priest families in houses or other facilities already owned by the diocese. This arrangement can be mutually beneficial financially, though it requires flexibility on the part of the married priest's family. Other dioceses have taken a proactive approach to housing, working with newly ordained married priests and their wives to find a house they like, then structuring a housing allowance based on that purchase. Two dioceses have followed an interesting variant of this strategy: The diocese invited the clergy couple to select a house of their liking, which the diocese then purchased outright. The diocese owns the house and provides long-term maintenance and upkeep and an allowance to cover utilities, while the couple, and particularly the wife, is assured of a lifetime right of residence. This strategy tends to increase the satisfaction of the clergy couple with their housing situation, since they have the assurance of stable residence in a house and neighborhood of their choosing. At the same time, it neatly addresses two financial support problems at once: housing, and liability for the wife's residence if her husband predeceases her. For the diocese, the greater part of the cost of housing is fixed at the time of purchase, and it can expect to recoup much of the cost when it eventually sells the house.

The deployment and compensation challenges that a married priest presents to a bishop are most frequently met by one of two strategies: either by tacitly skirting the canonical restrictions so that the married priest effectively functions as a parish pastor, or by placement in a Church-related institution with resources and financial structures in place to employ a married man. About an equal number of the Pastoral Provision priests serve under each arrangement. While all of the Pastoral Provision priests celebrated Mass regularly in a parish under some arrangement, two-thirds (66 percent) of them reported that a majority of their workweek was spent ministering in a parish; half (49 percent) of them were in parish ministry full-time. Two-thirds of those working full-time for a parish (36 percent of the total) functioned as the de facto pastor of the parish, usually with the canonical title of parish administrator. Of the half (51 percent) of the priests whose main job was not based in a parish, over half were educators, employed as a teacher or administrator in a Catholic university (33 percent) or high school (25 percent). The remainder served in a diocesan office (one in four) or hospital chaplaincy (one in six).

Into Full Communion, assuming inaccurately that none of the priests would serve in a parish, directs: "Since the Pastoral Provision requires that married priests exercise ministries that in principle do not involve the ordinary care of souls, the sponsoring bishop should determine whether the petitioner is suitable to serve in non-parochial ministries."[11] In practice, bishops have done almost no placement of married priests in non-parochial ministries outside diocesan bureaucracies. While most of the married priests who served in parishes or a diocesan office had been placed in their jobs at the initiative of the diocese, most of the ones who served in a non-diocesan institution, such as a hospital or independent Catholic school, had found their jobs on their own. Independent Catholic institutions employ more priests as chaplains and teachers than dioceses do, and dioceses increasingly use laypersons, not priests, in administrative positions.

Most of the priests in non-parochial ministry who had found their own job had done so in the interim between priesthoods. Since they had begun their job as a layperson, the priestly role, while compatible with or of added value to their work, was not essential to it. In two cases the married priest was placed in a diocesan institution before ordination and then subsequently was ordained in secret, with the expectation that he would continue in the same job as a priest. Married priests not in a parish were also often not included in diocesan deployment decisions, as they were perceived to be settled in their jobs; if they left their job, typically they were not placed by the diocese, but were on their own in finding a new one. In most cases, this independence was a happy arrangement for the priest, although some felt neglected and yearned to serve in a parish.

The married priests tended to remain in one job much longer than comparable celibate priests. The majority of the married priests, with an average of 17 years in the Catholic priesthood, were still in their first job since ordination. Celibate priests typically change jobs every five to seven years.[12] In part, this difference reflects the fact that the married convert priests were much older (age 49) on average when they entered Catholic priesthood than are priests in general (age 29). Most Catholic priests receive shorter job assignments early in their career, when they serve as curates (assistant pastors), than they do later, after they become pastors. The purpose is to give new priests experience in a variety of settings to help them grow as pastors. Very likely the Pastoral Provision priests, all seasoned pastors, were not perceived to need this type of experience as much.

Another factor is that it is much more complicated for a bishop to move a married priest. Since, as noted above, they are eligible for a narrower range of jobs, it is harder to find an appropriate placement for them. Plus, reassigning a married priest may involve a change of schools for children, the sale of one home and purchase of another, taking into account the interest and job of his wife, and other factors that root a family in a particular community to a much greater extent than a celibate priest who resides in a church rectory. For these reasons, a bishop, if he has already found a suitable place for the married priest, may be much more inclined to leave him there, rather than face the difficulty of moving him.

Predicting Ordination

Given these complications, it may not be surprising that the bishops were evenly divided on the question of their willingness to ordain a married priest. Just over half (56 percent) agreed that they would welcome the opportunity to do so. However, while concerns about money and mixed signals on celibacy have an effect, these were not the primary considerations affecting the bishops' willingness to ordain.

Figure 6.3 reports the strongest influences on the bishops' willingness to ordain, in descending order. The single item with the greatest effect on a bishop's disposition to ordain a married priest was his personal impression of the actual Pastoral Provision priests he had known. Nine in 10 (87 percent) bishops who agreed with the statement "I generally admire the Pastoral Provision priests I have known" reported that they would welcome the opportunity to ordain a Pastoral Provision priest in future, whereas none of the bishops who disagreed with this statement was willing to ordain a future Pastoral Provision priest. Similar strong effects on the bishops' willingness to ordain a married priest were related to statements of general support for the Pastoral Provision as a concept—that the bishop had a strong sense of support for the program, thought it should be expanded, believed that the conditions that led to creating it are still valid, and did not think it should be discontinued. The effect of concerns over celibacy and finances were secondary.

Assessing the separate influence of single items can, of course, be misleading, since the considerations affecting a decision like ordination often interact. A regression model that accounts for such combined influences revealed that just two factors accounted for a bishop's willingness to

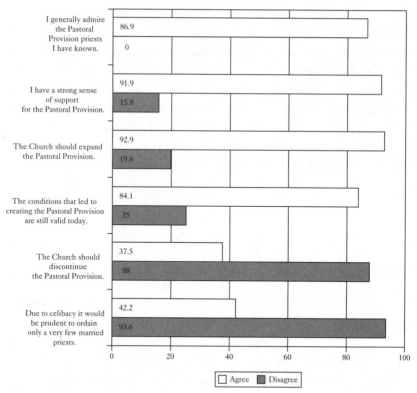

FIGURE 6.3 Views Affecting Willingness to Ordain a Married Priest, Comparing Percent Willing to Ordain by Agreement or Disagreement with Selected Items

ordain a Pastoral Provision priest. First, and most important, the bishop strongly supports the program in principle, as indicated by a strong sense of personal support and agreement that the Church should expand the Pastoral Provision. Second, the bishop disagrees with the proposition that only a few Pastoral Provision priests should be ordained; in other words, he is less concerned that ordaining a married priest would harm the rule of celibacy. The stronger these two factors are, the more likely a bishop is to be favorable toward ordaining a Pastoral Provision priest.[13]

It may seem ironic, but personal admiration for Pastoral Provision priests had little effect on the bishops' disposition to ordain. The reason is that such admiration is so pervasive—only 5 percent of bishops reported that they did not admire Pastoral Provision priests of their acquaintance—and the effect of this feeling is so strong. Because almost all bishops strongly admire Pastoral Provision priests, there is very little variation among them to be explained by this factor.

Given the risk and complication of a Pastoral Provision ordination, an expression of support or willingness to ordain on a survey item can be misleading. It is one thing for a bishop to check a survey box agreeing with the idea of welcoming a married convert Anglican priest. It is quite another, much more difficult, thing for a bishop to put the resources and peacefulness of his diocese on the line to actually ordain such a priest. As noted above, a bishop's willingness to ordain a married priest was overall not related—actually, it had a U-shaped relationship—to the number of married priests he had already had in his diocese.

I also explored how the fact that he already had married priests in his diocese affected a bishop's willingness to ordain a married priest. Just three factors, all expressing general support, were significantly related to having a married priest in the diocese. First, bishops who agreed that they generally admired Pastoral Provision priests were over 10 times more likely to have ordained one. Second, as already noted, bishops who already had a married priest in their diocese were much less likely to affirm that they would welcome ordaining an additional married priest. Finally, being well informed about Pastoral Provision priests also was strongly associated with having ordained one. Bishops who agreed that they had a good general understanding of the Pastoral Provision were about three times as likely to have ordained one as those who disagreed. This is most likely an effect, not a cause, of having done an ordination, since four of five bishops (80 percent) agreed that they did have a good understanding of the Pastoral Provision.[14]

Whether we are talking about intent or behavior, the crucial factors impelling bishops to ordain a Pastoral Provision priest are principled, not practical or ideological. Admiration of such priests is a given, and while practicalities and personal qualities are not absent from the bishops' thinking about Pastoral Provision ordinations, their decisions to ordain are mostly decided by abstract views on the value of the Pastoral Provision to the Church. Indeed, their principled commitment to such an ordination must be particularly strong in order to overcome the difficulties that are often involved.

In this respect, the bishops mirror the incoming priests, who enter the Catholic Church out of concern for doctrinal truth despite, in many cases, great personal inconvenience. Relatively few priests are sufficiently motivated to do that. Similarly, relatively few bishops may be motivated to negotiate the difficulties involved in ordaining them.

Conclusion: Exercising Risk and Caution

It is only by the concrete action of diocesan bishops that the grand ideals expressed in the Pastoral Provision come to fruition. While the Vatican—concerned for history and the global Church—encourages generosity in receiving married convert priests, bishops—concerned for the dioceses and parishes of their local community—are understandably cautious. The failure of a married priest may briefly embarrass the Church at large, but it can deeply trouble a diocese and can devastate a parish. A perception of unfairness or change on celibacy may complicate teaching a little for the global Church, but it can engender concerted controversy and disaffection among the clergy of a diocese.

We began by asking why there have been so few Pastoral Provision ordinations, despite the fact that bishops consistently express collective support for them. The answer is found in the fact that, although support for the policy is crucial, it is only one of several important factors. A bishop's support for the Pastoral Provision as a policy is not likely to lead to an ordination unless: (1) his support is particularly strong, enough to persist in overcoming the obstacles involved; (2) he admires Pastoral Provision priests he has known; (3) the clergy of his diocese are sufficiently receptive; (4) he has employment for the priest outside a parish or is willing to skirt restrictions to place him in a parish; and (5) he does not already have two or more of them in his diocese. It is also necessary, of course, for the bishop to be presented with a candidate—a matter on which I have no data.

Given these complex conditions and obstacles, perhaps the question should not be why Pastoral Provision ordinations have been so few but why there have been so many. In light of the difficulties and potential problems involved, it is remarkable that so many bishops have taken the risk to ordain a married priest, and that those ordinations have, in the vast majority of cases, turned out so well. That this is the case testifies to the faithfulness and idealism of the Catholic bishops—their ability to exercise risk as well as caution—which is more than a match for the corresponding qualities among the married priests themselves.

7

Are Married Priests Worse—or Better?

Introduction: Raising the Celibacy Issue

"I think it would be great if all priests could get married! Don't you, Father Paul?" The questioner, a writer in her early sixties, looked at me brightly across the restaurant table where we were grabbing a meal between the sessions of an academic conference. She obviously expected a quick affirmative reply. After all, here I was, a married Catholic priest—surely I would support an end to the rule of celibacy.

My lunch partner's question was a natural and common one. Like many Vatican II liberals, my questioner approached the issue of optional clergy celibacy with a vague sentimentality about marriage and sexual fulfillment that inclined her to favor it, without having thought seriously about the theological distinctions and justification for the practice of clergy celibacy. To be sure, Catholic conservatives who reject married clergy out of hand approach the issue with an equally sentimental set of notions about priesthood and sexuality. In the wake of the sexual revolution, changing norms on marriage, massive defections of priests who leave to marry, and persistent clergy pedophilia, it is hard for anyone to think clearly about clergy celibacy. Surely, existing married priests can shed some light on the subject.

The issue of celibacy comes up in numerous encounters by the married priests with people in the parish and community. Since everyone knows that Catholic priests cannot marry, the reception of these married men into the Catholic priesthood often raises questions—and eyebrows—for both Catholics and non-Catholics alike. Almost all the priests I interviewed, and all the wives without exception, reported that they had run into such questions. It was not unusual for them to have someone insist, upon first discovering that they were married, that they could not be actual or valid priests.

Just as the marriages of the Pastoral Provision priests are shaped by their status as clergy, so their priesthood is undeniably demarcated and defined by their status as married men. Marriage sets them apart from other priests and sharply limits their social and career prospects in the Church. They are restricted from serving as parish pastors, the central career role of a Catholic priest. In numerous small ways, the rhythm and experience of their lives as married men with families, living in homes in the midst of neighborhoods rather than in rectories, paying mortgages, buying school uniforms, and so on, will always be distinct from that of most priests. They enter the Church as outsiders to the extensive friendship networks that diocesan priests develop through shared seminary and early career experiences. Advancement to a higher position in the hierarchy is out of the question. Though no Church rule restricts it, no Pastoral Provision priest has ever been named a monsignor—the minimum honorific title above "reverend" that a priest can receive—nor is likely to be.

This chapter and the next examine the hotly debated issue of clergy celibacy in light of the experiences and perspectives of the Pastoral Provision priests. Although some of the debate over celibacy is theological, other questions are amenable to empirical study. In order to get at those issues, it will be helpful first to briefly examine the basics of the debate over celibacy.

The Paradox of Catholic Clergy Celibacy
Overview and Definitions

Catholic clergy celibacy is unique. Although monastic celibacy is found in many world religions, no other faith requires its congregational leaders to refrain from marriage. Local pastors, whom Catholics call "secular priests" (to distinguish them from priests who have also taken monastic vows), do not usually live in community with other priests, and are not withdrawn from ordinary life to pursue interior enlightenment; they live, at least in principle, in the same social and economic circumstances as the lay Catholics they are called to serve and lead. Yet they are committed to lifelong celibacy.

These celibate pastors, furthermore, typically lead large groups of adherents who are married, and who are encouraged to value marriage, family, and children as important spiritual goods. The tensions, both creative and hostile, generated by this juxtaposition may account in part for the unique salience and power of celibacy in Catholic life. Forgoing a family of their own, priests are in a certain sense part of every family in the parish. The priest joins with each family to sacralize the threshold moments of life: birth, coming of age, marriage, and death. By ancient custom, Catholic parents with many children address this man who will never have children as "Father."

The confusion that many people, even many Catholics, feel about clergy celibacy is heightened by a lack of awareness of some important, but subtle, distinctions. First, people often assume that, because celibacy is required of Catholic priests, it is essential to the priesthood; but Catholic thinking has repeatedly rejected this latter proposition. In ecclesiastical terms, celibacy is a discipline, but not a dogma, of the Church. Put another way, clergy celibacy is a rule of the Church, not a commandment of God. While Catholic thinking has sometimes gone so far as to affirm that there is an affinity between priesthood and celibacy, it has never taught that celibacy is essential or necessary, other than as a customary discipline, in order to be a priest.

Second, clergy celibacy is often conflated with a larger set of issues in the Catholic Church—its male-only priesthood, authoritarian structures of leadership, refusal to endorse homosexual relations, or prohibition of divorce or artificial contraception—generally by those critiquing Catholic practice and seeking reform.[1] Such general critiques may raise important issues to consider, but they fail to distinguish between matters on which the Catholic Church sees itself as open to change, such as celibacy, and settled doctrinal matters, such as the other items noted above. Such treatments unnecessarily confuse celibacy with other, more fundamental features of Catholicism, to the detriment of our ability to understand—and critique—the practice of clergy celibacy as understood by the Church itself.

Third, many people fail to distinguish between the case of a Catholic priest getting married and that of a married man becoming a Catholic priest. This subtle but crucial distinction goes all the way back to the earliest days of the Church. As far as we know, beginning around the second generation of Christians, no man who had entered what are today known as holy orders—that is, become a deacon, priest, or bishop—was subsequently allowed to marry. In the long history of the Church, there has never been an exception to this rule. As a condition of his ordination, every Pastoral Provision priest agrees that, if his wife predeceases him, he will not be permitted to remarry. This "secondary celibacy" is also required of the nearly 18,000 permanent deacons, almost all married, in the Catholic Church today.

On the other hand, since the earliest years of the Church, many men who were already married were allowed to receive holy orders. Indeed, this was the situation of most of the original 12 apostles chosen by Christ himself. This ancient tradition has persisted to the present day in Eastern Catholic Churches. Priests of these rites—which are legitimate expressions of the Catholic faith, in full communion with the Pope—are permitted to be married, though most do practice celibacy, which is necessary for advancement in the Church hierarchy beyond the status of a parish priest. The Latin Rite developed a tradition of celibacy for all clergy by the Middle Ages, and perhaps much earlier. In response to the Protestant challenges to clergy celibacy during the Reformation, the Catholic Church reaffirmed its commitment to a celibate clergy. While the issue of required clergy celibacy has not been at the root of any Christian division, in fact none of the other major divisions in Christianity, such as Orthodoxy or Protestantism, has continued it.

In the past century, as the Church has opened up to Protestantism in new ways, the Pope has occasionally allowed married Protestant clergymen who convert to the Catholic faith to be received into the Latin Rite priesthood. Pius XII began this practice with some married Lutheran convert priests following World War II. Since that time, there have always been a small number of active, validly ordained secular priests in the Catholic Church who are married. The Pastoral Provision merely regularized the consideration of such exceptions for Anglican clergy.

Ongoing Ambivalence

Throughout its long history, the Catholic Church has never fully embraced either clergy celibacy or clergy marriage. Although celibacy is not considered essential to the Catholic secular priesthood, it has been a nearly universal practice since the thirteenth century and was widespread for as much as a thousand years before that. While there are certainly theological questions involved, they have never been determinative, with the result that different and even contrasting policies have held sway in various eras, regions, and circumstances over the long history of Christianity.

This ambivalence begins with the Biblical record. Jesus was unmarried and commended celibacy, yet the New Testament refers to Peter's wife and the fact that she, like other church leaders' wives, accompanied him in his apostolic travels.[2] St. Paul recommends that Christian leaders refrain from marriage and seems to indicate that he was unmarried himself (or at least traveling apart from his wife), yet he explicitly permits marriage and counsels that a bishop should be a "husband of one wife" and have well-behaved children.[3]

In the third century, asceticism flourished as many Christians, subject to violent persecution, fled, literally, into the desert, to devote themselves to prayer and fasting in isolation or in celibate communities. These early attempts to escape the corrupting entanglements of the world, the flesh, and the devil (as they were later codified) eventually became formalized in the founding of monastic orders with vows of poverty, chastity (i.e., celibacy), and obedience. From this period on, all Christians had to choose between two contexts, or "states of life" (as the Church calls them): "secular" life or "religious" life, which requires celibacy. As the name implies, religious life was considered purer or more holy.

Priests, who have direct contact with the holy, were naturally expected to live in the holier state. Accordingly, it became the universal custom that when a man became a priest he was no longer permitted to marry.[4] This rule has continued to the present day without exception or serious challenge. Whether a married man could subsequently be ordained a priest, however, was another matter. On this there was a wide variety of practices in the far-flung regions of the Church, ranging from, in some dioceses or regions, the routine ordination of married men to, in others, the practice of ordaining only unmarried men, much like today.[5]

In 315, when the Emperor Constantine unexpectedly converted, Christianity was transformed almost overnight from an outlaw sect to the established religion of the Roman Empire. With the coming of permanent status and centralized administration, the Church began to regularize the immense variety of local customs and practices that had developed during the centuries of persecution. This was the era of the great Christological controversies, when regional synods were practically at war with one another, and bishops were often arrested, exiled, or murdered over theological differences.

Disputes often aligned with two centers of power that vied for supremacy in the fading empire: the Pope, in Rome, and the Emperor, in Constantinople. In the East, married Church leaders, with children, were more common and more accepted than in the West. Eventually, as with other issues of practice, such as Church governance and the use of icons, on which full agreement was not essential, the Church tolerated diversity. In the East, married men were permitted to be ordained, with some restrictions on advancement; in the West, only unmarried men could be ordained.

Although clergy celibacy was the established policy of the West by the seventh century, local variation persisted (as on many matters) until, in the twelfth century, a universal code of canon law was developed. It was not until the Second Lateran Council, in 1139, that the practice was codified for the entire Western Church. The rule proved difficult to enforce, and the Church went through successive periods of laxity and reform.

The Protestant Reformers of the sixteenth century rejected both monastic and clergy celibacy as unscriptural corruptions of the freedom of the Gospel. Luther and Calvin opposed both Catholic celibacy and radical Protestant celibate communities. The reformers also believed that sexual abstinence was impossible for men; to require it of priests would only lead to sexual sin and debauchery.[6] The ideal context for the Christian life was godly marriage. As did many of his clerical and religious followers, Luther married a former nun and fathered a family. The churches of the Reformation eventually replaced the ideal of clergy celibacy with that of the clergy wife.

The issue of married Catholic clergy is particularly sensitive in the United States because of the history of Eastern Rite immigrants over the past century. Unlike the Latin Rite, which prevailed in Western Europe, many of the Catholic countries of Eastern Europe have a long tradition of married clergy. By the late nineteenth century, when Eastern Catholic immigrants came in large numbers to the United States, the tradition of clergy celibacy of the Irish, Italian, and German Catholics of the Latin Rite was already firmly established and virtually universal. Growing tensions between the Eastern Catholics and the Latin Rite hierarchy, who had theological and pastoral objections to an influx of married clergy, led to an 1890 decision by the Pope to ban the ordination of married Eastern Catholic priests in the United States. This decision led a group of Greek Catholics to sever ties with Rome and align with the Russian Orthodox

Church, eventually growing into today's Greek Orthodox Church in the United States.

Subsequent Vatican decisions extended and reinforced the restrictions on married Eastern Catholic clergy. Concerned that a minority of married clergy might cause envy and unrest among celibate priests, in 1907 Pope Pius X issued an apostolic letter requiring celibacy for all priests serving in the United States—a policy that was widely ignored among Eastern Rite Catholics. Following a 1929 papal reaffirmation of the ban, in the 1930s groups of Ruthenian and Carpatho-Russian Catholics followed the Greeks in splitting from Rome. The Vatican position was that the Eastern Churches, which could exercise unique cultural traditions in their homelands, had to conform to the tradition or sensibility of the dominant Latin Rite Catholics in the United States. In the "melting pot" of immigrant differences, US Catholic clerical culture would remain exclusively celibate.

Since the late 1960s, in the wake of the Second Vatican Council, opinion among American Catholic laity on the issue of celibacy has diverged along liberal and conservative lines. Self-styled progressives have argued that the requirement of clergy celibacy is outmoded, repressive, and a barrier both to the priest's personal fulfillment and the ability of the Church to relate to the modern world. Self-styled orthodox elements, joined at times by the magisterium, have reasserted the symbolic or spiritual value of clergy celibacy, as well as its practical value for the work of the Church.

Shortly after Vatican II, support for optional celibacy among American Catholic clergy rapidly shot up to new heights. In their 1970 survey Greeley and Schoenherr found that over half (56 percent) of diocesan priests agreed that "celibacy should be a matter of personal choice for diocesan priests."[7] Dramatic differences in opinion by age suggested that clerical support for optional celibacy would grow even larger. Four-fifths (82 percent) of the priests under the age of 35 were in favor of optional celibacy (three-fifths "strongly agreed"), but only one-fifth (22 percent) of those over age 55.

Despite their own views, in 1970 almost all the priests anticipated an imminent relaxation of the rule of celibacy: over 9 in 10 (94 percent) thought that within 20 years "the present law of celibacy will be changed allowing priests to be married if they wish." Three-quarters (75 percent) of them thought it would happen within 10 years. A third (34 percent) of the younger priests (under age 35) reported that they would probably get married themselves if the rule were relaxed. As it became clear that the rule of celibacy would not be relaxed, thousands of priests resigned. In 1974 Schoenherr and Greeley wrote that in the face of a widespread desire to marry, "the cost of celibacy is currently a priest's principal consideration" in deciding to leave the priesthood.[8]

Support for optional celibacy among Catholic priests has remained high, even as the rate of resignations have waned. Subsequent replications of Greeley and Schoenherr's survey found that the level of support for optional celibacy was virtually unchanged in 1985 (53 percent) and 2001 (55 percent).[9] However, the age differences were the opposite of what they were in 1969, suggesting pending growth in support of the Church's present practice among the clergy. In 2001, optional celibacy was supported by over half (56 percent) of priests over the age of 55, but by a much smaller percentage (30 percent) of priests aged 35 and under. Two forces largely account for this conservatizing trend: the defection of many priests during the 1970s, and the growing influx of more conservative clergy since the 1980s.

Unlike the sixteenth century, when the celibacy debate was between Catholic and Protestant, today the debate is between Catholic and Catholic. It is Catholics who advocate most vocally for clergy marriage, typically as part of a cluster of issues—women priests, democratic church governance, less doctrinal rigidity—that have animated Protestants for generations. In this internal Catholic debate, where the disputants share a common framework of belief on most issues, theological arguments take a back seat to concerns about more earthly matters such as priestly satisfaction or institutional effectiveness. Theology is displaced, in part, by social science. This is all the more the case since one of the primary justifications for the practice of celibacy from the traditional side involves an explicitly empirical hypothesis.

The Catholic Argument: A Celibacy Advantage

One of the central arguments made by the Catholic Church in favor of clergy celibacy is that the demands of marriage impede a man's priestly ministry. A married priest is perceived to have two somewhat conflicting vocations that divide his loyalty and weaken his ability to serve the Church. This understanding is based on the Bible itself; St. Paul, addressing the church at Corinth, writes (in a verse quoted in the Catholic Catechism): "An unmarried man is anxious about the things of the

Lord, how he may please the Lord. But a married man is anxious about the things of the world, how he may please his wife, and he is divided."[10] Wives are competition for, or (at best) a distraction from, an otherwise single-minded focus on Christ and the Church, so it is best, says Paul, not to have one. This reasoning is explicitly reflected in Catholic canon law: "Clerics are ... bound to celibacy ... by which sacred ministers ... are able to dedicate themselves more freely to the service of God and humanity."[11]

Paul's comment is preceded by the unusual proviso that "I have no command from the Lord, but I give my own opinion," reflecting his personal observation and experience.[12] He is not advocating that married men should be anxious about the things of the world rather than those of the Lord, but observing, even conceding, that that is how they behave in practice. The same empirical conclusion has been generally affirmed by Catholics—sometimes in the face of principle. In a 1960s survey of Catholic priests, Joseph Fichter found that over half (54.2 percent) felt that married priests would be "less effective than the celibate clergy in the parish ministry," despite the fact that three-fifths (61.6 percent) of them also supported allowing priests to marry.[13]

Paul also makes clear that his advice about marriage and celibacy is time-dependent, prompted by the expectation that the end of the age will occur soon, during the lifetime of his hearers: "I would like to spare you [affliction]. I tell you brothers, time is running out. ... For the world in its present form is passing away."[14] Since two millennia have now passed without the coming of the envisioned end, it may be fair to ask whether the dynamics of marriage and Christian commitment may also be different.

To test this question convincingly requires examining comparable samples of celibate and married priests, which was impossible until the Pastoral Provision. The presence of these married priests scattered among the larger body of celibate ones provides a kind of natural experiment.

The Celibacy Advantage Examined

Are unmarried priests more "able to dedicate themselves freely to the service of God and humanity" than are married priests? Do unmarried men, without the demands of wives and children, simply have more available time and energy to devote to the service of God and parish?

Obviously, married priests do have to devote time to their families. But unmarried priests undoubtedly also experience conflicting commitments or distractions from their priestly ministry, including family concerns. The critical question is whether celibate priests do in fact engage in more prayer or priestly ministry than married ones.

As we saw in Chapter 5, family and parish demands often competed for the married priest's time and affection, but instead of distracting from the parish, those conflicts were generally resolved in favor of greater service to the parish. This is largely due to the wives' strong commitment to the parish and the Church, a commitment that both augmented and reinforced the ministry of their husbands. There is good reason to believe, therefore, that married priests may not be at a disadvantage in their availability for ministry, and may in fact have an advantage.

St. Paul's idea that a wife is a distraction from ministry could not have considered the nature of modern clergy marriages, and in particular the established social role of the minister's wife. When a wife makes it clear that she is most pleased when he is pleasing the Lord, the very dynamics that St. Paul feared would draw a man away actually serve to reinforce his commitment to serving the Church. Moreover, the wives, as we saw in Chapter 5, added their own service to that of their husband in many ways, from supporting church music to managing the parish office. The net service to the parish of this "two-for-one" arrangement might exceed the net service from any comparable unmarried priest.

With these reflections in mind, we can compare the behavior of unmarried and married priests.

Workload

The number of hours worked per week is a common measure of job commitment and relates directly to the amount of service provided by the worker. Those who are more devoted to God could reasonably be expected to spend more time ministering to the parish or other apostolate than do those who are less devoted.

Table 7.1 compares weekly hours worked by the married and celibate priests, repeating information already reported in Chapter 1 (Table 1.3). In order to make the comparison as conservative as possible, the data for celibate priests, but not for married priests, excludes retired priests. What the comparison shows is that while both groups of priests worked long hours, a sizable proportion of the celibate priests worked far fewer

**Table 7.1 Priests' Workweek, Comparing Married
and Celibate Priests**

	Celibate Priests*	Married Priests
	Hours worked each week	
Median	50	52
10% work more than	72	72
10% work fewer than	30	42

* Excludes retired priests.

hours than did the married priests. Only 10 percent of the married priests worked fewer than 42 hours per week, while the corresponding percentile for the unmarried priests was much smaller, at 30 hours; over a quarter (26 percent) of the celibate priests worked fewer than 40 hours per week (not shown). The median workweek of the married priests was two hours longer than that of their celibate counterparts. Possibly this difference is due to sampling or measurement variation, but it is clear that the celibate priests do not work significantly *more* hours than the married priests.

As discussed in Chapter 1, the substantially shorter workweek of many of the unmarried priests is reflected in a much higher number of reported days off than for the married priests. Figure 7.1 shows this. Nine in 10 celibate priests, compared to only 6 in 10 married priests, reported that they took at least one day off from work each week. Close to half (45 percent) of the celibate priests reported that they took two or more days off per week, an amount of rest that was possible for only 14 percent of the married priests. A quarter of the married priests reported that they regularly took part of one day, but not an entire day, off each week.[15] A fifth (22 percent) of the married priests, but only half as many (10 percent) of the unmarried priests, worked seven days a week without any day off.

In sum, in direct contradiction of the hypothesis that celibate priests will be more devoted than married priests, many celibate priests worked less, and most took more days off, than did married priests. This does not imply in any way that the celibate priests were taking their ease. They worked far longer hours, with fewer days off, than the average American or many other professionals. But the married priests worked still longer hours with yet fewer days off.

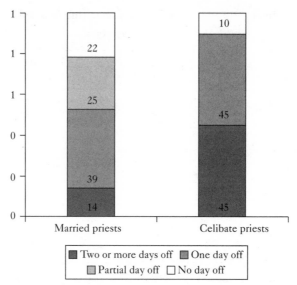

FIGURE 7.1 Weekly Days Off, Comparing Married and Celibate Catholic Priests (in Percent)

Prayer and Devotional Practices

A look at devotional practices also fails to support the idea that unmarried priests show greater devotion than do married priests. Figure 7.2 shows the comparison. The figure compares participation in three key priestly devotional practices: daily prayer of the Divine Office, also known as the breviary; confession at least once a month; and a retreat each year. Frequency of confession is a good general indicator of Catholic devotion; priests are enjoined to make confession at least once a month. Daily breviary prayer and an annual retreat are required of Catholic priests, and so form a particularly appropriate basis for comparison of the level of devotion of priests.

In Chapter 1 we saw that the devotional practices of the married priests were structured differently from those of celibate priests. The married priests were more frequent in the practice of devotions that could be performed individually or with little or no expense; on practices requiring extensive commitment of time and money—spiritual direction and retreats—the celibate priests had higher participation than the married priests. Figure 7.2 shows the two practices in which there was the greatest difference between the two groups of priests (breviary and retreats)— and the central practice (confession) on which there was essentially no

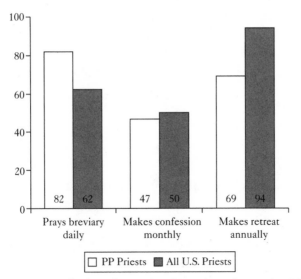

FIGURE 7.2 Frequency of Selected Devotional Practices, Comparing Married and Celibate Catholic Priests (in Percent)

difference. Four in five (82 percent) of the married priests, compared to less than half (48 percent) of the celibate priests, reported praying the breviary on a daily basis. About the same amount of married priests (47 percent) as unmarried priests (50 percent) made monthly confession. And almost all (94 percent) of the unmarried priests, but only two-thirds (69 percent) of the married priests, made a retreat each year.

While the structure of devotion is different, with married priests practicing some devotions more and some less than unmarried priests, the overall level of devotion in the two groups of priests is very similar. There is no suggestion in the data that the unmarried priests demonstrate more devotion. Perhaps, however, it is marriage demands, and not a relative lack of access to infrastructure or support (as suggested in Chapter 1), that inhibit the married priests from going on retreats as often as the unmarried priests. To test this question, I restricted the married priest data to show only those who were pastors, and thus would likely have access to the same kind of support for attendance at retreats that are available to most unmarried Catholic priests. The proportions of the married pastors praying the breviary daily and making confession monthly were unchanged from the full sample of married priests, at 82 percent and 47 percent, respectively. But the proportion of them who made a retreat at least once a year increased from 69 percent of all married priests to 89 percent of the married pastors, only slightly less than the 94 percent of unmarried priests who made an annual retreat. It does appear, therefore, that it is not marital demands but lack of support, such as an allowance of time and money to devote to a retreat, that constricts the remaining married priests from more frequent participation in retreats.

By the same reasoning, it is appropriate to wonder why the married priests pray the breviary so much more faithfully than do the unmarried priests. On the canonical hypothesis, we would expect married priests to be especially inhibited in maintaining daily personal prayers in the home, a practice that directly conflicts with potential family time. Yet just the opposite is the case. If, in theory, marriage might inhibit some devotions, it might also encourage others. Could it be that their strongly devoted wives encourage the priest in his daily prayers, or help keep him honest about maintaining it? Or perhaps the priest and his wife pray the breviary together, encouraging by their marital community greater faithfulness in this devotional service to God and the Church?

Job Satisfaction and Orthodoxy

Job satisfaction is a highly reliable indicator of job commitment, since "[p]eople who are satisfied with their jobs usually develop high levels of commitment, whereas those who are less satisfied are also less commit-ted."[16] Greater orthodoxy or dogmatism is also associated with stronger commitment to the clergy role.[17] On both job satisfaction and orthodoxy, as discussed in Chapter 1, the married priests were decidedly not at a disadvantage.

Married priests reported greater satisfaction than did celibate priests on almost every measure. This is especially notable since Catholic priests overall report a very high level of satisfaction to begin with. Table 7.2 shows some representative comparisons, repeating selected information from Chapter 1. Job fulfillment was measured by asking the priests to what extent they felt that they were utilizing their skills and abilities in their present job. The married priests reported a slightly higher sense of job fulfillment and much greater happiness than did celibate priests. The happiness of the married priests, moreover, depended more strongly on being of use in their job than it did for the celibate priests.[18]

The married priests also derived greater satisfaction from adminis-tering the sacraments and preaching, both distinctive priestly functions. Likewise, on every measure of orthodoxy, traditionalism, or sacramental

Table 7.2 **Selected Measures of Job Satisfaction, Comparing Married and Celibate Priests (in Percent)**

	US Priests 2001	PP Priests 2007
Self-reported happiness: Very happy, pretty happy, or not too happy? % *"very happy"*	46	66
To what extent do you feel you are utilizing your important skills and abilities in your present assignment? % *"a great deal"*	41	44
Satisfaction due to the joy of administering the sacraments and presiding over the liturgy. % *"of great importance"*	94	100
The satisfaction of preaching the word. % *"of great importance"*	80	96

orientation, the married priests exceeded celibate priests in their support of the truth claims of the Catholic faith. More than 9 in 10 (92 percent) of the married priests, but fewer than 3 in 10 (28 percent) of the celibate priests, characterized their religious views as conservative. (For a full discussion of these differences, see Chapter 1.) To the extent that commitment to ministry is reflected in job satisfaction or dogmatism, the married priests did not demonstrate less commitment than did celibate priests.

The standard measures of ministerial commitment—workload, satisfaction, devotion, and dogmatism—fail to reveal any advantage of celibacy for commitment to the priestly role or ministry. On the contrary, on almost every measure, married priests are more active and committed to their ministry than are celibate priests. In terms of personal commitment and function of ministry, these findings suggest that the marriage confers, if anything, an advantage rather than a liability for priestly ministry.

As we saw in Chapter 4, the married priests' wives typically entered into marriage as a distinct ministry of their own, with a vocation to support and minister with their husbands. The evidence presented earlier, showing greater devotion and availability among the married priests, may reflect the effectiveness of the wives' marital support and co-ministry to enhance their husbands' priestly service and devotion. If so, it suggests that the restriction of priests from marriage, far from creating an advantage for ministry, may result in a material loss to the Church.

Married Priests on Married Priests
Reflections on Availability

What do the married priest couples themselves think about this question? They have frequently confronted the question of their own availability or effectiveness compared to that of a celibate man, and most have informed and reflective opinions on the topic. Each priest and wife were asked to respond in their own words to the following: "Some have suggested that, for practical reasons, married priests are generally less able to be fully devoted to the care of a parish than ones who are unmarried. Please briefly share your views, thoughts or experience on this issue." Figure 7.3 shows the responses, classified into those who generally agreed or disagreed with the suggestion.

Consistent with the objective findings above, the married priests and their wives disagreed, by a two-to-one ratio, with the idea that a married man could not be as fully devoted to the care of a parish as an unmarried man. Six in 10 (59 percent) of the priests and their wives disagreed with this proposition, though a sizable minority (29 percent) agreed with it. Fichter's study of married former Catholic priests now serving as Protestant ministers, replicating the identical question above, found that 80 percent of the ministers disagreed, with only 18.5 percent agreeing.[19] Significantly, in my sample the wives (at 73 percent) were much more

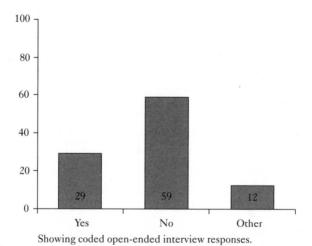

Showing coded open-ended interview responses.

FIGURE 7.3 Is a Married Man Less Able to Be Fully Devoted to the Care of a Parish? Combined Responses from Pastoral Provision Priests and Wives (in Percent)

likely to disagree with the proposition than were the priests themselves (at 49 percent).

The priests who disagreed often expressed their opinion emphatically, using words such as "horsefeathers," "preposterous," "ludicrous," and "crock." One priest asked, "Is there a place on this form for 'Hell, no'?" Fichter's respondents expressed themselves just as emphatically, with phrases such as "ridiculous," "hog wash," and "red herring."[20] This vehemence, among a smaller proportion than their wives, suggests that the priests giving the negative response in both samples were aware that they were confronting a common misperception.

In most cases, the written comments of the majority made clear that their response did not reflect an abstract opinion, but their own experience. A young, recently ordained married priest serving in a demanding chaplaincy said,

> I'm married, and I'm not boasting, but I'm working easily as hard as the other priests in the diocese, and somehow it's not a great conflict between family and ministry. I've never experienced that.

Another, older married priest reflected similarly that his commitment, while different, was comparable to that of the celibate priests he knew:

> It's a wonderful idea, but I don't see it practiced. I don't. ... I've been [a Catholic priest] for 23 years, and all the [celibate] friends that I have find alternate uses for their time. Where we would be having family time, they have friend time, and golf time, and hobby time, and travel time. And we don't go for a lot of that. I don't resent that, that's their—but why the trade-off? Why are we doing something that God didn't ask us to do? ... So, I just don't see it. I don't see them doing anything that I am not doing.

Some respondents suggested not only that they are equally available or devoted, but also that their experience of marriage offered an advantage. An older married priest who had raised four children while pastoring churches said,

> Horsefeathers! My experience has been just the opposite. There is a profound compatibility between marriage and holy orders.

Marriage opens a man to the whole world that the people in his pews live in. It opens him to serve them with compassion and charity, whereas the celibate world is closed off, and often it's an intrusion. A ministry of interruptions.

Likewise, another older priest, the effective pastor of a large parish, commented,

In theory [celibate priests] might be more available; in practice [a married priest] is just as available, because [celibate priests] tend to be very picky about their time off, and they also have other ways in which, as sort of single people, they're defending themselves against getting too involved.

Some respondents, especially some of the wives, were critical of the commitment of celibate priests. One wife, reflecting on 25 years as a Catholic priest's wife, said, "I have seen a number of priests who didn't work too hard. Some were lazy, some self-absorbed and uncaring of their parishioners."

A married priest's widow, also reflecting on a quarter-century of Catholic priestly ministry, offered a careful but also sentimental summation:

I could only speak for my own experience, ... I can't believe that [married priests] give less attention to a parish than a celibate priest. Because celibate priests often are not available after five o'clock. And they don't answer the phone. They're so busy telling us how hard they work and how tired they are that—I don't buy it. I've been around them enough to know that they just don't work that hard. ... The parishes and spiritual children who mourn [my husband's] loss since his death would be astonished at the idea that Father _____ was "generally less able to be fully devoted" to their care.

The former celibate Catholic priests, now married Protestant ministers, in Fichter's study offered similar comments on the question that were equally, if not more, pointed: "Tell this to the people who call the rectory and get an answering machine or parishioners in the hospital who look for their pastor but only get the chaplain of the day."[21]

Supporting Celibacy

Ironically, given these opinions and their own state of life, the married priests and their wives are about twice as opposed to the ordination of married priests as are celibate Catholic priests. About half of both the married priests (54 percent) and the wives (49 percent) opposed regularizing receiving married men in the priesthood, a position held by only a quarter (28 percent) of celibate Catholic priests. The position of the married priests on this issue reflected, in part, their general theological conservatism. Those who favored regularly opening up Catholic ordination to married men were more likely to deny the ontological character of the priesthood, that is, the belief that priests are different in their being than are laypersons, thus holding a more Protestant view of the matter.[22] Several priests supporting priestly celibacy explicitly made this distinction, commenting, as one did, "A Catholic priest is different than a Protestant minister." Those opposing a change in the rule of celibacy were also more likely to believe that married priests could not be as devoted as unmarried ones ($r = .29$). The corresponding correlation for the wives was much stronger ($r = .50$), consistent with their more practical and less theological approach on many issues.

Nonetheless, the married priests and wives were about evenly split on the question of priesthood and marriage. Their individual views were likewise balanced or measured. Few expressed an unqualified position on the topic, and almost none reported having experienced scandal or rejection from church members as a result of being married. Rather, their views mostly reflected a practical consideration of the difficulties or strengths that come with ministry as a priest family. Family stress, lack of income, high demands on scarce family time, and the absence of any defined role for wives and children in the Catholic Church figured largely in their assessment of the merits or demerits of a married priesthood. On this issue, the married priests and their wives largely see themselves as exceptions that prove the rule.

Conclusion

Catholic teaching documents and canon law repeatedly justify clergy celibacy by suggesting that celibate priests are personally more committed, devoted, available, or effective as ministers than a married man could be. I have found no evidence to support this claim. In every comparison where there was a difference, the married priests scored as high or higher on commitment, availability, effectiveness, and so on, than did celibate priests.

A major reason for the advantage of married priests lies in the character of their wives. The arguments in favor of clergy celibacy assume that a wife will necessarily be a detraction and distraction from ministry for a priest; but in fact the opposite is the case. The support of their wives for their priestly ministry (examined in detail in Chapter 4) enables the married priests to be even more effective priests than they would be otherwise.

Clergy celibacy is an institutionalized practice, and, as with marriage, the best justification for it may not lie in the quality of its enactment in particular instances, but in its institutional effects on social order. The institution of marriage, in other words, may still be a good thing for society, even if most individual marriages do not live up to the ideal. By the same argument, the institution of clergy celibacy may still be a good thing, even if most individual celibate priests do not live up to its ideals. In the next chapter, I will take up an older sociological defense of clergy celibacy, not often heard today, based on its institutional and social benefits. What effect would the practice of clergy marriage rather than celibacy have, not on the person of the priest, but on the Church as an institution and on society as a whole?

8

Why Clergy Celibacy?

Introduction: Engaging the Classical Debate

We have seen that being married does not cause priests to be less devoted to their churches. But the classic justification for clergy celibacy has never been based on issues of personal devotion or commitment but on social or institutional effects. Are there social benefits of clergy celibacy?

In sharp contrast to classical and early modern treatments, contemporary discussions of celibacy rarely consider this question. Almost all recent discussions of clergy celibacy consider the question almost exclusively as a personal virtue and discipline. Beyond perhaps a vague acknowledgment that its development had something to do with property and inheritance, one is hard pressed to find any awareness or consideration of its institutional or social logic. This is surprising, since what is at issue is not the personal practice of lifelong continence or chastity—most opponents of clerical celibacy are not thereby advocating premarital sex, and approve of some forms of celibacy, such as the voluntary celibacy of those in religious life—but the institutional requirement that clergy must live in such a state. Since this is a question of institutional policy, not personal spirituality or discipline, it seems that a consideration of the institutional causes and effects of the practice would be in order.

From the sixteenth century through as late as the mid-nineteenth century, scholarly treatment of Catholic clergy celibacy focused on just such an argument, considering what today would be called the social structural advantages and disadvantages of the practice in a kind of cost/benefit analysis. The eminent nineteenth-century Protestant historian Philip Schaff provides a classic summary of the Protestant position in his *History of the Christian Church*: "Whatever may have been the advantages of clerical celibacy, its evils were much greater."[1] Catholic authors of the era tended to come to the opposite conclusion, of course. But both sides engaged in a similar form of argument, both acknowledged advantages as well as disadvantages of the practice, and both agreed on what many of the pros and cons are.

To some extent, this rhetorical form persists today in the handful of extant secular social science discussions of clergy celibacy, which tend to interpret the practice as a means by which the Church, as a total or "greedy" institution, unfairly takes advantage of the devotion of young men to oppress and dominate them for its own interests.[2] This interpretation does not exactly form an argument, since it either assumes the negative, or takes no position, on the question of whether the benefits to the Church outweigh the personal sacrifice of the clergy. In this chapter I will extend this analysis by identifying the structural—that is, institutional and social—disadvantages and advantages of both clergy marriage and clergy celibacy. In sociological terms, I am moving from the micro to the macro—or more precisely, meso—level of social analysis. My purpose is not to form a definitive judgment, but to illustrate and re-state the terms of the debate in the modern context.

A Structural Comparison of Clergy Marriage and Celibacy
Disadvantages of Marriage
Mobility

A celibate priest may not be more available to his parishioners, but he is certainly more available to his bishop. This is particularly evident with regard to the ease by which the priest can move from one place of ministry to another. Things are inevitably more complicated for families, which are more deeply rooted in the community and require greater stability. The clergy wife is an asset in many ways, but this is not one of them.

The career choices of the married priests were clearly constrained by the needs of wife and family. The married priests were less mobile. The assignments of Catholic priests are typically rotated about every six years; but the average placement of a married priest was more than twice as long. One in 10 of the wives reported a dispute or disappointment with the bishop over issues related to the parish rectory. Three priests told stories of significant distress after they were required to move in the middle of a school year, while others related the kindness of their bishop in refraining from imposing such moves. In either case, the married priests are less easy to move.

Most of the married priests and their wives are aware of this and recognize decreased mobility as an inherent limitation of married life. Several of the wives discussed the issue in concrete and dramatic terms. One wife, whose husband served in a large Midwestern diocese, explained,

> When [my husband] was serving as a pastor, he was gone all the time to meetings and such. But that was just part of the job. And that was okay with me. [But] unmarried priests can move easily from one end of the diocese to the other. [Our diocese] is pretty big. You have from the inner city to extremely rural. If a family were to move like that, it wouldn't be as easy at all. That is a difference.

Another wife, with three children, whose husband holds two jobs in a large Eastern diocese, visualized:

> I can well imagine Father So-and-so being transferred from one end of the diocese to the other, and his wife in tears going to see the bishop and saying, "But the sixth-grade class has promised Suzie that she'll have the lead in the school musical." Or something like that. Clergy are simply not as mobile if they have families. And the bishop needs to be able to tell the clergy on July first, pack your bags and rotate one parish, or whatever he's going to do. I see the wisdom of his need to do that.

Loneliness

It may seem strange to list loneliness as one of the disadvantages of clergy marriage. The opposite—that allowing Catholic priests to marry would *alleviate* problems of loneliness—has often been suggested. Evidence suggests, however, that the particular kind of loneliness experienced by a priest is not alleviated by marriage.

As discussed in Chapter 6, both the married priests and their wives felt isolated because of the limitations on their relationships with parishioners. Just as their marital relationship is circumscribed, and in some ways restricted, by the demands of the job, so the relationships of a priest and of his wife to parishioners are limited by the responsibilities of marriage. Marriage didn't save them from loneliness, it often precipitated it.

The marriage, in a sense, creates a barrier to deeper relationships with parishioners. In the same way that corporate wives must be careful not to harm their husband's careers, it is risky for a pastor's wife to share feelings that involve her husband and family with parishioners. By the same token, a married pastor must be careful not to bring family tensions into the parish, and must be particularly careful not to let supportive relationships with parishioners displace those with his family. He must be mindful, beyond certain limits, not to treat his family as parishioners, but also not to treat parishioners as family. Ironically, an unmarried priest, precisely because he has not formed a personal family, is freer to develop familiar (family-like) relationships with parishioners.

Advantages of Marriage

Empathy

The idea that marriage constitutes a disadvantage for a priest's ministry would come as a surprise to most Catholic laypersons. Married priests heard frequently from laypersons that a married priest better understands their own experience of marriage, and so can provide better counsel to married couples. A married priest is also often perceived as more approachable in general, since he, as one parishioner put it, "understands what we're going through in life." Many of the married priests and their wives mentioned this perception. One priest expressed a common sentiment:

> Many people will say to me, I like having a married priest, especially if I go to counsel or confession, because I think that he can relate to some of the things I'm going through better than a celibate priest can.

The wife of a highly erudite married priest, a college professor, observed,

> A lot of people have commented on my husband's homilies, or have commented privately to me, that he's talking about real things. By which I think they mean that it relates to families and bills and teenage children—things that are the realities of their lives, in a different way.

This perception acknowledges the contribution of celibacy to the creation of a clerical caste. The historian Leslie Tentler notes: "A celibate clergy is by definition a group set apart. A priest's manner of life, indeed his very life course, differs from that of nearly all laity."[3] Though priests, married and celibate, may deny the importance of the distinction between them, to laypersons it is often obviously concrete. A married priest knows what it is like to help the children with homework, juggle funds to pay the mortgage, and try to get the family out of the house and to church in time for Mass. In ways that are significant to them, the celibate priest stands over against them, while the married one stands with them.

The perception of a special competence in marriage and family ministry is sometimes also shared by priests or bishops, who have consequently assigned married priests to marriage preparation or marriage-related diocesan committees. However, almost all the Pastoral Provision priests disagree with the idea, and often, with some irony, find themselves defending the competence and accessibility of their celibate counterparts. The "comeback" related by the following priest on this issue was mentioned by many others as well:

Sometimes people do say that they feel a married priest can relate better to their issues, because he's experienced what they experience. But my comeback is always, just think, that means a priest who is not married has a better relationship with the many singles in our church and widows or widowers. So they can relate better to ... those loneliness issues and all those issues that you have with that segment of our ecclesial body. ... I might have more to bring to the table of a family, but those guys have more to bring to the table dealing with the single issues and widow or widower issues.

Another married priest, who was a trained marriage counselor himself, pointed out:

I remind people that in marriage counseling one of the big problems is that the marriage counselor always has the danger of projecting his own experience on married couples. ... The marriage counselor above all has to try to remain objective, especially if he or she is married ... now the celibate priest has a big advantage there: he has nothing to project, and I think can look at [the situation] in a detached way that is scarcely possible for a married man.

At the same time, the married priests themselves are aware of the isolation of their celibate brothers from the manner of life of their parishioners and from themselves. Many observed that most priests have no idea of the financial and time pressures that families face. If pastoral ministry is about representing the people to God as well as representing God to the people, then effective ministry involves empathy as well as authority. Whether warranted or not, laypersons tend to see the features of life that they share with married priests as a more potent bond of empathy than the distinctive manner of life of celibate priests.

Disadvantages of Celibacy

Sex Abuse

The widespread and ongoing discoveries of horrific sex abuse of minors by US Catholic priests raises anew the question of whether the rule of clergy celibacy contributes to sexual misbehavior by priests. This is, as noted above, a claim that has been made by Protestants since the Reformation, though recently it has also been made by Catholics. Following the 2002 media exposure of sexual abuse among American Catholic clergy, many Catholics argued that permitting priests to marry would probably reduce such abuse. Defenders of celibacy have countered this concern by pointing out, correctly, that the known incidence of sexual abuse among married Protestant clergy is no different from that among Catholic priests.[4]

The Pastoral Provision priests and their wives speak with particular insight on these issues, both as married men among celibates and as converts who have experience with both married Protestant clergy and celibate Catholic clergy. I asked each priest and his wife for their thoughts on the claim that "married priests are less likely than celibate ones to engage in sexual misconduct, particularly the abuse of minor children." Seventy percent of the respondents answered in the negative, with most referring to statistics showing high rates of abuse in families or among Protestant clergy, or citing their own knowledge of recurring sexual misconduct in the Episcopal Church. Many felt that the misbehavior of Catholic priests received more publicity than similar behavior by Protestant clergy. A quarter (25 percent) of the respondents felt that married men are less prone to scandalous abuse involving children, although not necessarily sexual infidelity altogether. These views were, most often, based on their own experience.

Among the 96 priests who have been ordained under the Pastoral Provision, two have allegedly engaged in sexual misconduct involving a minor child or children. Recognizing the limitations of the data, this would compute to a prevalence of child sex abuse among the married priests of just over 2 percent. The exhaustive study of Catholic clergy sex abuse by the John Jay College of Criminal Justice in 2004, commissioned by the US bishops in the wake of the 2002 scandal, reported the prevalence of alleged sex abuse among all Catholic priests since 1950 to be close to 4 percent. However, the vast majority of the abuse they found occurred before 1980; among celibate priests ordained since 1980, as all the married priests have been, the proportion alleged to be engaged in child sex abuse has been only about 2 percent.[5] Other studies, restricted to a more recent time frame and/or a narrower sample, have produced even smaller estimates.[6] Depending on which estimate one uses, it is possible to say that the married priests are either less likely, equally likely, or more likely to engage in child sex abuse. The small sample data here can only be suggestive at best, but the fairest statement seems to be that the married priests appear to be about equally as likely to have engaged in child sex abuse as all Catholic priests ordained during the same period have been.

Homosexual Prevalence and/or Subculture

A direct consequence of the rule of celibacy is that, for centuries, the Catholic priesthood has been one of a very few socially acceptable roles for homosexual men. Whereas unmarried males were often stigmatized, priests were admired. Priesthood provided Catholic men who were both religious and homosexual with an honored status and identity that was not dependent upon conformity to heterosexual norms. Consequently the priesthood probably attracted somewhat more than its share of gay men.

Today, as far as we can determine, that continues to be the case. Even by the most conservative and reliable estimates, the proportion of Catholic priests who are homosexual is about 10 times that of the general male population.[7] It is impossible to know for certain that this concentration was higher in the past since very few gay men were open about their sexuality. And celibacy renders sexual orientation moot, as far as behavior, since abstinence is the same for everyone.

In recent decades these dynamics have changed as gay men have become more open about their sexuality. Donald Cozzens, a prominent seminary rector, in a controversial 2000 book, raised the concern that friendship networks of gay priests and seminarians in most dioceses or seminaries in the United States had become an exclusive subculture or clique "who interact continually with each other and seldom with outsiders, and who develop shared experiences, understandings and meanings."[8] Such cliques had become so pervasive, including among seminary faculty, Cozzens argued, that they tended to marginalize heterosexual seminarians or priests. Cozzens argued that "straight men in environments populated by a significant number of gays experience a sense of destabilization. They wrestle with a certain self-doubt, a feeling that they don't fit in. On both psychic and spiritual levels, they are not 'at home.' "[9]

Cozzens's concerns echoed those made by psychoanalyst A. W. Richard Sipe in a series of influential books on the sexuality of Catholic priests.[10] Using institutional and expert reports, Sipe found that during the 1980s, compared to the 1960s, "the reporting of homosexual behaviors increased significantly and the reliable estimates almost doubled." The difficulties were concentrated in a minority of dioceses with high concentrations (the estimates were between 42 percent and 75 percent of active homosexual clergy). The main cause of this situation, Sipe alleged, was a shift away from the structure of highly regulated seminary life beginning in the early 1970s, which led, in the closely confined all-male environment of the Catholic seminary, to the development of homosocial organizations in some seminaries that encouraged "relationships with sexual objects."[11] The secrecy of the confessional and a culture of official denial hindered church authorities from addressing the problem.

Subsequent research has confirmed Cozzens's and Sipe's concerns. In surveys of priests, a majority ordained over the past 20 years responded "yes" when asked if there was a homosexual subculture in their seminary.[12] On a 2003 survey of newly ordained priests, a fifth of those responding to an open-ended question on homosexuality in the priesthood believed that "[m]ore priests are homosexual than the public knows, and the priesthood is becoming homosexual."[13] Hoge and Wenger, reporting on survey data, interviews, and focus groups with Catholic priests, related that "many priests recognize the existence of homosexual subcultures" in their seminary and diocese.[14] "Most problems with homosexual subcultures occur in the seminary. Some priests expressed concerns about promiscuity, a predatory attitude toward young seminarians, and an unwillingness to address these issues on the part of the seminary faculty."[15] Almost all of the priests quoted in the interviews they cite acknowledged that the homosexual groups in the seminary were sexually active, not celibate.

In formal Catholic teaching, the presence of homosexual men in the priesthood is problematic on its face, and so their prevalence constitutes a disadvantage of celibacy. Catholic teaching holds homosexuality to be a morally disordered inclination that is not conducive to godliness and human well-being. Though persons, through self-denial and self-control, can achieve Christian maturity in spite of the condition, it is not a recommendation for Church leadership. Catholic norms formally prohibit any known homosexual man from being ordained.[16]

Cozzens and Sipe are not concerned about the presence of homosexual priests per se, but rather that seminary homosexual subcultures may undermine the practice of celibacy. "Some of these gay networks or subcultures are using the priesthood as a cover for their sexual acting out," Cozzens warns.[17] Sipe includes seminary homosexual activity among other violations of celibacy, concluding that only 40 percent of priests actually practice celibacy.[18] Both suggest that the ideal of celibacy may be too costly to achieve in practice in the modern world.

Neither Cozzens nor Sipe appear to be aware that their concerns and conclusions echo long-standing Protestant critiques of the Catholic rule of celibacy. Protestant critics generally have been skeptical that many men actually practice celibacy, and see the concentration of homosexual men who dissent from celibacy as a sign, not merely that formation practices need reform, but that celibacy itself is unworkable.

For the early Protestant reformers, the absence of marital sex, which provides a legitimate outlet for irrepressible sexual urges, must lead to a variety of sexual sins, among which homosexuality was prominent. In 1520 Martin Luther wrote: "The pope has as little power to command [celibacy], as he has to forbid eating, drinking, the natural movement of the bowels or growing fat. No one, therefore, is bound to keep it; but the pope is responsible for all the sins which are committed against this ordinance, for all the souls which are lost thereby, for all the consciences which are thereby confused and tortured."[19] Luther here reflected the influence of Andreas Bodenstein von Karlstadt, another German reformer, who "wrote that sexual renunciation promoted homosexuality and . . . masturbation."[20]

Whatever conclusion one draws from it, the evidence of practicing homosexual subcultures in Catholic seminaries, confirming Protestant apprehensions about the practice of celibacy, must be counted as a disadvantage of celibacy today. Whether or not marriage confers an advantage in resisting sexual misbehavior on an individual clergyman, the problematic culture of Catholic formation, to the extent that it involves a dissenting homosexual subculture, places those formed into celibacy today at a distinct disadvantage regarding sexual maturity. Not only by virtue of having a legitimate natural sexual partner, but also by avoiding the perilous formation of modern celibate seminarians, the married priests of this study may well be the most sexually balanced and innocuous group of clergy in the United States. Only time will tell whether this situation is unique to the past few decades, has already subsided and been corrected, or is an ongoing feature of the Catholic priesthood.

A Totalizing Experience

Married priests, we noted above, have a daily life experience more like that of laypersons than unmarried priests generally do. For many of the same reasons, unmarried priests also have a much more absorbing experience of the Church. Coining a distinction that has since become standard for sociological analysis, Erving Goffman described some modern institutions that demand a high level of involvement as "total institutions." Such institutions permit or require a much greater level of involvement and personal investment by those who participate in them. Goffman explains:

> A basic social arrangement in modern society is that the individual tends to sleep, play, and work in different places, with different co-participants, under different authorities, and without an overall rational plan. The central feature of total institutions can be described as a breakdown of the barriers separating these three spheres of life.[21]

For Goffman, traditional Catholic religious communities are prime examples of total institutions. Hall and Schneider noted, in an early study of Catholic priests' careers, that the parish setting in which most priests work, though not as absorbing as a religious community, nonetheless fulfills the central features of Goffman's criteria for a total institution: "[T]he parish priest works, eats, and lives in the church-rectory building complex of his parish, which represents a physical environmental factor forcing him into a high degree of involvement in the Church system."[22] While "[t]he Roman Catholic parish does not represent a completely total institution for the priest," as does a religious order, they observe that "[t]he separation of the barriers between sleep, play, and work is probably less evident for priests than for most other professionals."[23]

An important element of the totalizing experience for a priest, Hall and Schneider note, is his commitment to a life of celibacy, "which reduces the chances that he will experience social commitments that will rival his commitment to the Church."[24] Greeley and Schoenherr (1971) found that, for most priests, the majority of their friends were other priests—meaning that, even when they escape from the parish, much of the relaxation that priests do is in the company of other members of the same institution. With the decline in the number of priests since the 1970s, parish rectories have emptied, leading to greater integration and merger of office and living areas as parishes seek to make efficient use of space. For the same reason, more pastors live alone, and devote more of their working day to parish liturgies and meetings, both of which reduce casual contact with non-parishioners. For the married priests, of course, the contrary is true, bringing a wider exposure to non-clerical friends and cross-cutting commitments. The restriction from serving as pastors, moreover, removes most of them from the absorption of rectory life.

The more totalizing experience of celibate priests has its positive side. It certainly can further the interests of the institution, and create a stronger sense of community, than is possible with more independent actors. Yet it does contribute to a sense among laypersons, as noted above, that priests are not able to understand their concerns. From the standpoint of the priest himself, there is a point beyond which attachment to the Church institution does not appear to be healthy or conducive to maturity. Almost every book on clergy spiritual or psychological growth recommends that priests develop balance, seek outside interests or friends, take vacations, and so on, to gain valuable distance and perspective on their lives in the Church. Such measures, it appears, are more necessary for celibate than for married priests.

Advantages of Celibacy

The perpetuation of a celibate clergy over time faces a distinct challenge: the Church must continually recruit new priests from among the laity. Ministry cannot become the family business. The challenge of continual recruitment, however, turns out to have significant benefits for the Church. As early modern discussions of celibacy recognized, it may have benefits for society as well.

Institutional Renewal

Discussions of the current Catholic clergy shortage rightly link it to celibacy but fail to discern the full dynamics of celibacy and clergy recruitment. It is certainly true that the prospect of never marrying prevents many young men from choosing to be priests. What usually follows is the somewhat simplistic suggestion that permitting marriage would open up the priesthood to more candidates, and thus ease the clergy shortage. While this may (or may not: the evidence is inconclusive) happen in the short term, such a change would also fundamentally alter the nature of the priesthood and may eventually change the nature of the Church itself. A shortage of priests is not merely an accidental result but is a fundamental effect of the rule of celibacy, by which it has a strong constitutive influence on the Church. The current shortage of priests is not a temporary or unique situation, but only an intensification of the perpetual dynamics of clergy recruitment that are fueled by the rule of celibacy.

Celibacy creates a kind of permanent potential shortage of priests, as the presbyterate must be reconstituted each generation. This situation is opposite to that of the Judaism of Biblical times, in which the priesthood was hereditary and priests correspondingly had a duty to marry. In modern churches with a married clergy, to the extent that occupations tend to be inherited, the sons and daughters of priests provide a ready supply of new ministers. In today's labor market, characterized by a high degree of occupational mobility and declining inheritance of occupation, such an effect is relatively small; about one in 10 Protestant ministers today is the son or daughter of a minister.[25] On the other hand, in today's context of greater emphasis on sexual liberty and expression than in the past, the direct effect of celibacy in suppressing the number of aspirants for the Catholic priesthood, relative to Protestant ministry, may be greater than in the past. In any event, as is well known, compared to Protestant churches, the Catholic Church has very few clergy applicants today.

The perpetual need to recruit new Catholic clergy creates a dynamic of dependency, in which the clergy must appeal to the laity. This dynamic counteracts, to some extent, the tendency toward clericalism, or segregation by orders, that is natural in any institution with highly differentiated ranks, such as the distinction between laity and clergy. The nineteenth-century French historian Guizot observed:

Doubtless celibacy, in placing the Catholic clergy in an entirely spe- cial situation, foreign to the interests and common life of mankind, has been to it a chief cause of isolation; but it has thus unceasingly forced it into connection with lay society, in order to recruit and renew itself therefrom.[26]

The need for new vocations is manifest in many Church initiatives: in retreats and dinners organized to introduce young men to clerical life, often with the active involvement of senior Church leaders; in the focus on adolescents, particularly adolescent males, as altar servers; in the retention of gender distinctions in most formal liturgical roles; and in the emphasis in the Church on marriage and marital fertility, the encouragement of large families, and the sacralizing of family life.

The need to recruit new vocations also imposes certain institutional limits on the infidelity—in the sense of a failure to uphold orthodoxy—to which the clerical class of all religions are prone. The prospect of asso- ciation with a faithless class will tend to obstruct the successful entrance into the clergy of precisely those religiously sincere and idealistic young men who are most likely to take on a celibate life. In theory, then, the less faithless the priesthood is, the better recruitment should be. And this is something we can test empirically.

Since men enter the priesthood by means of a single bishop or dio- cese, and bishops and localities vary in traditionalism and fidelity, those bishops or dioceses who display these qualities in greater degree will, on this thinking, tend to attract more, and more successful, applicants to the priesthood. Archbishop Curtiss of Omaha, a traditionalist, argues:

> The dioceses and religious communities which promote orthodoxy and loyalty to the Church ... [and] call young men to ordained priesthood despite the opposition of those who rail against a male, celibate priesthood ... are the dioceses and communities which will enjoy increasing numbers of candidates and will disprove the forecasts of decline in vocations everywhere in the Church because of their successes locally.[27]

Recent social scientific studies have provided ample evidence in sup- port of these claims. In a 2001 study, the economist Andrew Yuengert, using data for all US dioceses, examined the effect on ordination rates of whether the bishop expressed a traditional, orthodox perspective of the faith, compared to a progressive, revisionist view. He found that the rate of ordinations in dioceses with the most traditional bishops was 73 percent higher than the average, while in dioceses with the most progressive bishops the ordination rate was 31 percent below the average. As a reason for this effect, Yuengert suggests that a more traditional bishop "may present a vision of the role of the priest that is more attractive to potential recruits."[28]

In what has been called the "supply-side" theory of religious groups, the sociologist Rodney Stark and collaborators have proposed that, in a situation of pluralism, more demanding religious groups will become stronger by offering more satisfying or authentic religious goods. In terms of individual participation, Finke and Stark asserted, "[r]eligious organizations are stronger to the degree that they impose significant costs in terms of sacrifice and even stigma upon their members."[29] When applied to the internal differences among Catholic dioceses, this thesis leads to essentially the same claim (though for somewhat different reasons) as made earlier: that due to the high cost of celibacy, more orthodox dioceses are likely to attract more candidates for the priesthood. Finke and Stark tested this prediction by comparing the ordination rates of six dioceses with a traditional orientation with eight comparable dioceses with a progressive diocesan culture. They reported: "The differences are quite astonishing. The traditional dioceses are far more successful at attracting young men to the priesthood."[30] In fact, the traditional dioceses produced four times as many priests, adjusted for size, as did the progressive dioceses. One of the reasons that the difference was so pronounced, they suggest, is that "young men from elsewhere are attracted to the seminaries in the traditional dioceses, thus inflating their rates."[31]

Finke and Stark argue that traditional settings are more successful in attracting priest candidates because they convey greater secular personal rewards, that is, role clarity, status and power, which compensate for the high sacrifices that candidates make to become a priest.[32] This may well have an effect, although a crude comparison of ordination rates falls short of convincing proof of this. A somewhat closer look, in fact, suggests that differences on the demand side—that is, differences between conservative and progressive priests or priest applicants themselves—are at least as important as the diocesan culture or bishop in explaining increased ordinations. Using the 2002 Los Angeles Times survey of Catholic priests, I was able to examine items relevant to this question. Table 8.1 shows the results.

Table 8.1 Comparisons of Priests in Traditional and Progressive Dioceses (in Percent)

	Diocesan Culture, Per Finke and Stark (2005)		
	Traditional (88)	Progressive (36)	Other (1,679)
Bishop's views on morals *(% too liberal)*	4.7	20.0	2.9
Bishop's views on morals *(% too conservative)*	24.4	2.9	19.3
Choose the priesthood again? *(% probably or definitely not)*	9.2	5.9	7.3
Life as priest turned out better, worse or as expected? *(% worse than expected)*	10.2	5.9	7.2
Might leave the priesthood? *(% somewhat or very likely)*	10.5	2.9	4.9
Advise a young man to enter seminary today? *(% no)*	6.9	5.6	8.8
Advise a young man to enter seminary today? *(% no, doctrinally liberal priests only)*	19.6	0	17.4
Advise a young man to enter seminary today? *(% no, doctrinally conservative priests only)*	3.6	21.7	3.8

Source: Los Angeles Times Survey of Priests (2002). Diocesan culture classification (traditional or progressive) is from Finke and Stark (2005): 271, Table 7.6.

Since the survey reported each priest's diocese, it was possible to compare priests from each of the two groups of dioceses (traditional and progressive) identified by Finke and Stark. Although there was no direct measure of a diocese's traditionalism, the respondents did rate the conservatism or liberalism of their bishop, a closely related measure.[33] The first two rows in Table 8.1 show that these ratings corresponded reasonably to Finke and Stark's traditional/progressive classification of dioceses. In progressive dioceses, one in five (20 percent) of the priests rated their bishop as "too liberal" and less than 3 percent (2.9 percent) thought he was "too conservative." In traditional dioceses it was the opposite: a quarter (24.4 percent) of the priests thought their bishop was "too conservative" and less than 5 percent (4.7 percent) thought he was "too liberal." These findings confirm the general accuracy of Finke and Stark's classification.

The next three items in Table 8.1 compare traditional and progressive dioceses on measures of satisfaction with the priesthood. If Finke and Stark's thesis that priests in traditional dioceses enjoy greater communal or status rewards were true, one would expect to find higher satisfaction among priests in traditional dioceses. But this is not the case. On each of these items, the priests in traditional dioceses reported less satisfaction in the priesthood than those in the progressive dioceses. About one in 10 of the priests in the traditional dioceses reported that if they could choose again, they probably or definitely would not choose to be a priest; life as a priest turned out worse than they expected; and they were likely to leave the priesthood. The proportion of priests giving these negative responses are all much lower in the progressive dioceses. Perhaps most tellingly, more priests in the traditional dioceses said that they would not advise a promising young candidate to enter the priesthood today. This item applies directly to the encouragement of ordinations, and indicates that the cultural support for priests in traditional dioceses is not noticeably stronger than in progressive ones. The advantage of traditional dioceses in ordinations does not appear to result from providing the kind of status rewards that produce more satisfied priests.

The reason that traditional dioceses ordain more priests is due not only to the character of the diocese, but also to the character of the men who seek ordination. The survey asked each priest to locate his own "views on most matters having to do with religious beliefs and moral doctrines" on a range of responses: very liberal, somewhat liberal, middle of the road, somewhat conservative, or very conservative. Overall, about three in 10 priests identified themselves as either conservative (29 percent) or liberal (32 percent), and almost four in 10 considered themselves doctrinally moderate (39 percent). The culture of the diocese, whether traditional or progressive, had very different effects depending on the priest's own liberalism or conservatism. As the bottom two rows of Table 8.1 show, doctrinal conservatism or liberalism sharply distinguishes the willingness of a priest to advise a young man to enter seminary, and in opposite directions according to the culture of the diocese. In traditional dioceses, a fifth of liberal priests (but only 4 percent of conservative priests) will decline to advise a promising young man to enter the priesthood; in progressive dioceses, a fifth of conservative priests (but no liberal priests) will do the same. Similar, though less sharp, distinctions are observed on the other satisfaction measures.

Accordingly, traditional and progressive dioceses have tended, at least in recent years, to ordain priests who are compatible with their distinctive theological differences. The difference is not slight. Since 1982 progressive dioceses have been three times as likely to ordain a liberal priest as a conservative one, and conservative dioceses have been 2.4 times as likely to ordain a conservative priest as a liberal one. Figure 8.1 shows the trend. Traditional dioceses are also somewhat more likely to ordain a moderate priest. Clearly, a conservative candidate for the priesthood is much more likely to achieve ordination in a conservative diocese than in a liberal one. Traditional dioceses, it appears, are not more attractive to *all* priest candidates, but only to conservative candidates.

At this point, two other factors complete the account of the increased ordinations in traditional dioceses. First, as discussed in Chapter 2, since the 1960s the Catholic priests being ordained have grown consistently more conservative. Second, the "demand" for ordination by conservative priests has not been matched by the "supply" of dioceses favorable to doing so. The *average* proportion of conservative priests ordained by a Catholic

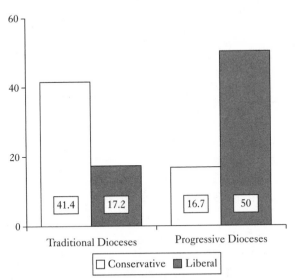

FIGURE 8.1 Doctrinal Conservatism/Liberalism of Priests Recently Ordained in Traditional and Progressive Dioceses (in Percent)

Source: Los Angeles Times Survey of Priests (2002). The odds on ordaining a priest compatible with the diocesan culture is 2.4 (41.4/17.2) for traditional dioceses and 3.0 (50/16.7) for progressive dioceses.

diocese during the 1990s was only 30.2 percent. When 42 percent or more of candidates seek ordination from dioceses that will only ordain 30 percent of them, on average, the distribution of ordinations by diocese has to become skewed. More candidates will have to be ordained in those dioceses that are willing to do so. This crowding of conservative candidates was magnified by the fact that in the American Catholic Church in the 1990s, relatively few dioceses were willing to ordain so many conservative priests. During that decade only 12 percent (12.3 percent) of dioceses ordained at least the proportion of conservative candidates who were seeking ordination (42 percent). The result was that a few dioceses ended up ordaining a comparatively large number of priests, who were disproportionately conservative, while most dioceses ordained very few. The distinguishing factor in Catholic priest ordination rates is not traditionalism versus progressivism as contrasting diocesan cultural contexts of status or social support, but simply the willingness to support and receive conservative priests.

One way to test whether the association of conservatism and ordinations is a matter of diocesan cultural supply or, as I am alternatively suggesting, of candidate demand, is to compare dioceses with higher and lower ordination rates to see which factor actually distinguishes the two groups. Figure 8.2 presents the results. The high-ordaining dioceses were classified using data provided by CARA, which identifies the top 20 US dioceses in number of ordinations, adjusted for size of diocese, for each of the five three-year periods from 1993 to 2009.[34] Dioceses that were listed in the top 20 for at least three of the five periods were considered genuinely high-ordaining dioceses; these dioceses have shown a consistent ability to generate higher numbers of ordinations. As my analysis above predicts, only a few (14) dioceses were consistently high-ordaining in this way.

Were the high-ordaining dioceses unusually receptive of conservative priests? As Figure 8.2 shows, the answer is an emphatic "yes." The high-ordaining dioceses were, as a group, over five (5.7) times more likely to ordain a conservative priest than a liberal one, a level of acceptance of conservative priests that is over four (4.4) times larger than the norm among dioceses that did not have high numbers of ordinations. This preference for conservatism in ordinands is even higher than among Finke and Stark's "traditional" dioceses. Yet the high-ordaining dioceses are not notably traditional. Only one of the six traditional dioceses identified by Finke and Stark is also on the list of consistently high-ordaining

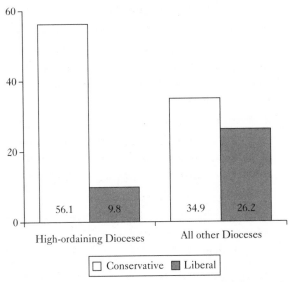

FIGURE 8.2 Doctrinal Conservatism/Liberalism of Priests Recently Ordained in High-Ordaining Dioceses (in Percent)

Source: Los Angeles Times Survey of Priests (2002). The odds on ordaining a conservative rather than a liberal priest is 5.7 (56.1/9.8) in high-ordaining dioceses and 1.3 (34.9/26.2) in all other dioceses.

dioceses.[35] Nor are the remaining dioceses, which are not consistently high-ordaining, notably progressive or liberal. There is, in fact, a small preference for conservative priests in most of the low-ordaining dioceses. Obviously, if one considers only especially traditional and liberal dioceses, the traditional ones will have more ordinations than the liberal ones. But a diocese did not have to be notably traditional to have more ordinations, nor notably progressive to have fewer. The large majority of Catholic dioceses, and Catholic bishops, both high-ordaining and low-ordaining, are neither notably conservative nor liberal, but tend to moderation on such measures.

In sum, traditional elements in the Church attract more priest candidates because, in contrast to a generation ago, priest candidates today are largely and increasingly conservative in their religious orientation. Conservative dioceses or bishops reap more ordinations primarily because they are willing to ordain (or less likely to screen out) more conservative candidates; but other dioceses and bishops, who are willing to tolerate or support candidates who may be more conservative than themselves, do this also.

These findings confirm Archbishop Curtiss's prediction of an affinity between ordinations and orthodoxy, with the qualification that the process he observed is not a unique or temporary product of the current cultural situation but reflects a more general sociological process in the Church. From the standpoint of the religious situation following Vatican II, the reassertion of traditional beliefs and practices among new priest candidates has been both unexpected and countercultural. It stands firmly athwart the liberalizing currents and cultural accommodation in the Church that followed Vatican II, and comes to those buoyed by the ideal of bringing the Church closer to the modern world as some surprise, perhaps even a regression from the advances of the Council. Yet the turn to orthodoxy among young men seeking to be priests has been strong, persistent, and global, and is likely to grow.

What does all this have to do with married priests? As I have suggested, this trend is driven in part by the requirement of clergy celibacy. If (on Finke and Stark's theory) religious demands are met because of the compensation of religious rewards, those for whom the rewards are most salient or real will be the most likely to accept high religious demands. Neither damnation nor blessedness has much power to motivate or stimulate the devotion—or celibate discipline—of those who do not believe in their reality or efficacy. By imposing a very high religious demand, the rule of celibacy selects for those priest applicants who believe and enact most fully the claims of the Church.

This institutional mechanism is indifferent to whether the return to fidelity is from what is today considered a liberal or conservative direction, and it operates more powerfully the stronger the tension between the culture and the faith. When the faith is most in disrepute, the cost of becoming a priest is the highest, and men of higher fidelity and countercultural commitment are made priests as candidates decline overall. Disrepute also stimulates a greater emphasis on holiness among ordination gatekeepers. In the extreme case, when there is open persecution of the Church, the risk of death adds to the cost of celibacy (which enables such risk) to select for heroically zealous priest candidates; in this way the blood of the martyrs becomes the seed of the Church.

Married men are less susceptible to all of these sociological forces. This is easy to see in the extreme case: Married men, with wives to care for and families to raise and protect, are obviously less available for martyrdom. But married men are also much more entangled with the majority culture generally. As noted above, the life course and living conditions of celibate priests are set apart from the laity, while married priests live in a manner similar to that of most laypersons. This difference for married priests, which their parishioners may see as a source of empathy, can also be a source of more ready accommodation to a hostile culture.

The married priests of the Pastoral Provision are certainly not given to cultural accommodation; nonetheless, they provide strong evidence for this point. The exemplars of clergy accommodation are not the less than 1 percent of Episcopalian clergy who left in reaction, but the more than 99 percent of Episcopalian priests, mostly married, female and male, gay and straight, who function happily and effectively, for the most part, in the Episcopal Church. Catholic laypersons are similar to Episcopalian laypersons in many (though not all) of their views on changing cultural values, such as on marriage, gender, and sexual orientation, and both groups have grown more liberal since the 1960s. But while the married clergy of the Episcopal Church have also grown more culturally accommodating along with their laity, the celibate clergy of the Catholic Church have moved in the opposite direction. Confronted with changing cultural values that challenge traditional religious norms, the Episcopal Church, with married priests, has for the most part adapted and changed its practices; the Catholic Church, with celibate priests, has for the most part resisted, and reasserted its traditional practices.

A Rationalizing Social Force

If the Catholic Church adopted a married priesthood, what effect might this have on society at large? If, as almost every understanding of society attests, marriage and family are central to social order, then those who do not participate in these institutions necessarily stand somewhat apart from mainstream social processes. Almost every society, including our own, meets single adults above the traditional age of marriage with stigma and marginalization. Reciprocally, an institution predicated on precluding marriage can be expected to influence society toward greater acceptance of singles. Apologists for clergy celibacy through the nineteenth century made just such a case, in the startling claim that clergy celibacy promoted the rise of social and political freedom and equality, contributing to what we today would understand as the rationalization of the West.

For much of the history of the West, when the Catholic Church was an unrivaled and dominant social force, the dynamic of clergy recruitment due to celibacy, discussed earlier, had extensive effects on the social and political order at large. Guizot, a French collaborator of Schaff, cited earlier, who separately published his own dissent from Schaff's hostile treatment of celibacy, argues that the recruitment dynamic of clergy celibacy helped Western culture to resist establishing a theocratic oligarchy such as had crippled political freedom in other parts of the world:

> In all parts of the world where a clergy made itself master of society, and forced it to submit to a theocratic organization, the government always fell into the hands of a married clergy, of a body of priests who were enabled to recruit their ranks from their own society. Examine history; look to Asia and Egypt; every powerful theocracy you will find to have been the work of a priesthood, of a society complete within itself, and which had no occasion to borrow of any other.[36]

The theocratic impulse in Christianity, which arguably reached its height in the Gregorian era (sixth century), was countered not only by the absence of heirs but also by the continual demand imposed by celibacy, which Gregory also set on a firmer and more universal basis, to re-establish the clergy anew in each generation. Due to celibacy, the priesthood

> was compelled to seek at a distance, among all stations, all social professions, for the means of its duration. In vain, attachment to their order induced them to labor assiduously for the purpose of assimilating these discordant elements; some of the original qualities of these newcomers ever remain; citizens or gentlemen, they always retained some vestige of their former disposition, of their early habits ... this necessity, which was always arising, did much more to prevent the success of the attempt at theocratic organization, than the *esprit de corps*, strongly supported as it was by celibacy, did to forward it.[37]

Although celibacy, as noted above, created a certain separation of the clergy from the laity, it also prevented the development of a distinct clergy caste, which requires restricting entry on the basis of hereditary characteristics. On the contrary, Guizot notes, the Church

> has constantly maintained the principle that all men whatever their origin are equally privileged to enter her ranks, to fill her

highest offices, and to enjoy her proudest dignities. The ecclesiastical career particularly from the fifth to the twelfth century was open to all. The Church was recruited from all ranks of society, from the lower as well as the higher, indeed most frequently from the lower. When all around her fell under the tyranny of privilege, she alone maintained the principle of equality of competition and emulation; she alone called the superior of all classes to the possession of power.[38]

For Guizot, the development of political equality and democratic freedoms in Western culture represent an appropriation by the allegedly secular political institutions of the Enlightenment of the religious ideals embodied in the rule of clergy celibacy. In many ways, the Catholic Church itself did not begin to understand this until Vatican II's declaration on religious freedom.

Balmes, a Spanish contemporary of Guizot, does not hesitate to link his insight to the rise of a middle class with political rights:

We are not ignorant of the numerous declamations against religious celibacy which have proceeded from the mouths of the pretended defenders of the rights of humanity; but is it not strange that they forget, as M. Guizot justly observes, that celibacy is exactly what has prevented the Christian clergy from becoming a caste? . . .

Let us suppose that the Church had not opposed such an abuse [i.e., clergy marriage] with all her force, and that the custom had become general; . . . and see whether there would not have been formed an ecclesiastical caste along with that of the nobility, and whether both, united by the bonds of family and common interest, would not have opposed an invincible obstacle to the ulterior development of the plebeian class, plunging European civilization into that degradation in which Asiatic society now exists.[39]

The submissiveness of the Church of England to the Queen, who selects its head, and of the Russian Orthodox Church to the ruling regime in Moscow suggest that Balmes may be correct in his claim that the married priests of an established religion are likely to resist social change and to align with the ruling interests against the working class and poor. Whether or not this particular point is pertinent to the United States, where church and state are separate, Balmes's main idea is sound and more credible today than when he wrote it 150 years ago.

In current discourse, a small but eminent minority of theologians and social scientists have asserted the notion that liberal political virtues such as equality and tolerance, not to mention reason itself, are part of the West's Christian inheritance.[40] Key to the sociological and historical argument for the Christian foundation of secular rationality is the role of celibate communities in routinizing and ordering life according to abstract principle rather than kinship and clan. Though the principal actors were monastic orders, the celibacy of the secular clergy also contributed to Western cultural development, not only by adopting monastic forms of rationality but also by adapting the ascetic ideal to less rarified states of life that were not oriented to otherworldly perfection but to this-worldly (secular) social engagement. The influence of clergy celibacy in this extended sense can be seen, for example, in the Catholic ideal of marriage, with its emphasis on self-denial and self-giving (and periodic sexual abstinence). Likewise, for Weber the Protestant inner-worldly asceticism which led to the ascendancy of Western capitalism included a "sexual asceticism" within marriage "which differs only in degree, not in fundamental principle, from that of monasticism."[41]

As it has contributed to rationalization, the Catholic practice of clergy celibacy has also contributed to the closely related process of globalization. The universality of the rule of celibacy, established prior to modernity and maintained intact in spite of the difficulties of doing so in a wide variety of societies and cultures, furthers the global disposition of Catholicism, which crystallizes in the relation of Catholicism to the nation-state. The perception that clergy celibacy is definitional of Catholicism recognizes this global character, which is in part what makes the Catholic Church a catholic (as opposed to only a national) church. Olson discerns this effect by its absence in the Eastern Orthodox rejection of universal clergy celibacy: "This attitude toward celibacy reflects in part the tendency of individual Eastern Orthodox Churches to practice independence from each other by forming bodies that more or less correspond to the national states in which they exist."[42]

These reflections converge on the recognition that clergy celibacy has functioned, and probably still functions, as a rationalizing force in Western culture. With the decline of the dominance of Catholic Christianity, clergy celibacy no longer has a direct social effect, but it retains a distinct cultural force in promoting an ascetic, rational, way of life. It is unlikely that the moral and social force of such asceticism is unrelated to the ability of the Catholic faith to retain an ethic of self-denial for its members and to advocate for morally strict public institutions in spite of widespread rejection of Catholic moral prescriptions by both non-Catholics and Catholics alike. The loss of clergy celibacy would represent a certain concession, not only to the individual demands of nature, but to the disordering decline of rationality, the dominance of interest over principle, which increasingly, and perhaps perpetually, militates against political and social order in late modernity.

Obviously, married priests cannot attest directly to the institutional and social effects of celibacy. They may, however, indirectly attest to the ascetic ideal of the Catholic priesthood by highlighting those Protestant clergy who were eligible to convert but who decided not to do so. What is significant in this regard is not the presence and assimilation of married priests in the Catholic priesthood, but the fact that, despite formally welcoming policies including exemptions from celibacy, there are so few of them. Though it is not possible to know for sure, the very small number of convert priests suggests that for every married priest who did convert, there is likely a much larger number who were discouraged or excluded from converting by the natural demands of career, marriage, and family. We know that, for those who did convert, their conversion often involved marital or family stress, including struggles with job and financial support, and in every case they forfeited career prospects, security, and seniority. Their wives, moreover, are sacrificially supportive of their priestly ministry, and they converted by an internal, rational process of response to perceived truth. The priests who completed the journey to become married Catholic priests, then, are exceptions not only to the rule of Catholic clergy celibacy but also, and primarily, to the accommodating effects of Protestant clergy marriage.

Conclusion

The disadvantages of celibacy are largely personal and individual, while the advantages are largely institutional and social. Perhaps US priests have not always represented the best effects of celibacy in recent decades. The largest, aging cohort of priests, those in their fifties and sixties, have witnessed abusive violations of celibacy and defections to marry to an unusual degree, and are rapidly being replaced by much more stable and orthodox younger cohorts. A prime mechanism in this unanticipated recovery of Catholic fidelity appears to be the rule of celibacy, which screens out candidates who are unwilling to make this sacrifice for their faith. The evidence suggests that, in the face of cultural accommodation, the expectation of celibacy may serve sociologically to restore strict fidelity to the Church, just as the practice of marriage by clergy may tend to undercut and weaken doctrinal exclusiveness over time.

The comparison of married and celibate clergy cannot resolve the question of clergy celibacy, which is a matter of theological and religious conviction, but it can offer insight into the issue by considering the experience and roles of married priests. The married priests of the Pastoral Provision are explicitly ordained as exceptions to the rule of celibacy in order not to call the rule itself into question. Given that marriage and children are highly valued in the Catholic faith, the requirement of clergy celibacy is itself somewhat exceptional. That there are then exceptions to this exception is perhaps not so, well, exceptional.

Priestly celibacy does not suggest, by intent or effect, that there is anything deficient about marriage. On the contrary, the sacrifice of celibacy has merit just to the extent that marriage is affirmed as a positive good that is surrendered for the sake of the kingdom of God. In the same way, priestly marriage does not imply, by intent or effect, that there is anything wrong with celibacy for priests. On the contrary, the condition of marriage for some priests makes clear the deficits and advantages of celibacy for most Catholic priests. Just as the relatively few celibate clergy show the value of marriage for laypersons, so the relatively few married clergy show the value of celibacy for the majority of Catholic priests.

If the rule of celibacy can help reassert the Church's tradition despite the untraditional views and behavior of celibate priests themselves, it may also have a culturally rationalizing effect despite the individual irrationality of forgoing marriage and offspring. The Pastoral Provision priests affirm this possibility by negation, as ones who have, but rarely, made a similarly irrational choice. As those who have engaged the irrationality of conversion in order to reconcile with religious truth despite marriage, they confirm the commitment of those who have engaged the irrationality of forgoing marriage to serve the truth, as well as the unique cultural force of an institution that operates by such commitment. In this way, as well, the married priests are found to be exceptions that prove the rule.

Conclusion

THE FUTURE OF MARRIED PRIESTS

AS I HAVE NOTED throughout the book, the presence and experience of these married priests inevitably prompts questions, for most observers, about future prospects for married priests and Anglican comity in the Catholic Church. Indeed, the 1980 Vatican document originally communicating the Pastoral Provision anticipated "concern for the sensitive areas of ecumenism and celibacy."[1] After three decades, these are still the central issues to be addressed in assessing the Pastoral Provision. Will the Pastoral Provision or a similar arrangement continue or expand? Will an Anglican common identity continue or default to some other ecumenical arrangement? And, of most interest, are married Catholic priests likely to become more common, or not, in years to come?

A Foot in the Door?

"A lot of people are going to see this as a foot in the door," said the spokesman for the US bishops when the Pastoral Provision decision was first announced in 1980. "A precedent-shattering breakthrough like this has got to have enormous implications."[2] Many people wonder whether the Pastoral Provision has had this effect. Has this limited pastoral exception to clergy celibacy made it any more likely that the rule itself will be relaxed or abolished?

Media accounts of the Pastoral Provision priests explicitly frame the story in terms of this question. To take just one example, a 2005 *ABC News* story reporting the ordination of a Pastoral Provision priest in Boston was headlined "Married Priests May Be Tests for Catholic Church," and featured contrasting interviews with the convert ordinand and a celibate seminarian under the heading "Pros and Cons of Celibacy." Catholic advocates of optional celibacy have pointed even more explicitly to the Pastoral Provision priests as a wedge. FutureChurch, an organization that promotes married and female priests in the Catholic Church, met the news of an expanded reception of Anglican converts with an announcement that began: "We're surprised and pleased to see Vatican flexibility in permitting married priests for Anglican converts, but we need the option of a married priesthood in the Latin rite of the Catholic Church too."[3] Promotional material published by FutureChurch lists the Pastoral Provision as the latest development in a timeline of anti-celibacy initiatives dating back to the founding of the Catholic Church.[4]

More deliberate scholarly reflection has largely concurred. A recent academic study attributing the sex abuse crisis to the Catholic hierarchy's misuse of power protests: "Pope John Paul II allowed married Episcopalian priests to convert and enter the Roman ministry. It is a situation that makes mandatory celibacy even more unfair to Catholic men who enter the priesthood and are required to remain forever unmarried."[5] The conservative canonist Edward Peters argues that, despite magisterial assertions to the contrary, the "expanding use of 'pastoral provisions' and 'personal ordinariates'" is a step toward a retreat from clerical celibacy. Given "the pressure being exerted against clerical celibacy by the ordination of married men and deacons and priests under various recent mechanisms ... one must conclude that Western *clerical* celibacy is in an unprecedented crisis."[6]

The Pastoral Provision priests and their wives generally meet such attention with chagrin. They are less likely than are most celibate priests to support optional celibacy; and even if they favor a change in the rule of celibacy, they are almost universally opposed to the confluence of liberal issues of which optional celibacy is often a part. They are also resistant to getting caught in a fruitless controversy that is not central to their lives. "I don't want to become a poster child for optional celibacy," one priest said, voicing an almost universal opinion among the married priests.

Indeed, many married priests professed some degree of irritation with these kinds of questions, and consequently took steps not to unduly display their unique status. The clergy couples were careful not to hold hands in the church foyer or act too familiar in the sacristy. Partly out of concern for such misunderstanding, the Pastoral Provision guidelines themselves call for the priests to be discreet and to avoid undue publicity. Almost all the priests (there were two exceptions) confirmed that they avoid press exposure. Such attempts make little difference, however, because it is not the personal behavior or characteristics of the priest or wife involved, but their mere presence among the clergy, that sparks questions.

The Future of the Pastoral Provision

The equivocal nature of the decision establishing the Pastoral Provision actually resulted in two tracks of married priests entering the Catholic Church. For Anglican priests reconciling individually with Rome, without accompanying an Anglican congregation, the "pastoral provision" for retaining an Anglican corporate identity was only theoretical. Over 90 percent of the men received under the Pastoral Provision have been of this type. Other than being married, these men have served in Latin Rite dioceses and parishes the same as any other Latin Rite priest. These priests, beginning with Father Parker, willingly conformed to the Latin Rite (though often, as noted earlier, holding their noses at the liturgy), being inserted into diocesan structures, if not the presbyterate, relatively seamlessly.

A small minority, under 10 percent, of the married priests converted as pastors of Anglican congregations that wanted to reconcile with the Catholic Church. In permitting Anglican congregations to retain a "common identity" and "ethos," Catholic leaders were clearly concerned to make an accommodation that would enrich the Church, if they thought in those terms, by adding to its already extensive diversity of cultural and liturgical expressions. The married pastors of Anglican Use parishes have often envisioned enriching the Catholic Church in another sense, by exemplifying a superior liturgy, spirituality, and form of pastoral care that would be attractive to Latin Rite Catholics and a model for improvement of the Latin Rite. At times they have exhibited an entrepreneurial spirit that has not always been well received by the hierarchy.

In becoming Catholic, the individual petitioners have largely left Anglicanism behind to humbly learn what it is to be Latin Rite Catholic. The Anglican Use pastors have explicitly, and sometimes aggressively, brought Anglicanism with them to help restore, as they see it, a patrimony that Catholicism has lost. Over the three decades of applying the Pastoral

Provision, the tension between these two understandings of the place or mission of Catholic Anglicanism has never been resolved.

Numerically, the Pastoral Provision program for married priests has not flourished. Ordinations of individual petitioners have been few and have taken place in a small fraction of American dioceses. The Anglican Use parishes have also been few, small, and marginal. On the other hand, bishops and parishioners served by married priests are, on the whole, very pleased with them. There has been no hint that married priests scandalized Catholics, though they have often presented bishops with practical problems of placement and remuneration. Both bishops and priests have grown much more conservative in the 30 years since the Pastoral Provision was established; but they still support, on balance and within limits, the idea of ordaining married Episcopalian convert priests.

Overtaken by the Ordinariate: Ecumenical Implications

Any concern over the programmatic sparseness of the Pastoral Provision was rendered moot, however, when in late 2012 Pope Benedict issued the Apostolic Constitution *Anglicanorum Coetibus*, enabling the formation of permanent communities of Anglican identity within the Catholic Church, and established the Ordinariate of the Chair of St. Peter for this purpose in the United States, with similar bodies in England and Australia. With this action, the decision of Church leaders was clear: the essential elements of the Pastoral Provision would become permanent, and resources and leadership would support their expansion. The coming of the Ordinariates brings new implications for the questions of ecumenism and celibacy that were raised by the Pastoral Provision.

The 1980 establishment of the Pastoral Provision was shaped by a desire not to damage the ongoing ecumenical dialogue that the Catholic Church was having with Anglicanism. It was largely to avoid presenting a direct challenge to the Anglican Communion that the CDF did not at that time establish a more permanent Anglican jurisdiction; it ruled that Anglican converts would only be received as individuals, not as groups, avoiding undue publicity. Sensitivity to ecumenical relations with the Episcopal Church also guided some of the more particular policies for administering the Pastoral Provision—for example, the rule that a convert Anglican priest could not serve in the same city in which he served as an Anglican priest, or the tacit presumption, made explicit in 2009, that there should not be more than two married priests in a diocese.

In 1980, of the three dozen national churches that comprised the Anglican Communion, only the Episcopal Church had ordained women, a move which precluded closer communion with the Catholic Church, and there were signs of resistance among the Episcopalian bishops, including the Presiding Bishop, which encouraged the hope that the decision to ordain women may have been retracted or limited. However, as time progressed, other Anglican Churches joined in ordaining women, and the Episcopal Church moved on to ordain women bishops, then practicing homosexual priests and bishops; by 2004, it became abundantly clear that there was no longer any hope of reconciliation between Rome and the Anglican Churches.

It was this realization, as much as anything else, which enabled the establishment of the Anglican Ordinariates, in order to provide a permanent welcome in the Catholic Church for Anglicans who wanted to reconcile with the Catholic Church. The Ordinariates boldly establish what the Pastoral Provision refrained from enacting: a permanent church organization that stands as a continuing challenge to Anglicanism.

The Ordinariates, in this sense, fulfill the original promise that the Pastoral Provision hesitated to complete. The Pastoral Provision provided for parishes of an Anglican common identity only half-heartedly, with a vague and uncertain canonical status that made it difficult, despite the best efforts of its proponents, to build a corporate identity. The US Ordinariate provides a robust structure, essentially a non-geographical diocese, to incorporate, nurture, express, and preserve the traditional liturgy, music, and pastoral governance that means so much to Anglicans, while restoring full communion with the Holy See. The Ordinariate is both the fulfillment and the end of the Anglican Use in a literal sense, as almost all of the existing Anglican Use parishes have joined the Ordinariate, which will be the locus for the formation of any new Anglican identity communities going forward.

A Successful Failure

It is not yet clear whether the Pastoral Provision will continue as a separate program, though it seems likely that its function will be consolidated, in large part if not completely, with the Ordinariate. The program might find new life in expanding accommodation to non-Anglican Protestant groups, as the recent reception of a former Lutheran priest convert suggests; or as a support to the Catholic bishops of the United States, if they began to

receive convert married priests of other religious groups by ordinary petition more frequently.

Did the Pastoral Provision pave the way for the Ordinariate? Probably.
The married priests of the Pastoral Provision demonstrated that married
priests could function well, even happily—certainly without scandal or
confusion—in Latin Rite parishes, even under the disabling restriction
that they could not normally serve as pastors. The Anglican Use communities established, despite their marginalization and lack of jurisdiction,
the viability of this form of worship and community. The Ordinariate, by
permitting its ordinands to pastor parishes and by forming a stable jurisdiction for convert Anglican communities, explicitly attempted to correct
these limitations in the Pastoral Provision. The Ordinariate, we might
say, is a reboot of the Pastoral Provision with improvements: a Pastoral
Provision 2.0. While the Pastoral Provision program may end, its purposes will live on in the Ordinariate.

The Future of Married Priests

Will the Pastoral Provision likely lead to a more regular reception of married priests in the Catholic Church? Yes and no. Although, generally
speaking, the experience of married priests in ministry has been positive, it has also not been superior to that of celibate priests in such a way
that would suggest any compelling pastoral or sociological reasons to
change the rule itself. Marriage has both advantages and disadvantages
for priestly functioning. And while there is a well-developed theology of
the affinity of celibacy with priesthood, there is, at least as yet, no corresponding theology of the affinity of marriage with Catholic priesthood.

The Pastoral Provision and the more recent Ordinariate were instituted
with great care to avoid challenging the rule of celibacy. Officially, married
priests are received under the Pastoral Provision as individual exceptions
to celibacy. A married priesthood, moreover, is explicitly not a permanent
feature of any resulting Anglican identity in the Catholic Church: whether
in persisting Anglican Use congregations or the US Ordinariate, future
candidates for the priesthood put forward by those communities must
observe celibacy.

The ordination of married men, in this sense, was envisioned to be
a temporary extremity, to enable the establishment of a more durable
Anglican community within the Catholic Church in which exceptions

to celibacy would no longer be needed. In accord with this, the Pastoral Provision itself was never intended to be permanent, but explicitly instituted as "not definitive, but ... granted *ad tempus non determinandum* ("for an indefinite time").[7] There was a reasonable expectation that, after the initial reaction by Anglo-Papalists to the 1976 ordination of women, few members of future cohorts of Anglican priests, having grown up in a more secularized Episcopal Church, would want to leave it for Catholicism. As it happened, there has been a continuing trickle of Anglican priests seeking to convert, due to subsequent further secularizing changes by the Episcopal Church. The 2012 Ordinariate responded to this continuing demand by establishing a permanent structure to carry forward the practice of ordaining married priests for Anglicanized Catholic communities. It is still conceived as a temporary practice, in that future priest candidates from the Ordinariate must be celibate; but there is a significant difference in that the Ordinariate itself is not a temporary jurisdiction. The Pastoral Provision, we might say, was conceived as a temporary program allowing for temporary exceptions to celibacy; but the Ordinariate was established as a permanent program allowing for temporary exceptions to celibacy.

The practical result is that the Ordinariate establishes, for the first time, a permanent arrangement for the incorporation of married priests into the Catholic Church. The expectation for the Ordinariate, as it was for the Anglican Use part of the Pastoral Provision, is that eventually it will have a celibate priesthood composed of men who grew up in Anglican identity communities. Only time will tell if the Ordinariate will produce its own celibate priesthood; but the Anglican Use experience gives us reason to doubt that it will. After three decades, no Anglican Use community has yet put forth a celibate candidate for the priesthood to serve Anglican Use parishes.

On the other hand, there are good reasons to expect that married convert priests, even if only a small number, will continue to be received for the foreseeable future. Unlike the Pastoral Provision, which has only received convert priests from historic Anglican churches (to date only the Episcopal Church and the Church of England), the Ordinariate receives convert married priests from Continuing Anglican churches as well, resulting in a larger pool of potential applicants. Furthermore, the Ordinariate not only receives priests linked to a converting Anglican congregation, but can also ordain priests entering the Catholic faith as individuals, on terms that are very similar to those of the Pastoral Provision.

Ordinariate priests, of course, could be considered somewhat "walled off" from mainstream Catholicism. They serve an exclusive class of culturally distinct Catholic parishes, like priests in a Uniate rite such as the Melkites or Ukrainian Catholics. Persons baptized and confirmed in another rite of the Catholic Church are not normally eligible to join the Ordinariate.[8] Unlike the Uniate rites, however, there has been no conflict over or restrictions imposed on their use of married priests as pastors. And mainstream Latin Rite Catholics will have greater exposure to the married priests of the Ordinariate. Unlike the Uniate rites, Ordinariate priests are, officially, priests of the Latin Rite; every Ordinariate priest is ordained by a local Latin Rite diocesan bishop. Clergy ordained for the Ordinariate are "available to assist the Diocese in which they have a domicile" when needed, may serve on that diocese's Presbyteral Council, and are encouraged to maintain good relations and participate in priestly events—retreats, convocations, and so on—of the local diocese.[9]

The initial numbers suggest that US Ordinariate priests will be serving quite a bit in Latin Rite dioceses. Most of the communities comprising the Ordinariate are very small. As of mid-2013, the Ordinariate reported having about 30 congregations comprising about 1,600 parishioners, an average of only 53 members per congregation.[10] Four of the congregations were described as "large"; two of these four had about 125 members each.[11] Not surprisingly, most Ordinariate priests reportedly "rely on income generated from work in Catholic institutions such as schools or diocesan offices" or assisting parishes in their local Latin Rite dioceses.[12] At least for the near term, regular Latin Rite Catholics will have the experience of ministry from the married priests of the Ordinariate. In the long term, the Ordinariate institutionalizes the ongoing practice of married priests serving in the American Catholic Church.

From Rigidity to Pastoral Understanding

For the leaders and decision-makers of the Catholic Church, the problem of priesthood and marriage arises not only with respect to married convert priests of the Pastoral Provision or the Ordinariates, but also, and perhaps more intensely, with regard to men who resigned the priesthood in order to marry. As I mentioned in Chapter 1, there are as many as 25,000 such men in the United States. In auguring the future prospects for married priests, recent developments in the treatment of these resigned priests are instructive.

The resigned priests' experience of rejection by the Church is often cited in contrast to the acceptance of married convert priests. What is not generally known is that the Church's treatment of men who have resigned the priesthood has become far more pastoral and nuanced in recent years. As a recent Vatican-authorized report reveals, many, perhaps most, resigned Catholic priests today perform valued service for the Church, and some, even some who have married, have been welcomed back into the priesthood.[13]

Men who leave the Catholic priesthood may petition to be officially dispensed from its obligations, thereby being restored to good standing in the Church. About half of resigned priests do make such a petition. Although some present difficult complications, most petitions are granted; during the 1970s, when most priests who resigned did so specifically to marry, 95 percent of dispensation petitions were granted. The Vatican report discloses that many resigned priests "have been taken in by bishops to fulfill ecclesiastical roles, and, once a dispensation has been received, to teach religion classes, or in any case to work in institutions under ecclesiastical authority."[14]

A substantial number of other resigned priests have come to regret their resignation, and on petition have been returned to the priesthood. According to Vatican records, of the 69,063 men who left the priesthood from 1964 to 2004, 11,213 (16 percent) have subsequently been returned to priestly service. This includes "priests who have left the priestly ministry and married, but, once free from the marriage bonds, ask to be readmitted to the exercise of the ministry. . . . [In recent years] the Church has modified its legislation in order to accompany better those who had consecrated their lives to its service and later made other choices. New procedures have been established that offer a guide . . . , and the majority of the cases are concluded with the granting of pontifical clemency."[15] Clearly, though it may have been so in the past, it is neither fair nor accurate today to characterize the Catholic Church as harsh and dismissive toward resigned priests.

The concluding summary of the report, which poignantly relates the recent change in attitude of Church leaders toward resigned priests, is worth quoting at length:

[W]hile the legislation in force in the matter of celibacy has not been modified, the Church's praxis has been significantly changed, in the sense of going to meet the desire of men who have abandoned the ministry for the most varied reasons and now desire to resume the mission for which they have prepared for years and which still holds value and significance for them. The rigidity of a former time, which harshly judged and condemned any abandoning of the priesthood, has been tempered by a pastoral praxis that is certainly more understanding and "maternal.". . . While fully respecting those who decide to serve the Lord better in a different state of life that they have embraced after realizing that they were not suited for the priestly life, the Church cannot help but rejoice at every return to the priestly ministry, finding once again a person willing to serve with all of his being the ecclesial community and the cause of the Gospel.[16]

In this very significant development, essentially the same generosity that is embodied in the Pastoral Provision accommodations is now extended to men who have left the priesthood to marry. Certainly the rigid condemnation of resigned priests of a former time is paralleled by the former rigid condemnation of Protestants during the same era. In regard to both convert Protestant and resigned Catholic clergy, the accommodation extends as far as can be done without conceding anything the Church teaches or creating misunderstanding regarding the rule of celibacy. Just as many dispensed priests have found appropriate service as teachers and catechists, so also have many clergy converts, including former Anglican priests, who are not candidates for Catholic ordination.

As we saw with the Pastoral Provision, the emerging generosity toward resigned priests reflects the continuing influence of the Second Vatican Council. In the same way that, following Vatican II's emphasis on the freedom of conscience, the Pastoral Provision was enabled, in part, by understanding Protestants' differences with Catholicism in a more nuanced and relatively tolerant way, so the choices of resigned Catholic priests appear to be understood in a more nuanced and relatively tolerant way, enabling, in part, their restoration. Like the Ordinariate, the new, softer attitude toward resigned priests who have married also suggests that Catholic leaders may have developed beyond the emotional reaction to priestly marriage of a former time when, even when it was canonically permitted, it was seen as something scandalous and negative. The history of the prohibition of married Eastern Catholic priests in the United States since 1890 does not hide the fact that the foreseen scandalizing of Latin Rite

Catholics and the resentment of their priests, not a considered theology of celibacy or marriage, were the primary issues involved.

Since his election in March 2013, Pope Francis has signaled yet further pastoral openness to married priests. One of his earliest decisions was to permit individual married priests to join the Ordinariates, established to receive converting Anglican congregations, that Benedict had begun just a year earlier. This ruling opens the door for married priests from a wide range of traditional Anglican groups (not just the Episcopal Church) to come into the American Catholic Church, even if they are not accompanied by a congregation that seeks to convert. Since Ordinariate clergy, who can be pastors, are technically part of the Latin Rite and can be assigned to serve Latin Rite parishes, this change also allows greater flexibility for married priests to serve as pastors on par with celibate priests. Some Pastoral Provision priests, in fact, have been received into the Ordinariate with the prospect of pastoring a parish. Then, in November 2014, Pope Francis quietly lifted the 114-year-old ban on married Eastern Catholic priests serving outside their rite's home country, opening the door for Catholics of the Melkite, Coptic, Ukrainian, and other Eastern rites in the United States to be served by married pastors.

In the Pastoral Provision, the Ordinariate, the new openness to the restoration of resigned priests, and Francis's new approval of married pastors, we can see a general movement from rigidity to pastoral understanding among Church decision-makers that suggests a greater openness to accommodate anomalies of all types—including married priests. This does not necessarily portend any alteration in the rule of celibacy, a question that is subject to a different set of considerations altogether, but it does suggest that growing toleration and comfort with the experience of priests who are married is likely to continue going forward. Gradually, Catholic leaders are coming to recognize that being celibate is not the only way to be a priest. This may be the ultimate legacy of the married priests of the Pastoral Provision.

Conclusion

The priests of the Pastoral Provision, with the possible exception of some of the more avid proponents of the Anglican Use, did not become Catholic with the idea of changing the Church. Their concern in reconciling with Rome was primarily for their own salvation and the integrity of their ministry, and for the most part they have little desire to become entangled in Church politics. They emphatically deny any desire to change the Church's rule of celibacy; nor do they intend either to advance or to retard ecumenical relations with Anglicans. Indeed, although we have found many similarities among them, and they share a common life situation, they are not, sociologically, a group. Other than a common participation in the Pastoral Provision program, they do not have any collective identity, do not seek to pursue common goals, and most of them do not know one another.

If, as Pope Saint John Paul II said, a priest is a sign of contradiction, the married priests of the Pastoral Provision are a bundle of contradictions.[17] They reject authority to find authority, leave home to come home, innovate on the basis of tradition, and take risks out of an excess of caution. Newcomers to the Catholic priesthood, they more fully believe its teaching, practice its priestly devotions, work harder at serving it, and are happier doing so, than priests born Catholic. Their wives subordinate their identity to find their identity, boldly asserting their right to be submissive.

For these priests and their wives, the Catholic faith has been a project to be achieved, not an inheritance to be assumed. They have paid a great price to obtain what many Catholics take for granted. For many cradle Catholics, their sincerity and zeal are moving and inspiring—when it is not annoying. The absolutism of their faith can challenge the tacit dissent of many American Catholics and, in a sense, relativize the Church. The Catholic faith that was stronger than their attachments to the Episcopal Church may also turn out to transcend the present practices of the Catholic Church.

Appendix

This appendix presents technical analyses and supporting material for the various arguments and evidence presented throughout the book. Section titles note the chapter, if any, to which the material is particularly pertinent. These materials are gathered here so as to be readily available to the reader who is interested in such detail, without distracting the reader who is not.

I. STUDY DESCRIPTION AND METHODS

This book tells the story of the 72 married Pastoral Provision priests serving in the Latin Rite Catholic Church and their wives. Based on 115 interviews and three written surveys, augmented by archival and historical research, it recounts their unusual and difficult journey from Anglicanism and their life in the Catholic Church, examining their resulting roles and functions as priests and as married men. The study also relates, as necessary background, the story of the establishment of the Pastoral Provision and the processes by which its priests are assessed, placed, and funded; it explores the related socio-theological issues of conversion, celibacy, and liturgy; and it profiles the views of the US Catholic bishops and, for the first time, the wives of these married priests.

In 2007 the Ecclesiastical Delegate in charge of administering the Pastoral Provision in the United States, Archbishop John Myers of the Archdiocese of Newark, New Jersey, commissioned my research team at the Catholic University of America to engage in a retrospective study of the Pastoral Provision. It had been 25 years since the first priests were ordained under the program, and it was time to take stock.

For the next two years we collected data on the priests and their wives from multiple sources, but primarily from the subjects themselves through structured interviews. The gathering of data was guided by four main goals: to obtain feedback on the Pastoral Provision process and experience; to gather comprehensive demographic information; to replicate questions from other national priest surveys for comparison; and to get the views of the priests themselves on issues related to the Catholic Church and married priests. To achieve these goals we designed a survey questionnaire that would also serve as an interview protocol to stimulate and guide open-ended discussion; see Section VII.

We sent a copy of the questionnaire to each of the 72 active Pastoral Provision priests with a request to interview them in order to get their answers to the survey questions as well as other opinions. This was followed by a phone or email contact within two weeks to schedule an interview, and two additional follow-up contacts if needed. Sixty-two of the priests granted an interview, answering all or most of the survey and/or offering other opinions. Five priests filled out and returned the survey but declined to be interviewed. The remaining five were sent a follow-up survey after three months, but did not return them or otherwise respond. The resulting overall response rate from the priests was 93 percent for this full-population census.

Information for the five non-responding priests in the sample, and for other Pastoral Provision priests who were not in the sample due to being deceased or unmarried, was obtained where possible from church records, archives, and media accounts. In this way we were able to obtain at least minimal demographic data—for example, date of birth, date of Episcopalian ordination, and date of Catholic ordination—on all 96 priests who had been successfully involved in the Pastoral Provision since its inception. In some cases, we also augmented or corrected interview data from archival records.

Sixty of the 62 priests interviewed were currently married (two were widowed). At the time of the interview we asked their permission to interview their wives; 55 of them agreed or said they had no objection. We then sent a questionnaire and interview request to these wives and followed up to schedule an interview, as we had done with their husbands. The wives' questionnaire was somewhat shorter than the one for the priests, but replicated many of the same questions for comparison; see Section VIII. Forty-four of the contacted wives agreed to an interview; one additional wife completed and returned the questionnaire without an interview, for a total of 45 responses from the wives. In this way, response was obtained from 82 percent of the contacted wives, or 73 percent of all possible wives in the sample.

For additional background, we also interviewed several other persons with various perspectives on the Pastoral Provision or on married priests, including four bishops (two who had ordained married priests and two who had not); one married Catholic priest who had been ordained via ordinary petition; and four men who had applied to be ordained under the Pastoral Provision but had either not been approved or had subsequently decided not to be ordained. We did not complete questionnaires or compile any data for analysis from these interviews, which were largely inductive and open-ended.

In 2009, following a preliminary report, Archbishop Myers funded an additional mail survey of the US Catholic bishops to assess their views on the Pastoral Provision program at that point. The short questionnaire for this survey is found in

Section IX. A total of 156 of the 271 active US bishops (58 percent) returned a questionnaire, most of them with additional written comments.

The comparative frequencies for all closed-end questions on the priests and wives surveys discussed in this book—also comparing their answers, where data are available, to all US priests—are reported in Section VI. The reader interested in the "raw" data at any point is encouraged to consult these tables, which also contain additional technical information. Other information pertaining to each set of data—priests, wives, and bishops—in the overall study is presented in the respective chapter reporting on that sample.

II. TECHNICAL DATA ON PRIEST SURVEYS (CHAPTER 1)

To enable the findings presented in Chapter 1, I replicated many items from a 1969 national survey of US Catholic priests, directed by Andrew Greeley and Richard Schoenherr for the National Opinion Research Center. This was the largest survey study of American Catholic priests ever performed, both in terms of the number of cases obtained (5,110) and the number of questions asked (the questionnaire was 46 pages long).[1] As such, it has formed a benchmark for most subsequent research on US Catholic priests. Numerous local or targeted surveys of priests have replicated questions from the Greeley and Schoenherr study, as have national surveys administered by Hoge (with various collaborators) in 1985, 1993, and 2001.[2] Since, unlike Greeley and Schoenherr, the surveys since 1985 did not ask directly about pertinent doctrinal and moral issues, to obtain more recent data on these items I used two nationally representative surveys of Catholic priests administered by social scientists on behalf of the *Los Angeles Times* newspaper in 1993 and 2002.[3]

All six of the survey projects referenced above used a similar sampling methodology: first, they randomly drew a sample (ranging from 50 to 120) of dioceses from the Official Catholic Directory (OCD); then they mailed survey questionnaires to a random sample of the priests in those dioceses, based on names reported in diocesan directories or, in the absence of a diocesan directory, published in the OCD. While there may be some bias in question design and interpretation on these surveys, there is little discernible bias in sampling design or in the raw survey data itself.[4]

For a few items not covered by the six surveys above, I drew on more limited surveys of Catholic priests administered by or on behalf of the National Catholic Educational Association (NCEA), the Committee for Applied Research in the Apostolate (CARA), and the Archdiocese for the Military Services (AMS). In order to compare the views of priests with those of Catholic laypersons, I drew on a wide range of other population surveys, such as the General Social Survey and polling or tracking surveys by Gallup, Pew, and news organizations. While motivated by different questions, organizations, and theoretical orientations, all of the comparative survey data used or referenced in Chapter 1 are derived from national random samples that are statistically representative of the population, as the case may be, of US priests or US Catholics, and are cited fully at the point of use.

III. TECHNICAL COMMENTS ON MARRIED PRIEST SCREENING PROCEDURES (CHAPTER 2)

While a competent psychological evaluation can provide valuable information about a candidate's mental health and stability, its value as a screening mechanism for the risk of sexual or criminal misconduct is highly questionable, and of particularly little use for the Pastoral Provision priests. Estimates of the predictive validity of unstructured psychological assessments, that is, clinical assessments that are not specifically designed to screen for misconduct or criminal behavior and are not performed by clinicians who specialize in risk assessment, range from "highly inaccurate" to "dismal."[5] Structured psychological risk assessments (such as the MAST, CAST, and DSFI required of Pastoral Provision candidates) are a little better, having a perceivable correlation (less than .30) with average risk of offending, but are still of negligible value in predicting individual risk.[6] Recently, in a comparison of offending rates with diagnostic outcomes on the PCL-R (Psychopathy Check List—Revised), a screening instrument widely used in forensic settings, and which has higher aggregate predictive validity for offending than any of the instruments administered to Pastoral Provision priests, Cooke and Michie concluded that "prediction of future offending cannot be achieved in the individual case with any degree of confidence."[7] In contrast to psychopathic assessments, "actuarial analysis" that takes into account age, former offenses, addictions, and other non-psychological stress factors has been found to have strong predictive validity for misconduct of varying types. Clinical assessment is so poor a predictor of misbehavior that the combination of actuarial analysis with structured clinical assessment is more error prone than an actuarial approach only—to the extent that the former can no longer be forensically defended in court.[8]

These findings suggest that the use of a clinical interview to screen for criminal or sexual misconduct is misguided, and may well do more harm than good. To be sure, it is conceivable (though I'm not aware of any evidence for it) that a general psychological evaluation or personality assessment may help predict compatibility with the functions of ministry, and thus persistence in the priesthood. But while such information may be of great value for a man in his twenties considering the priesthood as one among several possible life courses, for a middle-aged man with already 17 years in the priesthood it would seem to be largely moot. On the other hand, the Pastoral Provision priest candidate has something highly pertinent to the prediction of misconduct that a young seminarian does not: a history. It is unrealistic, as well, to try to predict marital stability without assessing the wife, or assessing marital satisfaction from her perspective, as well as that of the candidate priest.

I am not able to find any body of research or practice that even conceives of accurately assessing a marriage with information from only one partner.

These considerations lead to several suggestions for ways in which the screening process for married priests could be improved. First, the general psychological interview and personality profile should not be used to screen for misconduct, as distinct from psychological pathology. Second, any assessment of misconduct risk should be based primarily on "actuarial" criminal and background checks. A criminal background check should be required as a matter of course; today such a clearance is required in many Catholic dioceses, even to volunteer in a parish. It would also be well worth the minimal effort involved to engage in some level of stricter scrutiny of the candidate's background and history as a priest. The candidate's former parishes or other work settings and ecclesiastical superiors could provide valuable information regarding possible misconduct or irregularities. Third, if they are used, structured risk assessments, such as the MAST, CAST, and DSFI, should be administered and evaluated by a specialist in forensic risk assessment. Fourth, the priest's wife should also receive a general psychological evaluation and possibly other assessments, which would include her views and assessment of the stability of the marriage, independently and apart from her husband.

IV. DESCRIPTION AND METHODS: BISHOPS SURVEY (CHAPTER 6)

The bishops' questionnaire, which is reproduced in Section IX, was developed and administered by a research team at Catholic University and supported by funds from the Office of the Ecclesiastical Delegate of the Pastoral Provision, Archbishop John Myers of Newark. In February 2009, using lists provided by the US Conference of Catholic Bishops, we sent questionnaires to all 271 active US Catholic bishops. Four questionnaires were returned undeliverable for address problems or other reasons. A total of 156, or 58 percent, of the bishops returned a completed questionnaire. This is a creditably high response for a survey of this type, especially considering that we used no incentives or follow-up, and is consistent with other similar surveys of the US bishops. Surveys of the bishops in 2000 (by Catholic University's Life Cycle Institute) and 1987 (by the NCCB Office of Research) yielded responses of 59 percent and 63 percent, respectively. There was a notable difference in response according to the type of episcopal position held by the respondent: 125, or 65 percent, of the 194 diocesan bishops, but only 27, or 37 percent, of the 74 auxiliary bishops responded to the questionnaire. A similar disparity was found in 2000 and in 1987.

The questionnaire asked a variety of questions about specific aspects of the bishops' support or reservations toward the Pastoral Provision and issues that they take into account when considering ordaining a married priest. Their responses to the most important closed-end items, in which the bishop selected a response from the categories "strongly agree," "agree," "neutral/no opinion," "disagree," or "strongly disagree" are reported in Table 6.1. Many bishops also wrote in comments and thoughts in their own words, in response to open-ended questions about the restrictions placed on priests ordained under the Pastoral Provision, why so few have been ordained, and the most important strengths and weaknesses of the program.

We asked each bishop how many married priests were serving currently or had ever served in his diocese. Comparison of their responses with the known actual distribution of married priests allowed us to check the accuracy of the sample and the information provided by the bishops. Sixty-three percent of responding bishops reported that their diocese had never had a married priest, a number somewhat smaller than the actual proportion of 74 percent. On the other hand, the concentration of married priests in dioceses that did ordain them is very similar to the actual skew; and the total number of married priests serving currently that can be computed from the bishops' reports is 72, which is very close to the actual number (at the time of the survey) of about 70. These comparisons suggest that the survey information provided is reasonably accurate, but that bishops with more experience of the Pastoral Provision were somewhat more likely to have responded to the survey. The nonresponding bishops may have felt that their opinions were simply less valuable to the survey since they had not had experience with a married priest. During the survey administration we received several queries by email or letter from bishops or their staff on just this point. If, however, the nonresponding bishops were more likely to be opposed to the Pastoral Provision, the survey findings might overstate somewhat the level of support for the Pastoral Provision.

V. COMPENSATION ANALYSIS COMPARING MARRIED AND CELIBATE PRIESTS (CHAPTER 6)

This section compares the cost to a parish to support a celibate priest with the cost to support a married priest. A fair comparison of the cost of support in the two cases requires estimating, as accurately as possible, the dollar value of a wide variety of in-kind supplies and services, a procedure which necessarily involves a certain amount of assumption and possible error. Value estimates are also complicated by the large overlap of personal and professional lives of Catholic clergy. A number of professional activities subsume personal expenses, for example meals and retreats. Rectories are often physically attached to parish offices, and it is not always clear where one ends and the other begins. There are substantial expenses related to housing and services that parishes generally pay to support celibate priests, which are not accounted as compensation to the priest and are commingled with other parish expenses, but which married priests must pay out of their salary. Complicating clergy compensation further are unique provisions of the income tax code which reflect the ongoing transition from the benefice system to one of cash compensation. IRS rules require the monetizing of certain customary allowances so that their value can be taxed as income to the priest, even though he receives no money to pay the tax. Clergy, moreover, are considered employees for purposes of income tax but self-employed for purposes of social security tax, leading to additional complications.

Notwithstanding these complications and the attendant uncertainty they bring, this section attempts to analyze the compensation of married and celibate priests in order to compare them as accurately as possible. The recent collection of extensive detailed information on Catholic clergy compensation makes such a comparison possible with a much higher degree of confidence that might have been the case as little as a decade ago. The numbers referenced throughout the analysis are presented in Table A.1.

The celibate clergy compensation amounts (lines 1–5) in Table A.1 report the results of a comprehensive survey of priest compensation conducted in 2008 by the National Federation of Priests Councils (NFPC), the data from which are compiled in a 120-page reported titled "The Laborer is Worthy of His Hire."[9] Ninety percent of U.S. Catholic dioceses provided the NFPC researchers with data on salaries, benefits, and in-kind provisions for their clergy. Compensation practices and amounts varied widely from diocese to diocese, and thus (like any average) the numbers reported in Table A.1 do not represent the actual cost of, or a recommendation for, the compensation or support of any particular priest. The amounts reported for married clergy in Table 3.1 are from the 2007 survey of Pastoral Provision priests that is reported throughout this book. As already noted, about half (49 percent) of the Pastoral Provision priests served full-time in a Catholic parish, that is, in a role comparable to the vast majority of regular Catholic priests. Table A.1 includes data only for these parish-based married priests. With some adjustments, the table reports national averages.[10]

Cash Allowances

Almost all (90 percent or more) of the parish-based married priests reported that, like almost all regular Catholic priests, in addition to their cash stipend they received a basket of allowances including fully paid health insurance; pension or retirement account contributions; use of a parish-owned car or reimbursement or an allowance for use of their personal vehicle for parish business; and allowances for continuing education, retreats, and ministry expenses. They also reported receiving, like all Catholic priests, Mass stipends or stole fees amounting to about 2 percent of their annual income. These credits and allowances are included in the average compensation amounts reported in the first row of Table A.1.

For these generally universal compensation elements, the average amount for married priests in 2007 was $57,933, which is 1.6 times higher than the $36,441 average amount received by celibate priests.[11] The additional $21,492 paid to married priests, on average, on the most recognizable elements of clergy compensation, corresponds,

Table A.1 Support Expenses for Celibate and Married Priests Compared

Support Item	Average Expense for Married	Average Expense for Celibate	Difference M - C	Ratio M:C
(1) Average compensation	$ 57,933	$ 36,441	$ 21,492	1.6
(2) SECA reimbursement	560	2,240	–1,680	
(3) Auto insurance allowance	383	1,035	–652	
(4) Food allowance	414	3,454	–3,040	
(5) Adjusted average compensation	59,290	43,170	16,120	1.4
Non-compensation housing expenses				
(6) Utilities and public services	0	2,365*	–2,365	
(7) Household furnishings and equipment	0	1,222*	–1,222	
(8) Household operations	0	669*	–669	
(9) Liability insurance	0	537	–537	
(10) Housekeeping supplies	0	434*	–434	
(11) Support adjusted for housing expenses	59,290	48,397	10,893	1.2
(12) Staff: Housekeeping, cooking and laundry	0	6,266	–6,266	
(13) Household operations and supplies offset	0	–334	334	
Total priest support expense	$ 59,290	$ 54,329	$ 4,961	1.1

Sources: Celibate clergy figures are based on Daly (2008), reporting 2007–2008 average amounts reported on the National Diocesan Salary Survey. Married clergy numbers are from the 2007 survey of Pastoral Provision priests. Average compensation includes stipend, housing, health insurance, pension, and any cash allowances and in-kind benefits in addition to those broken out in the table.

* = Data from Bureau of Labor Statistics' Consumer Expenditure Survey.

as noted above, to the widespread perception that married priests are compensated more highly or cost the Church substantially more than do celibate priests. However, this simple comparison vastly overstates the net difference in costs in the two cases. This is largely due to two factors, which, since they are not easily visible, are often overlooked: celibate priests typically receive additional compensation allowances that the married priests do not; and there are substantial expenses related to housing and services that parishes pay directly, not by way of compensation, to support celibate priests, but which married priests must pay out of their parish compensation.

Clergy, considered self-employed for most tax purposes, are designed "statutory employees" by the IRS for social security (SECA/FICA) tax, as noted above. The result is that, unlike regular employees whose employer is required to pay half of the social security tax, leaving the employee liable for a tax of only 7.65 percent, clergy must pay a full 15.3 percent of their income in SECA tax. For many priests, this amount is much more than their income tax liability. As a result, almost all Catholic dioceses reimburse the priest the amount of the employer share of this tax; many reimburse the entire tax. Survey data provided by the National Federation of Priests Councils reports the average SECA reimbursement in 2007 to be $2,240. By contrast, only a fourth (25 percent) of married priests reported receiving a SECA reimbursement. Likewise, the large majority of celibate priests, but only just over a third (37 percent) of married priests, received an auto insurance allowance; and only one in eight (12 percent) married priests reported receiving a food allowance or in-kind supply, a benefit reported to the NFPC at an average value of $3,454 for celibate priests nationwide in 2007. In 2007 celibate priests received an average of $7,669 for these additional allowances, while married priests received only $1,825. When the disparity in these allowances are taken into account, the adjusted average compensation for married priests, at $59,290, drops from 61 percent to only 37 percent higher than, or 1.4 times, the corresponding $43,170 average compensation of celibate priests.

Housing Allowance

The most extensive differences in compensation between married and celibate priests, however, have to do with the cost, and attribution of the cost, of housing. These differences are related to the very different housing situations of the two types of priests. Virtually no celibate priests live in their own home; the 2008 NFPC compensation survey reported that 92 percent of priests lived in a parish rectory or other house maintained by the parish. By contrast, the large majority (68 percent) of married priests who serve parishes lived in a home that they own and maintain. A careful analysis of housing expenses and allowances reveals that, for reasons related to the tax code and to the usual living arrangements of celibate priests, diocesan priest compensation structures generally understate the true cost of resident priests' housing to the parish, which then tends to inflate the apparent difference in cost between celibate and married priests. When all the expenses associated with priests' housing, not just those reported for compensation purposes, are accounted for, the apparent cost disparity between the two types of priests is greatly reduced.

The "housing allowance" of a priest who lives in a rectory is not an actual cash payment, but the estimated value of residing in the rectory, a number that is provided to him for the purpose of reporting his income for tax purposes. The IRS requires that the housing allowance be stipulated in advance and evaluates its accuracy relative to the fair market value of comparable housing. Thus, unlike cash housing allowances for persons who live in their own residences, which can be justified by expense records, the rectory housing allowance amount does not reflect the actual cost of maintaining the rectory or any associated in-kind services.[12]

Since the priest does not receive this money, but must (as noted above) pay social security taxes of 15.3 percent on it, it is to his advantage (and, when the parish reimburses his social security tax, to the advantage of the parish) that the estimate be as conservative as possible. In 2007, accordingly, the average annual taxable housing allowance for a celibate diocesan priest residing in a rectory in the United States was $8,202, or $684 per month, an amount that was comparable to, albeit about 20 percent lower than, the 2007 US average shelter cost of $835 per month.[13] This comparatively low amount is defensible when one considers the type of housing priests receive, abstracted from other benefices and considerations. Priests typically reside in shared quarters, including a shared bathroom, except for a single bedroom, which is private—a form of housing that would be on the low end of any range of shelter prices.

Of course, the cost of room or "shelter" alone is only part of the entire cost of owning and maintaining a house, and far less than what it costs the parish to maintain the rectory in which the priests reside. In its analysis of spending patterns that contributes to the estimation of the Consumer Price Index, the Bureau of Labor Statistics (BLS) identifies, in addition to shelter, the cost of four distinct components of housing expenditures in the United States: utilities, household furnishings and equipment, household operations, and housekeeping supplies. The BLS measures, based on thousands of detailed reports of expenses, form a clear basis for comparison of the financial commitments of the two groups of priests. Utilities includes the cost of electricity, natural gas, fuel oil, as well as public services like garbage collection. At over $3,400 per year on average, it is by far the largest component of housing costs after shelter. Household furnishings and equipment, at an average of over $1,700 per year, includes not only furniture but also appliances, carpet, and such large-ticket items as furnaces and air conditioning. Household operations and housekeeping expenses, averaging just under $1,600, include routine repair and maintenance expenses as well as periodic capital maintenance like replacing a roof or windows, cleaning products, and services like pest control or security. Because the CPI computations, for technical reasons, do not include the cost of property liability insurance, that cost is included separately, showing the 2007 average cost for such insurance reported by the National Association of Insurance Commissioners. [14]

The typical celibate priest who resides in a parish rectory does not pay these expenses.[15] The fact that only the value of shelter is attributed to him as taxable compensation does not negate the other real expenses involved in housing, which must be paid by the parish on his behalf, and which married priests, who live in their own home, must pay directly out of their compensation. Moreover, unlike shelter alone, there is no reason to suppose that these other housing costs are likely to be lower for parish rectories than for other US residences. To the extent that parish rectories tend to be larger and older, thus less energy-efficient, than the typical home, a good case could be made that the costs related to maintaining a rectory are probably larger than average. Lines 6–10 of Table A.1 report the average expenditure per priest for these housing costs, as measured by the BLS, in 2007. Since in 2007, according to the Official Catholic Directory, there was an average of one and one-half resident priests per parish rectory, the table reports two-thirds of the US average expenditure per housing unit.[16] When these additional costs of housing are included, the average excess cost to maintain a married priest is reduced to under $11,000, about half of what it originally appeared to be, with a ratio of married to celibate priest compensation of only 1.2. But there is one more class of differences in cost, which is directly related to the difference between the celibate and married state of life.

Housekeeper/Cook and Other Staff

Most Catholic parishes employ persons to perform services for the rectory or the parish priests that are typically done by the husband or wife in middle-income American households, including yard care, ice and snow removal, routine maintenance, and/or laundry, cooking, and cleaning. A comprehensive survey of Catholic parish staffing in 2010 found that the average Catholic parish employed a paid staff of eight persons, half of them full-time. Over a fifth (21 percent) of Catholic parishes reported employing a rectory housekeeper/cook to provide "cleaning, cooking and/ or laundry services for persons living in rectory."[17] Averaged over all parishes, these costs amount to $3,192.50 per resident priest.[18] Including the cost of these services to a parish is directly pertinent to this comparison, since these are precisely the services that wives provide without monetary compensation in a traditional marriage arrangement.

More than a fifth (23 percent) of responding Catholic parishes employed a housekeeper/janitor whose duties included "cleaning bathrooms, washing windows and trash removal" in the church and other buildings, and a quarter (25 percent) employed at least one maintenance worker to perform semi-skilled maintenance and repair work on parish buildings and grounds. Half of the parishes employed either a groundskeeper whose duties included "caring for lawn, trees, shrubs and flowers; mowing, trimming, raking and watering; ice and snow removal; and collecting and disposing of leaves and litter" and/or other types of maintenance personnel whose duties included such tasks.[19] These percentages are not additive and certainly overlapped; many of the positions were part-time; larger parishes tended to have multiple staff in these areas, and many smaller parishes had none. On reasonable assumptions, however, Catholic parishes devoted an average of at least four hours per week of staff time for such tasks, at an estimated average annual cost per resident priest of $3,073.50.[20] (The services of parish employees no doubt offset some of the BLS-estimated "household operations" expenses that are not related to capital maintenance; accordingly, celibate priest expenses are reduced by the half the amount of this category in Table A.1.) By contrast, none of the married priests reported that the parish provided any maintenance, lawn care, snow removal, laundry, cooking, or cleaning services for their home.

Combining the housekeeper/cook and facilities staff costs results in a total average rectory-related staff expense of $6,266. When these parish staff expenses are acknowledged, the estimated average difference in the expense to a parish to maintain a married versus a celibate priest comes to only $4,961, a difference of less than 10 percent, or only 1.1 times as much.

There is, of course, a good deal of uncertainty and wide variation in this estimate. In some cases, the cost factors are estimated or imputed from sparse information, and the numbers compared represent national averages of local situations
that may be very different from the average. Smaller parishes without facilities or
housekeeping staff, or parishes with a larger number of resident priests, may well
have paid much less than the average to maintain a celibate priest.

VI. TABLES OF SURVEY RESULTS

This section includes detailed tables of findings from the Pastoral Provision priest
surveys of priests and their wives. Where possible, the responses of the married
priests are compared to the general population of US priests on similar questions.[21]
Only living Pastoral Provision priests are included. Percents reported may not total
exactly 100 due to rounding and/or nonresponse.

Table A.2 Description of Sample Members (in Percent)

	PP Priests	PP Wives	US Priests
Present age:			
39 or younger	2	4	8
40–49	6	9	15
50–59	29	28	24
60–69	33	41	24
70–79	20	15	21
80 or older	10	2	9
Mean age:	63.7	61.0	60.9
Race/Ethnicity: (L)			
White	97	98	92
Black	2	0	1
Asian	0	2	4
Other	1	0	2
Latino (may be of any race)	2	5	6
Highest Education Attained:			
B.A.	1	28	7
M.A./M. Div. or postgraduate	79	31	78
Doctoral Degree	17	2	14

Table A.3 Ordination Age and Tenure (in Percent)

	PP Priests	US Priests
Age at Anglican ordination		
29 or younger	58	
30–39	37	
40–49	3	
50–59	2	
Mean	30.0	
Age at Catholic priest ordination		
29 or younger	0	68
30–39	19	27
40–49	32	4
50–59	35	2
60–69	14	0
Mean	49.1	29.3
Years since first ordained		
1–10	0	12
11–20	2	15
21–30	61	18
31–40	33	24
41–50	3	22
51–60	0	8
61 or more	2	1
Mean	30.4	31.3
Years in Episcopal ministry		
1–10	29	
11–20	39	
21–30	26	
31 or more	6	
Mean	16.7	
Years in Catholic ministry		
1–10	22	
11–20	39	
21–30	33	
31–40	4	
41 or more	2	
Mean	17.5	

Table A.4 Family Background (in Percent)

	PP Priests	PP Wives	US Priests
Birth order**			
1st child	69	45	35
2nd	12	34	22
3rd	11	13	19
4th or later	8	37	24
Religion raised (baptized) in			
Episcopalian/Anglican	27	22	
Methodist	23	24	
Baptist	15	8	
Disciples of Christ	6	0	
Lutheran	6	10	
Catholic	3	20	
Presbyterian	2	10	
Other Protestant	18	6	
Family religious attendance as a child***			
Several times a week	29	14	13
Once a week	55	60	43
Monthly or more	11	9	23
Less than monthly	5	17	21

** Comparison data from a 1999 survey of Catholic priests serving as military chaplains (n = 452).

*** Comparison group is adult American Catholic males, from the 2008 General Social Survey.

Table A.5 Satisfaction with Catholic Priesthood (in Percent)

	PP Priests	PP Wives	US Priests
Taking all things together, how would you say things are these days? Would you say you are			
Very happy	66	49	46
Pretty happy	25	51	48
Not too happy	9	0	6
To what extent do you feel you are utilizing your important skills and abilities in your present assignment?*			
A great deal	44	—	41
Fairly much	36	—	36
To some degree	8	—	14
Comparatively little	8	—	7
Not at all	4	—	2

(continued)

Table A.5 (Continued)

	PP Priests	PP Wives	US Priests
Has your life as a Catholic priest [priest's wife] turned out ... (L)			
Better than you expected?	61	59	61
About as you expected?	25	26	28
Worse than you expected?	8	4	7
Not Sure	6	11	4
If you had the opportunity to make the choice again, would you become [support husband becoming] a Catholic priest? (L)			
Definitely yes	88	83	67
Probably yes	11	14	21
Neutral/No opinion	0	0	8
Probably no	0	3	3
Definitely no	2	0	1
How well would you say you have been received as a Catholic priest [priest's wife] by laypersons?			
Very well	93	73	—
Moderately well	6	27	—
Neither well nor poorly	2	0	—
How well would you say you have been received in the Catholic presbyterate by other priests?			
Very well	72	73	—
Moderately well	24	25	—
Neither well nor poorly	2	3	—
Moderately poorly	2	0	—
Very poorly	0	0	—

* Comparison data from a 1993 NFPC survey of Catholic priests.

Table A.6 Spiritual Practice (in Percent)

	PP Priests	PP Wives	US Priests
Compared to a year ago, would you say today you are **			
Closer to God		53	67	48
Further away from God		6	6	4
About the same		39	25	47
In the past year did you meet with a spiritual director? - % yes		38	32	61
Prays the *Liturgy of the Hours* (Breviary) daily*		80		62

(*continued*)

Table A.6 (Continued)

	PP Priests	PP Wives	US Priests
How often do you receive the sacrament of reconciliation (go to confession)?*			
Occasionally, rarely or never	16	47	19
Several times a year	38	42	37
About once a month	43	8	40
About once a week	4	3	10
How often do you pray the Rosary?*			
About once a month or less	31		42
About once a week	21		14
Several times a week	15		19
Every day	33		25
How often do you practice Eucharistic Adoration?*			
About once a month or less often	54		48
About once a week	25		20
Several times a week	15		18
Every day	6		14
How often do you practice a devotion to a particular saint?*			
Never or rarely	40		48
Less than weekly	13		15
About once a week or more often	48		37
How often do you make a retreat?			
Never	31		6
Once a year	58		54
Several times a year	12		40

* Comparison data from a 2005 survey of priests ordained five to nine years (*n* = 722).

** Comparison data from a 1999 survey of Military Archdiocese priests (*n* = 452).

Table A.7 Work Status (in Percent)

	PP Priests	US Priests
Hours worked each week**		
Median	52	49
10% work more than	72	72
10% work fewer than	42	28

(continued)

Table A.7 (Continued)

	PP Priests	US Priests
Days off each week**		
Two days or more	14	45
One day	64	45
No day off	22	10
Percent of work week spent ministering in a parish		
None	7	
1–25	22	
26–50	6	
51–99	16	
100	49	
Parish position		
Pastor	19	37
Administrator, priest-in-charge, etc., with faculties of a pastor	30	0
Assistant/Associate pastor	29	12
Retired	15	16
Non-parish position		
Educator	21	8
Chaplain	13	2
Diocesan administrator/officer	9	4
Other apostolate	7	21
Other, not Church related	2	

** Comparison data from a 1985 NFPC survey of Catholic priests. Excludes retired priests.

Table A.8 Views on Moral Issues (in Percent)

Do you think it is a sin. . . .	PP Priests	PP Wives	US Priests
. . . for unmarried persons to have sexual relations? (L)			
Always	84	73	53
Often	16	24	32
Seldom	0	0	8
Never	0	3	2

(continued)

Do you think it is a sin. . . .	PP Priests	PP Wives	US Priests
. . . for a woman to get an abortion? (L)			
Always	92	71	75
Often	8	24	19
Seldom	0	3	3
Never	0	3	1
. . . for married persons to use artificial methods of birth control? (L)			
Always	61	46	28
Often	27	32	25
Seldom	7	11	32
Never	5	11	9
. . . to engage in homosexual relations? (L)			
Always	90	77	49
Often	9	14	25
Seldom	2	6	15
Never	0	3	4
. . . to take one's own life if suffering from a debilitating disease? (L)			
Always	77	81	57
Often	18	11	17
Seldom	4	5	10
Never	2	3	6
. . . to use human cloning for medical research? (L)			
Always	95	94	45
Often	5	3	18
Seldom	0	0	16
Never	0	3	8
. . . to use the stem cells of fetuses for medical research? (L)			
Always	91	86	57
Often	7	9	17
Seldom	2	3	10
Never	0	3	6
. . . to use condoms as a protection against AIDS? (L)			
Always	67	47	31
Often	11	13	17
Seldom	13	22	18
Never	9	19	25

(continued)

Table A.8 (Continued)

Do you think it is a sin. . . .	PP Priests	PP Wives	US Priests
. . . to masturbate? (L)			
Always	64	60	30
Often	22	8	21
Seldom	10	16	28
Never	3	16	14
In your opinion, are the pope's views on moral issues generally . . . . (L)*			
Too liberal	2	3	1
Too conservative	6	15	33
About right	92	77	62
In your opinion, are the views of the bishop of your diocese on moral issues generally . . . . (L)			
Too liberal	10	—	3
Too conservative	2	—	18
About right	88	—	73

*This question referenced Benedict XVI when asked of the Pastoral Provision priests and wives in 2007, but John Paul II when asked of the US priests in 2002.

Table A.9 Ecclesial Issues (in Percent)

	PP Priests	PP Wives	US Priests
Would you describe your views on most matters having to do with religious beliefs and moral doctrines as			
Very liberal	0	3	4
Somewhat liberal	6	9	27
Middle of the road	2	12	37
Somewhat conservative	57	48	23
Very conservative	35	29	5
As an Episcopalian, which of the following best describes your churchmanship?			
High Church (or Anglo-Catholic)	85	—	—
Moderate/No preference	10	—	—
Low Church (or Evangelical)	5	—	—

(continued)

Table A.9 (Continued)

	PP Priests	PP Wives	US Priests
Do you think Roman Catholics must follow all the Church's teachings to be faithful, or do you think they may disagree on some issues and still be considered faithful?			
Must follow all teachings	57	53	35
May disagree and still be faithful	43	44	58
Overall, do you approve or disapprove of the way your diocesan bishop is handling his duties?			
Approve strongly	47	52	39
Approve somewhat	35	40	37
Disapprove somewhat	16	8	14
Disapprove strongly	2	0	6
How much confidence do you have in the Catholic Church in America today? (L)			
A great deal	48	47	53
Some	35	47	33
Not much	15	6	9
None at all	2	0	1
Would you favor or oppose the ordination of women as priests?			
Favor	9	11	46
Oppose	91	89	51
Would you favor or oppose the regular ordination of married men as priests in the Latin Rite?			
Favor	46	49	69
Oppose	54	49	28

Table A.10 Attitudes on the Priesthood (in Percents)

	PP Priests	US Priests
Ordination confers on the priest a new status of a permanent character which makes him essentially different from the laity within the church.		
Agree strongly	87	48
Agree somewhat	6	29
Uncertain or neutral	0	6
Disagree somewhat	6	10
Disagree strongly	2	7

(continued)

Table A.10 (Continued)

	PP Priests	US Priests
I feel that I am most a priest when I am saying (celebrating) Mass and hearing confessions.		
Agree strongly	70	41
Agree somewhat	14	32
Uncertain or neutral	4	4
Disagree somewhat	10	16
Disagree strongly	4	8
The Catholic Church needs to move faster in empowering lay persons in ministry.		
Agree strongly	10	38
Agree somewhat	16	35
Uncertain or neutral	16	11
Disagree somewhat	31	10
Disagree strongly	28	6
Celibacy should be a matter of personal choice for diocesan priests.		
Agree strongly	23	35
Agree somewhat	12	21
Uncertain or neutral	8	10
Disagree somewhat	17	10
Disagree strongly	40	24
I think it would be a good idea if the priests and/or laity in a diocese were to elect their own bishop.		
Agree strongly	2	22
Agree somewhat	4	25
Uncertain or neutral	6	15
Disagree somewhat	14	15
Disagree strongly	75	23

Table A.11 Sources of Priestly Satisfaction (in Percent)

Would you indicate how important each of the following is *as a source of satisfaction* to you as a priest?	PP Priests	US Priests
Ministering the sacraments and presiding over the liturgy.		
Great importance	100	90
Some importance	0	9
Little importance	0	1
No importance	0	0

(continued)

Table A.11 (Continued)

Would you indicate how important each of the following is *as a source of satisfaction* to you as a priest?	PP Priests	US Priests
Preaching the Word.		
Great importance	96	80
Some importance	4	18
Little importance	0	2
No importance	0	1
Respect that comes to the priestly office.		
Great importance	12	24
Some importance	47	46
Little importance	31	25
No importance	10	4
Engaging in efforts at social reform.		
Great importance	18	23
Some importance	51	49
Little importance	22	23
No importance	8	4
Opportunity to work with many people and be a part of their lives.		
Great importance	67	68
Some importance	31	27
Little importance	2	5
No importance	0	1
Spiritual security that comes from responding to the divine call.		
Great importance	60	51
Some importance	26	33
Little importance	6	13
No importance	9	3

SURVEY OF PASTORAL PROVISION PRIESTS

A STUDY BY THE CATHOLIC UNIVERSITY OF AMERICA COMMISSIONED BY THE U.S. ADMINISTRATION OF THE PASTORAL PROVISION
LIFE CYCLE INSTITUTE, THE CATHOLIC UNIVERSITY OF AMERICA, WASHINGTON, DC 20064, FALL 2006

DO NOT FILL OUT THIS QUESTIONNAIRE. It is intended to be completed by an interviewer who will contact you. We are sending it to you only for preview. You may want to make notes on it so that you will have your answer ready to hand when you are phoned. All information provided is strictly confidential and will be reported only anonymously and/or in aggregate form. THANK YOU for your time.

Background

A1. In what year were you born? _____
Counting from oldest to youngest, I was born number A2. _____ of A3. _____ children in my family of origin.

A4. Which best describes your main ethnic identification?

1. White   2. Black   3. Hispanic   4. Asian   5. Other _____

A5. Are you currently—married, widowed, divorced, separated, or have you never been married (circle correct response?

1   Married
2   Widowed
3   Divorced
4   Separated
5   Never Married (skip next question)

A6. Have you been married more than once (circle correct response)?   Yes   No

A7. On what date were you married (most recently, if more than one marriage)?

_____

A8. Please list, from oldest to youngest, the sex and age of each of your children (e.g. "male age 18, female age 13," etc.), if any:

Also ask: Which ones went to Catholic school? Are any of them priests/religious?

1. _____
2. _____
3. _____

4. _____
5. _____
6. _____

A9. Which of the following options best describes your current living situation? (Circle one number)

I live alone.	1
I live with at least one other priest.	2
I live with my wife and/or family.	3
Other: _____	4

A10. What type of housing do you currently live in? (Circle one number)

Rectory	1
Other Church-supplied housing	2
I rent an apartment.	3
I own my own house.	4

Religious/Spiritual Journey

We would like to get some background about your religious background and spiritual practice. Please fill in the blanks below.

B1. In what religious group or tradition were you first formally designated a priest or minister? _____

B2. When and where did this occur? Please note each successive ordination status (e.g. "deacon," "elder"), the year designated to that status, and the diocese or judicatory you served in:

Status: _____ Year: _____ Judicatory: _____ By whom ordained: _____
Status: _____ Year: _____ Judicatory: _____ By whom ordained: _____
Status: _____ Year: _____ Judicatory: _____ By whom ordained: _____
Status: _____ Year: _____ Judicatory: _____ By whom ordained: _____

B3. Prior to your first ordination or designation, what higher educational degrees or certifications, if any, did you receive, and when did you receive them? Start with your highest degree and work backward. (Prompt for Ph.D., D.Min., M.Div., B. Div.. B.A., High School Diploma)

Degree/Certificate	Year Received	Institution/Seminary

B4. In what year did you first become affiliated with the religious tradition you were first ordained in? _____

If the year is greater than year of birth(A1), ask:

B4a. What religion were you affiliated with before that? _____
B4b. Starting in what year? _____

If the year is greater than year of birth(A1), ask:

B4c. What religion were you affiliated with before that? _____
B4d. Starting in what year? _____

(Repeat until all lifetime religious affiliations are covered. Use the back of the paper for additional space if needed, and circle the word "OVER" here.)

B5. With what religion were your parents affiliated at the time of your birth?
Mother _____
Father _____

B6. When you were around 11 or 12, how often did *you* attend religious services then? (Circle the number of the closest response.)

1   Never
2   Less than once a year
3   About once or twice a year
4   Several times a year
5   About once a month
6   2–3 times a month
7   Nearly every week
8   Every week
9   Several times a week

B7, B8. In what year _____ and religious tradition _____ were you baptized?

B9, B10. In what year _____ and religious tradition _____, if any, were you first confirmed?

B11. Would you say you have been "born again" or have had a "born again" experience? _____

(If yes →) B11a. In what year did this happen? _____

B12. As compared to this time last year, would you say that today you are (circle one number)

Closer to God	1
Farther from God	2
About the same	3
Don't know/Can't say	4

B15. In the past month, how often have you prayed the Liturgy of the Hours (Divine Office) (circle one number)?

Never	1
Occasionally	2
At least once a week	3
Several times a week	4
Every day	5

B13. Using the responses below, how often do you do the following? (Write one number on each line)

Never or rarely	1
About once a year	2
Several times a year	3
About once a month	4
About once a week	5
Several times a week	6
Every day	7

_____ B13a. Receive the sacrament of Reconciliation.

_____ B13b. Meet with a spiritual director.

_____ B13c. Pray the Rosary.

_____ B13d. Make a retreat.

_____ B13e. Practice Eucharistic Adoration.

_____ B13f. Practice a devotion to a particular saint.

B16. In the past month, about how many times did you celebrate Mass each week?

_____

Professional Support and Satisfaction

C1. Now considering *all* your duties of any type, in a typical week about how many hours *total* do you work/minister

a. Monday through Friday?   _____ hours (total for all 5 days)

b. on Saturday?   _____ hours

c. on Sunday?   _____ hours

C2. About what percent of your workweek do you currently spend ministering in a parish? _____

(If zero percent, skip the next question.)

C3. Which of the following options best describes your current *parish* position? (Circle one number)

Pastor	1
Associate Pastor	2
Stipendiary Mass assistance	3
Other: _____	4

C4. Which of the following best describes your current *non-parish* position, if any? (Circle one number)

Chaplain	1
Diocesan Administrator	2
Educator	3
Other apostolate_____	4
Other non-Church-related work:_____	5

C5. Most weeks I have (check only one). . .

_____ two 24-hour periods that are entirely free from priestly duties ("two days off").

_____ at least one 24-hour period that is entirely free from priestly duties ("one day off").

_____ at least one 24-hour period that is mostly, but not entirely, free from priestly duties. On this day I spend on average about ____ hours working.

_____ none of the above.

C6. About what percent of your income comes from each of the following?

A parish (or diocese for parish duties)	_____
A diocese (for diocesan duties)	_____
Another Church-related institution	_____
Non-Catholic or secular employment	_____
Pension, savings, or investment	_____
Other	_____

C7. Please indicate the types of financial support, if any, you receive from your parish, diocese, or order. (Circle all that apply.)

Regular stipend	1
Church-supplied housing or housing allowance	2
Utilities allowance	3
Pension or retirement account such as 403B	4
Retreat allowance	5
Continuing education allowance	6
FICA reimbursement	7
Tuition assistance for children's Catholic school	8
Auto allowance or mileage reimbursement	9
Auto insurance reimbursement	10
Medical expenses reimbursement	11
Mass supply stipends	12
Other _____	13

C8. Was your conversion and/or Catholic ordination related to the entry of a congregation of people into communion with Rome?

Yes
No

C9. Have you ever served in an Anglican Use parish?

Yes, currently
Yes, but not currently
No

C10. As an Episcopalian, which of the following best describes your churchmanship?

High Church (or Anglo-Catholic)	1
Leaning toward High Church	2
Moderate, no strong preference	3
Leaning toward Low Church	4
Low Church (or Evangelical)	5

C11. Please indicate any fraternities or organizations you were a member of in the Episcopal Church, such as the Society of the Holy Cross, National Organization of Episcopalians for Life, etc.

_____

C11. Please indicate any other languages, besides English, you can converse in. (Circle as many numbers as needed.)

None, only English	1
Spanish	2
French	3
German	4
Other _____	5

C12. Taking all things together, how would you say things are these days—would you say you're very happy, pretty happy, or not too happy? (Circle one number.)

Very happy	1
Pretty happy	2
Not too happy	3

C13. To what extent do you feel you are utilizing your important skills and abilities in your present assignment? (Circle one number.)

Not at all	1
Comparatively little	2
To some degree	3
Fairly much	4
A great deal	5

C14. How well would you say you have been received as a Catholic priest by laypersons? (Circle one number.)

Very well	1
Moderately well	2
Neither well nor poorly	3
Moderately poorly	4
Very poorly	5

C15. How well would you say you have been received in the Catholic presbyterate by other priests? (Circle one number.)

Very well	1
Moderately well	2
Neither well nor poorly	3
Moderately poorly	4
Very poorly	5

C16. How well would you say you have been received in the Catholic presbyterate by your bishop and/or diocesan administration? (Circle one number.)

Very well	1
Moderately well	2
Neither well nor poorly	3
Moderately poorly	4
Very poorly	5

C17. If you had the opportunity to make the choice again, would you become a Catholic priest? (Circle one number.)

Definitely yes	1
Probably yes	2
Not sure	3
Probably no	4
Definitely no	5

C18. Has your life as a Catholic priest turned out ...? (Circle one number.)

Better than you expected	1
Worse than you expected	2
About as you expected	3
Not sure	4

C19. As you reflect on your conversion journey, what were the greatest losses, disappointments, or struggles you experienced (if any) in your transition into the Catholic Church and priesthood? Please briefly mention up to five, beginning with the most important.

1. _____
2. _____
3. _____
4. _____
5. _____

C20. As you reflect on your conversion journey, what were the greatest gains, encouragements, or satisfactions you experienced (if any) in your transition into the Catholic Church and priesthood? Please briefly mention up to five, beginning with the most important.

1. _____
2. _____
3. _____
4. _____
5. _____

Doctrinal, Moral, and Ecclesial Issues

These questions replicate ones that have been asked of national samples of priests, and are designed to compare the opinions of pastoral provision priests with those of all US priests.

D1. Do you think Roman Catholics must follow all the Church's teachings to be faithful, or do you think they may disagree on some issues and still be considered faithful? (Circle one number.)

Must follow all teachings	1
May disagree and still be faithful	2

D2. Would you describe your views on most matters having to do with religious beliefs and moral doctrines as. . . .

Very liberal	1
Somewhat liberal	2
Middle of the road	3
Somewhat conservative	4
Very conservative	5

D3. In your opinion, are Pope Benedict's views on moral issues generally. . . .

Too liberal	1
Too conservative	2
About right	3

D4. In your opinion, are the views of the bishop of your diocese on moral issues generally. . . .

Too liberal	1
Too conservative	2
About right	3

D5. How much confidence do you have in the Catholic Church in America today?

A great deal	1
Some	2
Not much	3
None at all	4

D6. Overall, do you approve or disapprove of the way the bishop who presides in your diocese is handling his duties?

Approve strongly	1
Approve somewhat	2

Disapprove somewhat	3
Disapprove strongly	4

D7. Would you favor or oppose the ordination of women as priests?

Favor	1
Oppose	2

D8. Would you favor or oppose the regular ordination of married men as priests in the Latin Rite?

Favor	1
Oppose	2

D9. Do you think it is always, often, seldom, or never a sin. . . .

1. For unmarried people to have sexual relations?	4	3	2	1
2. For a woman to get an abortion?	4	3	2	1
3. For married couples to use artificial methods of birth control?	4	3	2	1
4. To engage in homosexual behavior?	4	3	2	1
5. To take one's own life if suffering from a debilitating disease?	4	3	2	1
6. To use cloning for medical research?	4	3	2	1
7. To use stem cells of fetuses for medical research?	4	3	2	1
8. To use condoms as a protection against AIDS?	4	3	2	1
9. To masturbate?	4	3	2	1

D10. Here are some statements about assorted issues in the priesthood. Do you agree or disagree with them? After each, circle the number for the response that best fits your present thinking.

KEY TO RESPONSES

1 = Agree strongly
2 = Agree somewhat
3 = Uncertain or neutral
4 = Disagree somewhat
5 = Disagree strongly

A. Ordination confers on the priest a new status of a permanent character which makes him essentially different from the laity within the church. 1 2 3 4 5

B. I feel that I am most a priest when I am saying (celebrating) Mass and hearing confessions. 1 2 3 4 5

C. The Catholic Church needs to move faster in empowering lay persons in ministry. 1 2 3 4 5

D. Celibacy should be a matter of personal choice
for diocesan priests.   1 2 3 4 5

E. I think it would be a good idea if the priests
and/or laity in a diocese were to elect their   1 2 3 4 5
own bishop.

D11. There are many sources of satisfaction in the life and work of the priest. Would you indicate how important each of the following is *as a source of satisfaction* to you? (Circle one number on each line.)

As a source of satisfaction, this is of . . .

	Great Importance	Some Importance	Little Importance	No Importance
A. Ministering the sacraments and presiding over the liturgy	1	2	3	4
B. Preaching the Word	1	2	3	4
C. Respect that comes to the priestly office	1	2	3	4
D. Engaging in efforts at social reform	1	2	3	4
E. Opportunity to work with many people and be a part of their lives	1	2	3	4
F. Spiritual security that comes from responding to the divine call	1	2	3	4

D12. In your opinion, what are the most important problems facing the Catholic Church in the United States today? Please briefly mention up to five, beginning with the most important.

1. _____
2. _____
3. _____
4. _____
5. _____

Pastoral Provision Ordination Process

E1. On what date were you ordained a Catholic priest? (Please enter the month, day, and year) _____

E2. By whom were you ordained a Catholic priest? _____

E3. For which (arch)diocese or religious order were you ordained a Catholic priest?
_____

E4. In what diocese or religious institute are you currently incardinated?
_____

E5. When did you first inquire a Catholic source about the possibility of conversion? Here we would like to know when, if ever, you *first* asked questions about it. Please give the month and year, or exact date if you recall it: _____

E6. When did you first contact a diocesan vocations office, the US Pastoral Provision Administration, or other Catholic source, to begin the process to seek Catholic ordination under the Pastoral Provisions? Please give the month and year, or exact date if you recall it: _____

E7. When did you formally become a Catholic? Please give the month and year, or exact date if you recall it: _____

E8. When was your rescript dossier submitted to the Holy See? Please give the month and year, or exact date if you recall it: _____

E9. When did you receive word your rescript had been approved? Please give the month and year, or exact date if you recall it: _____

E10. When did you discontinue active ministry as an Episcopal priest? Please give the month and year, or exact date if you recall it: _____

E11. In what *paid employment* were you engaged from the time you left active ministry as an Episcopal priest until the time you were ordained a Catholic priest? Please list the positions and dates of employment, starting with the earliest:

   1. _____
   2. _____
   3. _____

Improving the Pastoral Provision Ordination Process

E12. Consider a scale of 1 to 10, where 1 is the absolute worst and 10 is the absolute best. All things considered, about where on this scale would you candidly rate (write in a number from 1 to 10, or a range of numbers) the support *you personally* received during your conversion transition period from

   . . . . the Episcopalian (or other) bishop/diocese/parish you left. _____
   . . . . your immediate family (spouse and children). _____
   . . . . your extended family. _____
   . . . . your friends. _____
   . . . . a Catholic parish. _____
   . . . . the US Pastoral Provision Administration. _____
   . . . . the Catholic diocese in which you were eventually ordained. _____

E13. Here are some suggestions that have been made for improving the effectiveness and support of the Pastoral Provision Administration for priests converting to the Catholic faith. In your opinion, how important is each suggestion? After each, circle the number for the response which best fits your present thinking.

KEY TO RESPONSES

5 = Very important
4 = Somewhat important
3 = Uncertain or neutral
2 = Somewhat unimportant
1 = Not important at all

A. Develop community and contact among Pastoral Provision priests (for example, by sponsoring or organizing dinners or retreats). 5 4 3 2 1

B. Educate Church leaders about, and advocate for, the needs of Pastoral Provision priests. 5 4 3 2 1

C. Maintain more personal contact with applicants during the period of waiting for a rescript. 5 4 3 2 1

D. More sensitivity to the needs of wife and family. 5 4 3 2 1

E. Define the process more clearly, and make available clear specific detailed information about what steps are involved. 5 4 3 2 1

F. Other: _____ 5 4 3 2 1

E14. Please share any other suggestions or comments you have for improving the effectiveness of the US Pastoral Provision Administration:

E15. Here are some suggestions that have been made for improving the effectiveness and support of Catholic diocesan vocations ministries for priests converting to the Catholic faith. In your opinion, how important is each suggestion? After each, circle the number for the response which best fits your present thinking.

KEY TO RESPONSES

5 = Very important
4 = Somewhat important
3 = Uncertain or neutral
2 = Somewhat unimportant
1 = Not important at all

A. Educate Church leaders about, and advocate for, the needs of Pastoral Provision priests. 5 4 3 2 1

B. Maintain more personal contact with applicants during the period of waiting for a rescript. 5 4 3 2 1

C. Better assistance in finding suitable employment during the transition period. 5 4 3 2 1

D. Other: _____ 5 4 3 2 1

E16. Please share any other suggestions or comments you have for improving the effectiveness of diocesan vocations ministries relative to the Pastoral Provision:

Related Issues

F1. People often ask, "Why did you convert?" or more specifically, "What issues, conditions, or experiences led you to leave the Episcopal Church and join the Catholic Church?" How do/would you respond to this question?

F2. Some have suggested that married convert priests of the Pastoral Provision are a model for the regular ordination of married men in the Latin Rite, or for the readmittance to active priestly function of priests who have renounced orders or been laicized in order to marry. Please briefly share your views, thoughts, or experience on these issues.

F3. Some have suggested that married priests are less likely than celibate ones to engage in sexual misconduct, particularly the abuse of minor children. Please briefly share your views, thoughts, or experience on these issues.

F4. Some have suggested that, for practical reasons, married priests are generally less able to be fully devoted to the care of a parish than ones who are unmarried. Please briefly share your views, thoughts, or experience on this issue.

F5. What, if anything, has surprised you about the Catholic Church?

F6. Finally, we want to give you a chance to express opinions in your own words that may not have been addressed elsewhere in the survey. Use the space below to elaborate on any of your answers above or share any other thoughts, experiences, or perspectives you may wish to relate. Attach additional paper if you need more space.

THANK YOU FOR YOUR TIME AND EFFORT IN COMPLETING THIS SURVEY.

Please keep this questionnaire for reference during your interview. If you do not wish to be interviewed, please fill the questionnaire out and return it to: Dr. Paul Sullins, Life Cycle Institute, Room 215, The Catholic University of America, Washington, D.C. 20064.

SURVEY OF PASTORAL PROVISION WIVES

A STUDY BY THE CATHOLIC UNIVERSITY OF AMERICA COMMISSIONED BY THE U. S. ADMINISTRATION OF THE PASTORAL PROVISION

LIFE CYCLE INSTITUTE, THE CATHOLIC UNIVERSITY OF AMERICA, WASHINGTON, DC 20064, FALL 2006

This document is intended to be completed by an interviewer who will contact you. We are sending it to you only for preview. However, if it is more convenient, you are welcome to fill it in yourself. Directions for self-administration: Please fill out this questionnaire and return it as indicated on the last page. Circle the number that best corresponds to your answer. If you prefer not to answer any particular question, just skip it. Please feel free to use additional paper to expand on your answer to any question. If any question is not applicable to you personally, enter "NA." All information provided is strictly confidential and will be reported only anonymously and/or in aggregate form. THANK YOU for your time.

Background

A1. In what year were you born? _____
Counting from oldest to youngest, I was born number A2. _____ of A3. _____ children in my family of origin.

A4. Which best describes your main ethnic identification?

1. White   2. Black   3. Hispanic   4. Asian   5. Other

_____

A5. Are you currently—married, widowed, divorced, separated, or have you never been married (circle correct response?

1   Married
2   Widowed
3   Divorced
4   Separated
5   Never Married (skip next question)

A6. Have you been married more than once (circle correct response)?   Yes   No

A7. In what year _____ were you first married?

A8. Please list, from oldest to youngest, the sex and age of each of your children (e.g., "male age 18, female age 13," etc.), if any:

1. _____
2. _____
3. _____
4. _____
5. _____
6. _____

A9.   What type of housing do you currently live in? (Circle one number)

Rectory	1
Other Church-supplied housing	2
I/we rent an apartment.	3
I/we own my/our own house.	4

A10.   What is your highest level of education? Start with your highest degree and work backward. (Prompt for Ph.D., D.Min., M.Div., B. Div.. B.A., High School Diploma)

1   Less than high school
2   High school diploma
3   Some college, but no degree
4   College graduate
5   Master's degree(s). In what field(s)?

_____

6   Doctor's degree(s). In what field(s)?

_____

A11.   In the past year, how many weeks did you work for pay, not counting work around the house, including paid vacations and sick leave? (Enter a number from 0 to 52) _____

A12.   (If greater than 0) Was this work full-time or part-time? 1 Full-time 2 Part-time

A13.   (If greater than 0) What was your work title or occupation? _____

A14.   In the past year, about how many hours *in a typical week* did you volunteer or help at the parish (or a ministry related to the parish) your husband serves (if applicable)? _____
If not zero, ask: What did you do?

Religious/Spiritual Journey

We would like to get some background about your religious background and spiritual practice. Please fill in the blanks below.

B1. What is your current religious affiliation? _____

B1a. In what year did you become (religion named in B1)? _____

B2a. What religion were you affiliated with before that? _____

B2b. Starting in what year? _____

If the year is greater than year of birth(A1), ask:

B2c. What religion were you affiliated with before that? _____

B2d. Starting in what year? _____

(Repeat until all lifetime religious affiliations are covered. Use the back of the paper for additional space if needed, and circle the word "OVER" here.)

B3. With what religion were your parents affiliated at the time of your birth?
     Mother _____
     Father _____

B4. When you were around 11 or 12, how often did *you* attend religious services then? (Circle the number of the closest response.)

   1   Never
   2   Less than once a year
   3   About once or twice a
         year
   4   Several times a year
   5   About once a month
   6   2–3 times a month
   7   Nearly every week
   8   Every week
   9   Several times a week

B5, B6. In what year _____ and religious tradition _____ were you baptized?

B7, B8. In what year _____ and religious tradition _____, if any, were you first confirmed?

B9. Would you say you have been "born again" or have had a "born again" experience? _____

     (If yes →) B9a. In what year did this happen? _____

B10. As compared to this time last year, would you say that today you are (circle one number)

Closer to God	1
Farther from God	2
About the same	3
Don't know/Can't say	4

B11. In the past 12 months, how often did you receive the Sacrament of Reconciliation (circle one number)?

Not at all	1
At least once	2
Several times	3
At least once a month	4
Once a week or more often	5

B12. At any time in the past 12 months did you have a spiritual director?
No
Yes

B13. In the past year, how often did you attend religious services (such as Mass) in a typical week? _____

B14. Please describe any devotions or spiritual practices you engage in on a regular or occasional basis (for example, Rosary, systematic Bible reading, Divine Mercy, Morning Offering, daily quiet time)?

Support and Satisfaction

C1. Taking all things together, how would you say things are these days—would you say you're very happy, pretty happy, or not too happy? (Circle one number.)

Very happy	1
Pretty happy	2
Not too happy	3

C2. How well would you say you have been received as a priest's wife by laypersons in the Catholic Church? (Circle one number.)

Very well	1
Moderately well	2
Moderately poorly	3
Very poorly	4

C3. How well would you say you have been received as a priest's wife by other priests? (Circle one number.)

Very well	1
Moderately well	2
Moderately poorly	3
Very poorly	4

C4. How well would you say you have been received as a priest's wife by your bishop and/or diocesan administration? (Circle one number.)

Very well	1
Moderately well	2
Moderately poorly	3
Very poorly	4

C7. If your husband had the opportunity to make the choice over again, would you favor his becoming a Catholic priest? (Circle one number.)

Definitely yes	1
Probably yes	2
Not sure	3
Probably no	4
Definitely no.	5

C8. Has your life as a Catholic priest's wife turned out . . .? (Circle one number.)

Better than you expected	1
Worse than you expected	2
About as you expected	3
Not sure	4

C5. As you reflect on sharing your husband's conversion journey, what were the greatest losses, impediments, or struggles you experienced (if any) as a result of his transition into the Catholic Church and priesthood? Please briefly mention up to five, beginning with the most important.

1. _____
2. _____
3. _____
4. _____
5. _____

C6. As you reflect on sharing your husband's conversion journey, what were the greatest gains, encouragements, or satisfactions you experienced (if any) as a result of his transition into the Catholic Church and priesthood? Please briefly mention up to five, beginning with the most important.

1. _____
2. _____
3. _____
4. _____
5. _____

Moral and Doctrinal Issues

These questions replicate ones which have been asked of national samples of Catholics, and are designed to compare the opinions of pastoral provision priests' wives with those of all US Catholics.

D1. Do you think Roman Catholics must follow all the Church's teachings to be faithful, or do you think they may disagree on some issues and still be considered faithful? (Circle one number.)

Must follow all teachings	1
May disagree and still be faithful	2

D2. Would you describe your own views on most matters having to do with religious beliefs and moral doctrines as. . . .

Very liberal	1
Somewhat liberal	2
Middle of the road	3
Somewhat conservative	4
Very conservative	5

D3. In your opinion, are Pope Benedict's views on moral issues generally . . ..

Too liberal	1
Too conservative	2
About right	3
Not sure	4

D6. How much confidence do you have in the Catholic Church in America today?

A great deal	1
Some	2
Not much	3
None at all	4

D7. Overall, do you approve or disapprove of the way the bishop who presides in your diocese is handling his duties?

Approve strongly	1
Approve somewhat	2
Disapprove somewhat	3
Disapprove strongly	4

D5. Do you think it is always, often, seldom, or never a sin . . ..

	Always	Often	Seldom	Never
1. For unmarried people to have sexual relations?	4	3	2	1
2. For a woman to get an abortion?	4	3	2	1
3. For married couples to use artificial methods of birth control?	4	3	2	1
4. To engage in homosexual behavior?	4	3	2	1
5. To take one's own life if suffering from a debilitating disease?	4	3	2	1
6. To use cloning for medical research?	4	3	2	1
7. To use stem cells of fetuses for medical research?	4	3	2	1
8. To use condoms as a protection against AIDS?	4	3	2	1
9. To masturbate?	4	3	2	1

D9. Would you favor or oppose the direct democratic election of diocesan bishops by the diocesan clergy and laity in the United States?

Favor	1
Oppose	2

D6. Would you favor or oppose the ordination of women as priests?

Favor	1
Oppose	2

D7. Would you favor or oppose the regular ordination of married men as priests in the Latin Rite?

Favor	1
Oppose	2

D4. In your opinion, what are the most important problems facing the Catholic Church in the United States today? Please briefly mention up to five, beginning with the most important.

1. _____
2. _____
3. _____
4. _____
5. _____

Improving the Pastoral Provision Ordination Process

E1. Consider a scale of 1 to 10, where 1 is the absolute worst and 10 is the absolute best.

All things considered, about where on this scale would you candidly rate (write in a number from 1 to 10, or a range of numbers) the support *you personally* received during your family's conversion transition period from.

. . . . the Episcopalian (or other) bishop/diocese/parish you left. _____

. . . . your family. _____

. . . . your friends. _____

. . . . a Catholic parish. _____

. . . . the US Pastoral Provision Administration. _____

. . . . the Catholic diocese in which your husband was eventually ordained.

_____

E2. Here are some suggestions that have been made for improving the effectiveness and support of the Pastoral Provision Administration for priests converting to the Catholic faith. In your opinion, how important is each suggestion? After each, circle the number for the response which best fits your present thinking.

KEY TO RESPONSES

5 = Very important
4 = Somewhat important
3 = Uncertain or neutral
2 = Somewhat unimportant
1 = Not important at all

B. Develop community and contact among Pastoral Provision priests (for example, by sponsoring or organizing dinners or retreats). 5 4 3 2 1

B. Educate Church leaders about, and advocate for, the needs of Pastoral Provision priests. 5 4 3 2 1

C. Maintain more personal contact with applicants during the period of waiting for a rescript. 5 4 3 2 1

D. More sensitivity to the needs of wife and family. 5 4 3 2 1

E. Define the process more clearly, and make   5   4   3   2   1
available clear specific detailed information
about what steps are involved.

F. Other: _____   5   4   3   2   1

E3. Please share any other suggestions or comments you have for improving the effectiveness of the US Pastoral Provision Administration in welcoming or orienting priests' wives and/or families:

E4. Here are some suggestions that have been made for improving the effectiveness and support of Catholic diocesan vocations ministries for priests converting to the Catholic faith. In your opinion, how important is each suggestion? After each, circle the number for the response which best fits your present thinking.

KEY TO RESPONSES

5 = Very important
4 = Somewhat important
3 = Uncertain or neutral
2 = Somewhat unimportant
1 = Not important at all

A. Educate Church leaders about, and advocate   5   4   3   2   1
for, the needs of Pastoral Provision priests.

B. Maintain more personal contact with appli-   5   4   3   2   1
cants during the period of waiting for a
rescript.

C. Better assistance in finding suitable employ-   5   4   3   2   1
ment during the transition period.

D. Other: _____   5   4   3   2   1

E5. Please share any other suggestions or comments you have for improving the effectiveness of diocesan vocations ministries in welcoming or orienting priests' wives and/or families:

Related Issues

F1. If you were not already Catholic, did you convert to the Catholic faith with or alongside your husband? If so, why? If not, why not? Please describe in your own words how your own religious/spiritual journey has interacted with your husband's conversion journey.

F2. Please describe how your husband's conversion journey has affected, if at all, your marriage and personal relationship.

F3. Some have suggested that married convert priests of the Pastoral Provision are a model for the regular ordination of married men in the Latin Rite, or for the readmittance to active priestly function of priests who have renounced orders or been laicized in order to marry. Please briefly share your views, thoughts, or experience on this issue.

F4. Some have suggested that, for practical reasons, married priests are generally less able to be fully devoted to the care of a parish than ones who are unmarried. Please briefly share your views, thoughts, or experience on this issue.

F5. Finally, we want to give you a chance to express opinions in your own words that may not have been addressed elsewhere in the survey. Use the space below to elaborate on any of your answers above or share any other thoughts, experiences, or perspectives you may wish to relate. Attach additional paper if you need more space.

THANK YOU FOR YOUR TIME AND EFFORT IN COMPLETING THIS SURVEY!

Please return to: Dr. Paul Sullins, Life Cycle Institute, Room 215, The Catholic University of America, Washington, D.C. 20064.

SURVEY OF US BISHOPS

A STUDY BY THE CATHOLIC UNIVERSITY OF AMERICA COMMISSIONED BY THE ECCLESIASTICAL DELEGATE FOR THE ANGLICAN PASTORAL PROVISION
DEPT. OF SOCIOLOGY, THE CATHOLIC UNIVERSITY OF AMERICA, WASHINGTON, DC 20064, SPRING 2009

After three decades, the Pontifical Council for the Doctrine of the Faith's Delegate for the Anglican Pastoral Provision is assessing its effectiveness and looking to its future. Would you take 10 minutes to fill in this brief two-page questionnaire and help us make our ministry as fruitful as possible? Thank you and God bless you.

Directions: Indicate the response that comes closest to your own opinion. Return the questionnaire in the envelope provided. If you prefer not to answer any particular question, just skip it. Do not indicate your identity in any way. Return the postcard separately.

1. Please check one: _____ Diocesan _____ Auxiliary
2. In your (arch)diocese how many Pastoral Provision priests . . . serve currently? _____ have ever served? _____
3. How much do you agree or disagree with each of the following statements?

	Strongly Agree	Agree	Neutral	Dis-agree	Strongly Disagree
A. I have a good general understanding of the Pastoral Provision.	5	4	3	2	1
B. I am kept up to date on recent developments regarding the Pastoral Provision.	5	4	3	2	1
C. I personally feel a strong sense of support for the Pastoral Provision.	5	4	3	2	1
D. I generally admire the Pastoral Provision priests I have known.	5	4	3	2	1
E. I have heard few objections to the Pastoral Provision from my priests.	5	4	3	2	1
F. The conditions that led to creating the Pastoral Provision are still valid today.	5	4	3	2	1

	Strongly Agree	Agree	Neutral	Dis-agree	Strongly Disagree
G. In light of the irregularity of such ordinations and the importance of the rule of celibacy, it would be prudent to ordain only a very few married Anglican converts.	5	4	3	2	1
H. In light of the shortage of priests, it would be prudent to ordain as many suitable married Anglican priest converts as possible.	5	4	3	2	1
I. I would welcome the opportunity to ordain a (or an additional) Pastoral Provision priest in my (arch)diocese at this time.	5	4	3	2	1
J. All else equal, I would rather ordain an older man whose children are grown than a younger man with young children.	5	4	3	2	1
K. While awaiting the Holy See's approval for the ordination, a diocese has no responsibility for financial support of the convert priest who has resigned his Anglican ministry.	5	4	3	2	1
L. The success of the Pastoral Provision would not call into question the rule of celibacy for priests in any way.	5	4	3	2	1
M. The Church should expand the Pastoral Provision, e.g., to other countries.	5	4	3	2	1
N. The Church should discontinue the Pastoral Provision.	5	4	3	2	1

Key to responses below: 4 = Very important; 3 = Somewhat important; 2 = Somewhat unimportant; 1 = Very unimportant

4. When considering the possibility of receiving a (or an additional) Pastoral Provision priest in your (arch)diocese, how important in your mind are each of the following practical concerns?

4	3	2	1	B. His reception by the presbyterate	Now please
4	3	2	1	C. His reception by parishioners	**CIRCLE THE**
4	3	2	1	D. The reception and role of his wife in the parish or diocese	**L E T T E R S** correspond-
4	3	2	1	E. The stability of his marriage	ing to your
4	3	2	1	F. Finding proper employment or placement	**two most**
4	3	2	1	G. Financial support for him and his family	**important**
4	3	2	1	H. Other (Specify): _____	concerns.

5. Far fewer priests than anticipated have been ordained under the Pastoral Provision in the past three decades (about 100 altogether). Please share any comments or reflections you may have about this.

6. Men ordained under the Pastoral Provision are restricted from remarriage, undue publicity, and serving as pastors. Please share any comments or reflections you may have about these stipulations.

7. What do you recommend as the best policy or practice regarding the pastoral care and reception of the priest's wife and children?

8. What do you see as the most important strength of the Pastoral Provision?

9. Please describe your most serious concern about the Pastoral Provision.

THANK YOU for your gift of time and care in doing this survey.

Please return in the envelope provided to: The Rev. Dr. Paul Sullins, Dept. of Sociology, Aquinas Hall 116C,
The Catholic University of America, Washington, D.C. 20064.

Notes

1. Max Weber, *The Theory of Social and Economic Organization*, 1st American ed. (New York: Oxford University Press, 1947), 88ff.

1. "Father Tom" is a pseudonym, and, as with all the profiles in this book, selected neutral details in the life history and views presented have been altered or conflated so as to ensure anonymity.

2. On Hoge's 2001 survey the average age at ordination for priests ordained since 1980 was 34, rising from 32 during the 1980s to higher ages in more recent years. Annual surveys of ordination classes from 1999 to 2009 found the average age consistently to be about 36. See United States Conference of Catholic Bishops, "Ordination Class Reports," accessed March 27, 2014, http://www.usccb.org/beliefs-and-teachings/vocations/ordination-class/.

3. For the age at ordination of US Catholic priests, the 1980–1989 and 1990–1999 rows of the table report the weighted average of the ages found on the 1993 and 2001 surveys of Catholic priests. The 2000–2009 row reports the average age from annual ordination surveys during that decade, as reported in Mary Gautier, Mary Bendyna, and Melissa Cidade, *The Class of 2009: Survey of Ordinands to the Priesthood* (Committee for Applied Research in the Apostolate, April 2009), http://www.usccb.org/beliefs-and-teachings/vocations/ordination-class/upload/Ordination-Class-of-2009-Report.pdf.

4. The question was: "Do you agree, or disagree, with this statement? The Catholic Church in the US should continue to welcome Episcopalian priests who want to become active Roman Catholic priests, whether they are married or single." In response, 72 percent of priests agreed strongly or somewhat; 14 percent disagreed strongly or somewhat; and 14 percent were neutral.

5. GianPaolo Salvini, "Priests Who 'Desert,' Priests Who 'Come Back,'" trans. Matthew Sherry, *La Civilta Cattolica* 3, no. 3764 (April 21, 2007): 149.

6. Ibid., 150.

7. William P. Daly, *Early Career Resignations from the Priesthood* (Chicago: National Federation of Priests Councils, 2001). Using data from a random sample of 87 US dioceses, Daley found the five-year resignation rate for diocesan ordinands to be 5.1 percent during 1980–1984, 7.3 percent during 1985–1989, and 9.0 percent during 1990–1994. The simple average of these rates is 7.1 percent. Since there were more ordinands in the later periods, and the proportion of resignations is increasing, this number very probably understates the true resignation rate during the entire period and extending to the present time; by comparison, Andrew Greeley and Richard Schoenherr, *The Catholic Priest in the United States: Sociological Investigations* (Washington, D.C.: Publications Office, United States Catholic Conference, 1972), p. 278, found that 4.6 percent of priests resigned in 1966–1969, with over half of the resignations occurring in the last two years of the period. This trend computes to a five-year resignation rate of 5.5 percent, or an effective five-year rate of 9 percent for 1968–1969.

8. This rough estimate is based on Richard A. Schoenherr and Lawrence A. Young, "Quitting the Clergy: Resignations in the Roman Catholic Priesthood," *Journal for the Scientific Study of Religion* 29, no. 4 (December 1, 1990): 463–481. To ensure a conservative estimate of attrition, I have taken their smallest estimate of attrition and extended it to the entire period.

9. Greeley and Schoenherr, *The Catholic Priest in the United States*, 280.

10. Salvini, "Priests Who 'Desert,' Priests Who 'Come Back,'" 150.

11. Greeley and Schoenherr, *The Catholic Priest in the United States*, 24.

12. This was the most recent data available. In Greeley and Schoenherr's 1970 survey, clergy reported similar hours worked and days off. Forty-five percent of priests at that time reported taking one day off a week; 10 percent took no day off. (These proportions were taken from the raw data tape, not the book.) This suggests that clergy workload and days off have remained fairly stable over the past half-century.

13. Due to the small number of cases, this number (and thus those reported for comparison) is a mean, not a median; the corresponding median is 61.5 hours.

14. The difference in median hours worked is significant at .05 for the comparison of all Pastoral Provision priests with the results of the 1985 priest survey. It does not appear to be significant for the comparison, restricted to married pastors only, with the corresponding reported survey results.

15. We used exploratory factor analysis with maximum variance rotation on the 12 questions about sources of satisfaction asked by Hoge and Wenger's 2001 survey. We included the two top-loading questions on each of the three dimensions, which are the six questions discussed in the text, on the Pastoral Provision priests survey. We also found a fourth dimension, related to pastoral

leadership role satisfaction, which we did not think would be pertinent due to the restrictions on the ministry of the Pastoral Provision priests. We did not anticipate that half of the Pastoral Provision priests would be serving as de facto parish pastors.

16. Cynthia Woolever and Keith Wulff, *U.S. Congregational Life Surveys*, 2001, The Association of Religion Data Archives, www.TheARDA.com. In these surveys of Protestant ministers, of 535 Presbyterian clergy, 75 percent of those married compared to 67 percent of those never married reported that they felt happy all or most of the time. Among 410 Lutheran clergy, the corresponding proportions were 79 percent and 68 percent.

17. Douglas T. Hall and Benjamin Schneider, *Organizational Climates and Careers: The Work Lives of Priests* (New York: Seminar Press, 1973).

18. This comparison is based on diocesan priests only. Due to a coding error regarding the skills variable on the 2002 *LA Times* priest survey data file, the 1993 survey data were used for this analysis.

19. Comparative priest data are derived from Dean R. Hoge, *Experiences of Priests Ordained Five to Nine Years* (Washington, D.C.: National Catholic Educational Association, 2006).

20. Greeley and Schoenherr, *The Catholic Priest in the United States*, 74.

21. These figures are also for diocesan priests only; religious priests have somewhat higher and less variable breviary practice. A 1990 survey of religious priests, by the National Survey of the Religious Life Futures Project (archived at www.theARDA.com), found that 62 percent reported praying the liturgy of the hours every day. This proportion is almost identical to that found by Greeley and Schoenherr—61 percent—among religious priests in 1970.

22. On issues where opinions among Catholics differ significantly by sex, I have compared the US priests and Pastoral Provision priests, who are all males, to lay Catholic males.

23. "Gallup Beliefs and Values Polls 2006–2008," accessed March 30, 2009, www.gallup.com. Respondents were asked of abortion: Regardless of whether or not you think it should be legal, please tell me whether you personally believe that in general it is morally acceptable or morally wrong. Opposition to abortion is much lower on questions about whether it should be legal and/or under what circumstances it should be permitted.

24. The latter question is more restrictive, indicating that, although the proportions reported in the chart are similar, opposition to abortion by regular priests is much stronger than among active Catholics.

25. "Gallup Polls May 6–9, 2002," May 16, 2002, www.gallup.com.

26. This undoubtedly understates the actual opposition to human cloning among regular US priests due to poor and highly misleading question wording. In summary reports, the *Los Angeles Times* published the question as asking whether it was acceptable "to use human cloning for medical research," but

what was actually asked in their survey instrument was whether it was acceptable "to use cloning—that is, copying DNA cells—in medical research that
could result in a cure for diseases such as Alzheimer's, Parkinson's or cancer?"
Note that, although the issue involved is human cloning (there is no moral
controversy over animal cloning for medical purposes), the item wording does
not specify "human." Further, the language of the question is biased toward a
supportive response: It speaks of the possible benefits of human cloning, but
does not mention that the practice destroys fetuses; and it restates "cloning" in
innocuous language ("copying DNA cells") that minimizes the complex biological procedures involved.

27. Frank Newport, "Catholics Similar to Mainstream on Abortion, Stem Cells"
(Gallup Research Reports, March 30, 2009), www.gallup.com. In 3,022 aggre-
gated phone interviews from 2006–2008, 53 percent of Catholics reporting they
were regular worshippers responded that "medical research from stem cells
obtained from human embryos" was "morally acceptable."

28. In annual Gallup polls in 2003–2009, the percentage of Americans responding that human cloning is "morally acceptable" has been consistent, at only
8–11 percent. When used without further qualification, "human cloning" is
understood by most respondents to refer to the production or birth of a complete human being by cloning.

29. The General Social Survey asks a question that is very similar to the one used
in the surveys being compared in this analysis: "What about sexual relations
between two adults of the same sex. Are these always wrong, almost always
wrong, wrong only sometimes, or not wrong at all?" In aggregate data from
2004–2008, 71.0 percent of Catholic males who attended Mass every week
or more often responded that homosexual relations are "always wrong." The
identical proportion was also found in a similarly worded question on Baylor
Institute for Studies of Religion, *The Baylor Religion Survey [machine-readable
data file]*, 2005, Association of Religion Data Archives, www.thearda.com.
Original analysis by the author.

30. This number reports on combined General Social Survey data from 2000–2008.

31. Edward O. Laumann, ed., *The Social Organization of Sexuality: Sexual Practices
in the United States* (Chicago: University of Chicago Press, 1994), 299. Only
2.4 percent of males reported currently identifiying as homosexual and actually having sex with other men. Among males age 35 and over (the age bracket
of 95 percent of Catholic priests) only 0.6 percent (six-tenths of one percent)
reported a persisting homosexual identity. The corresponding proportion on
the 2008 General Social Survey was 0.7 percent (seven-tenths of one percent).

32. The proportion of married men reporting a homosexual orientation on most
surveys that ask this question is well under one percent. On the most recent
such survey (to my knowledge), a panel of the 2008 General Social Survey
($n = 1,713$), none of the married male respondents reported having a homosexual

orientation. The fact that virtually none of the Pastoral Provision priests are homosexual may be one of the unacknowledged advantages, from the standpoint of Catholic Church leaders, of this class of clergy applicants.

33. Newport, "Catholics Similar to Mainstream on Abortion, Stem Cells."

34. Ibid.

35. General Social Survey, 2000–2008 aggregate data. The item asked, "Do you think a person has the right to end his or her own life if this person has an incurable disease?" Among persons who attend church every week or more often, 49.2 percent of Catholic males, 57.9 percent of Catholic females, and 64.8 percent of non-Catholic males responded "No."

36. David Moore, "American Catholics Revere Pope, Disagree with Some Major Teachings" (Gallup Research Reports, April 1, 2005), www.gallup.com. On this survey, 29 percent of Catholics who reported that they attended church weekly, when asked whether the next pope should or should not allow Catholics to use birth control, responded "should not."

37. Langer, Gary (Principal Investigator), *ABC News/Washington Post Poll*, October 9, 2003, American Religious Data Archive, www.thearda.com. Original analysis by the author.

38. Based on the 2000–2008 combined General Social Surveys. Question wording differs slightly.

39. D. Paul Sullins, "Institutional Selection for Conformity: The Case of U.S. Catholic Priests," *Sociology of Religion* 74, no. 1 (March 1, 2013): 56–81; Dean R. Hoge and Jacqueline E. Wenger, *Evolving Visions of the Priesthood: Changes from Vatican II to the Turn of the New Century* (Collegeville, MN: Liturgical Press, 2003); Andrew M. Greeley, *Priests: A Calling in Crisis* (Chicago: University of Chicago Press, 2004). Greeley, using the same data for all priests as the present study, presents an excellent, similar analysis of age differences, though it is confined to only three items and is pejorative of younger more conservative priests.

40. As determined by the chi-square test, at .05 significance level.

41. Although an adequate discussion of this point lies beyond the scope of the present study, priests ordained prior to the 1960s are retrocessively more conservative on the moral issues examined here, with the result that the longest-ordained priests, ordained in the 1940s and 1930s, are very similar in their views to the priests most recently ordained.

42. Sullins, "Institutional Selection for Conformity: The Case of U.S. Catholic Priests."

43. Anita Creamer, "Former Lutheran to Be Sacramento Diocese's First Married Catholic Priest," *McClatchy—Tribune Business News*, December 12, 2010, 817202798, ABI/INFORM Complete.

44. For a more complete discussion of this distinction, see Chapter 7.

45. Creamer, "Former Lutheran to Be Sacramento Diocese's First Married Catholic Priest."

46. Actually, by ordination cohort, for which age is a good proxy. See Sullins, "Institutional Selection for Conformity: The Case of U.S. Catholic Priests."

CHAPTER 2

1. Leo XIII (Pope), *Apostolicae Curae* [Encyclical Letter on the Invalidity of Anglican Orders], 1896.

2. Paul VI (Pope), *Gaudium et Spes* [Pastoral Constitution of the Second Vatican Council on the Church in the Modern World] (Vatican City, 1965).

3. Ibid., sec. 4.

4. Ibid., sec. 13.

5. Paul VI (Pope), *Lumen Gentium* [Dogmatic Constitution of the Second Vatican Council on the Church] (Vatican City, 1964), sec. 29.

6. Paul VI (Pope), *Sacerdotalis Caelibatus* [Encyclical Letter on the Celibacy of the Priest] (Vatican City, 1967), sec. 42.

7. Quoted in Anglican–Roman Catholic Joint Preparatory Commission, *The Malta Report*, 1968, sec. 2, http://www.vatican.va/roman_curia/pontifical_councils/chrstuni/angl-comm-docs/rc_pc_chrstuni_doc_19680102_malta-report_en.html.

8. Sacred Congregation for the Doctrine of the Faith, *The Ordination of Women: Official Commentary from the Sacred Congregation for the Doctrine of the Faith on Its Declaration Inter Insigniores ('Women and the Priesthood') of 15th October 1976 Together with the Exchange of Correspondence in 1975 and 1976 Between His Grace the Most Reverend Dr. Frederick Donald Coggan, Archbishop of Canterbury and His Holiness Pope Paul VI* (London: Catholic Truth Society, 1977), 27–28.

9. Congregation for the Doctrine of the Faith, *Observations on the Final Report of ARCIC—ANIMADVERSIONES*, 1982, sec. B.2.3, http://www.vatican.va/roman_curia/congregations/cfaith/documents/rc_con_cfaith_doc_19820327_animadversiones_en.html.

10. Sacred Congregation for the Doctrine of the Faith, *The Ordination of Women*, 26.

11. Peter Stanford, *Cardinal Hume and the Changing Face of English Catholicism* (New York: Continuum, 1999), 92.

12. Mary Tanner and Andrew Faley, "Anglican-Roman Catholic Relations: A Kick Start?" (Society for Ecumenical Studies, May 30, 2007), 2, sfes.faithweb.com/0705sfesagmanglicancatholic.pdff.

13. Ibid., 3.

14. Society of the Holy Cross, "Rule of Life," n.d., sec. 7.ii, http://www.sscamericas.org/resources/rule.html.

15. For a more detailed account of these developments, see D. Paul Sullins, "The History and Development of the Anglican Pastoral Provision," *The Catholic Historical Review* (forthcoming), 103 (2017).

16. Franjo Seper (Archbishop), Prefect of the Sacred Congregation for the Doctrine of the Faith, "Letter to Archbishop Quinn Outlining the Pastoral Provision, July 22, 1980," in *Into Full Communion: Pastoral Provision for Former Clergy of the Episcopal Church* (Office of the US Ecclesiastical Delegate for the Pastoral Provision, 2009), 11–13, http://www.pastoralprovision.org/.

17. Ibid., 11.

18. Ibid., 13.

19. Ibid., 11.

20. Kenneth Woodward, "The First Married Priests," *Newsweek*, September 1, 1980, 67.

21. "Washington Dateline-PM Cycle," *Associated Press*, August 20, 1980.

22. Ibid.

23. "Vatican to Allow Ordination of Dissident Episcopal Priests," *Washington Post*, August 21, 1980.

24. "Vatican to Allow Ordination of Dissident Episcopal Priests."

25. Woodward, "The First Married Priests."

26. "Anglicans Admitted into Catholic Church on 'Common Identity,'" *Religion News Service*, August 20, 1980.

27. "Vatican to Allow Ordination of Dissident Episcopal Priests."

28. "Episcopal Bishop Criticizes Action by Roman Catholics on Dissidents," *New York Times*, September 29, 1980.

29. Ad Hoc Committee for Convert Married Ministers, "Report in Response to Bishop Marshall's Memo and Outline," Unpublished manuscript (September 16, 1977), 1, Archived at the American Catholic History Research Center, The Catholic University of America.

30. Bernard Law (Bishop), "A Progress Report to the Sacred Congregation for the Faith from Its Ecclesiastical Delegate for the Pastoral Provision," December 1982, 3, Archived at the American Catholic History Research Center, The Catholic University of America.

31. Franjo Seper (Archbishop), Prefect of the Sacred Congregation for the Doctrine of the Faith, "Letter Outlining the Pastoral Provision."

32. Ibid., 15.

33. Ibid., 17.

34. John Paul II (Pope), *Ad Tuendam Fidem* [Apostolic Letter Motu Proprio to Protect the Faith], 1998.

35. John Paul II (Pope), *Pastores Dabo Vobis* [Post-Synodal Apostolic Exhortation on the Formation of Priests in the Circumstances of the Present Day], 1992.

36. Franjo Seper (Archbishop), Prefect of the Sacred Congregation for the Doctrine of the Faith, "Letter Outlining the Pastoral Provision," 21.

37. Committee on Priestly Life and Formation, *Program of Priestly Formation* (US Conference of Catholic Bishops, 2006). *Into Full Communion* contains a detailed description, outline of studies, and recommended readings for each of the eight areas.

38. These are rough estimates, based on a combination of self-reports, correspondence, and file records maintained by the ED.

39. There is no reliable information on the incidence of such screening, which is by its nature highly confidential; however, such decisions appear to be very rare.

40. Franjo Seper (Archbishop), Prefect of the Sacred Congregation for the Doctrine of the Faith, "Letter Outlining the Pastoral Provision," 25.

41. Ibid. An earlier section of the manual (p. 21) states, confusingly, that criminal background checks of the candidate priest and his wife are required.

42. Ibid., 20.

CHAPTER 3

1. As with all the profiles in this book, Father James is a pseudonym, and some background details and material in the life history and views presented have been altered or conflated so as to ensure anonymity in this small population. The name "Father James" was chosen as an homage to Father James Parker, who was involved in founding and administering the Pastoral Provision and was the first married priest ordained under the program. None of the material presented has any connection to Father Parker, whose own life history and conversion story is recounted in James Parker, "The Reverend James Parker: A Married Catholic Priest?" in *The New Catholics: Contemporary Converts Tell Their Stories*, ed. Dan O'Neill (New York: Crossroad, 1987), ch. 16.

2. Peter Marsden Smith, Michael Hout, and Jibum Kim, *General Social Surveys 1972–2010 [machine-readable data file]* (Chicago: National Opinion Research Center, 2010), Thirty-three percent of all respondents in these data since 1972 have reported changing religious affiliation. In addition, 44 percent of Americans surveyed in 2009 by the Pew Forum on Religion and Public Life reported switching affiliations.

3. Reginald W. Bibby and Merlin B. Brinkerhoff, "The Circulation of the Saints: A Study of People Who Join Conservative Churches," *Journal for the Scientific Study of Religion* 12, no. 3 (September 1, 1973): 273–283, doi: 10.2307/1384428; D. Paul Sullins, "Switching Close to Home: Volatility or Coherence in Protestant Affiliation Patterns?" *Social Forces* 72, no. 2 (December 1, 1993): 399–419, doi: 10.1093/sf/72.2.399.

4. Smith et al., *General Social Surveys 1972–2010 [machine-readable data file]*, combined data 1972–2008.

5. Ibid., combined data 1972–2008. The 2008 Pew Religious Landscape Survey, a large-sample (n = 35,505) survey designed to measure religious affiliation precisely, reveals, in similar numbers, that 5.5 percent of those raised Episcopalian are now Catholic, and 0.64 percent of those raised Catholic are now Episcopalian.

6. Stephen Joseph Fichter, "Shepherding in Greener Pastures: Causes and Consequences of the Dual Transition of Celibate Catholic Priests into Married Protestant Ministry" (Ph.D. Dissertation, Rutgers University, New Brunswick, NJ, 2009), 94, Table 6.

7. As of January 1, 2008, the reference date for data collection in this study. See Appendix, Part V for details. Total clergy amounts are from the *Yearbook of American and Canadian Churches* (New York: National Council of Churches USA, 2006).

8. These crude numbers lack important qualifications that would be necessary to produce an acceptably precise measure of the proportion of clergy switchers in each denomination. For example, the denominators of the rates (total clergy in each group) should be adjusted for age and retirement; Episcopal priests retire, on average, much younger than do Catholic priests. If the Catholic priest defections are in line with national trends, the large bulk of these switches occurred in the 1970s, with the effect that the actual current defection rate would be much lower than reported here.

9. According to Kenedy and Sons, ed., *The Official Catholic Directory* (New Providence, NJ: P. J. Kenedy & Sons, Publishers, Annual), for the years 2007–2011, the average annual number of adults baptized is 48,023 and adults received into full communion (converts whose previous baptism in another church is recognized by the Catholic Church) is 82,139, a total of 130,162 converts annually.

10. This designation is by Albert J. Menendez, *The Road to Rome: An Annotated Bibliography* (New York: Garland, 1986), xi.

11. Findings reported are from James D. Davidson (Principal Investigator), *Catholic Pluralism Project Survey [machine-readable data file]*, 1995, Association of Religion Data Archives, www.thearda.com; results from this survey are reported in James D. Davidson, *The Search for Common Ground: What Unites and Divides Catholic Americans* (Huntington, IN: Our Sunday Visitor, 1997).

12. For example, the massive 2007 American Religious Landscape Survey (n = 88,292) administered by the PEW Research Center found that Catholic converts were significantly more likely than cradle Catholics to send their child to a religious education program (60 percent vs. 50 percent); to pray "several times a day" (37 percent vs. 31 percent); to be an "official member" of the church (71 percent vs. 67 percent); to participate at least monthly in church-related community volunteer (22 percent vs. 19 percent) or social (30 percent vs. 24 percent) activities; to attend church weekly or more often (43 percent vs. 41 percent); and to report that religion was "very important" to them (59 percent vs. 55 percent). Like most surveys of religious adherents, on this one "converts" are only a secondary analytical category, identified post hoc by comparing respondents'

reported religious affiliation as a child with their current religious affiliation. By contrast, the Catholic Pluralism Project survey, which is the basis for the findings reported in the text (see note 11), included an explicit question asking respondents to identify as a convert. This feature makes it particularly useful for our purposes in this study, and may also account in part for the larger and more extensive effects reported.

13. Colleen Carroll, *The New Faithful: Why Young Adults Are Embracing Christian Orthodoxy* (Chicago: Loyola Press, 2002), 4.

14. Ibid., 168. Here Carroll is citing, evidently with agreement, Paul Griffiths, a Catholic convert academic.

15. Menendez, *The Road to Rome*, ix.

16. Patrick Allitt, *Catholic Converts: British and American Intellectuals Turn to Rome* (Ithaca, NY: Cornell University Press, 1997); excellent summary accounts of Catholic intellectual converts in the past centruy and a half are also provided by Joseph Pearce, *Literary Converts: Spiritual Inspiration in an Age of Unbelief* (San Francisco: Ignatius Press, 2000); and Charles P. Connor, *Classic Catholic Converts* (San Francisco: Ignatius Press, 2001).

17. Allitt, *Catholic Converts*, 5.

18. Menendez, *The Road to Rome*, xiii.

19. John Tracy Ellis, *American Catholics and the Intellectual Life*, 1st ed. (Chicago: Heritage Foundation, 1956), 51–52.

20. Catholic Church in England and Wales, "Liturgical Calendar | National Calendar for England II," accessed August 15, 2013, http://www.liturgyoffice. org.uk/Calendar/National/England2.shtml#May4.

21. William J. Gordon-Gorman, *Converts to Rome* (London: Sands, 1910). Gorman enumerates 4,896 converts by elite status, position, or profession prior to conversion, and 1,388 converts who have entered the Catholic priesthood or religious life, without reporting the amount of overlap between the two lists. The number 5,000 estimates an almost complete overlap, thus almost certainly understating, conservatively, the total number of converts.

22. Ibid., 2.

23. Allitt, *Catholic Converts*, 5.

24. David Newsome, *The Parting of Friends: The Wilberforces and Henry Manning* (Grand Rapids, MI: Leominster, UK: Eerdmans; Gracewing, 1993), ix.

25. Best-selling books in this genre are Mark P. Shea, *By What Authority? An Evangelical Discovers Catholic Tradition* (Huntington, IN: Our Sunday Visitor, 1996); Stephen K. Ray, *Crossing the Tiber: Evangelical Protestants Discover the Historical Church* (San Francisco: Ignatius Press, 1997); and David B. Currie, *Born Fundamentalist, Born Again Catholic* (San Francisco: Ignatius Press, 1996); collections of such conversion accounts are presented in *Surprised by Truth: Eleven Converts Give the Biblical and Historical Reasons for Becoming Catholic* (San Diego: Basilica Press, 1994), which has sold over 300,000 copies.

26. As quoted by W. Bradford Wilcox, "A River Runs to It: A New Exodus of Protestants Streams to Rome," *Crisis Magazine*, May 1999.

27. Scot McKnight, "From Wheaton to Rome: Why Evangelicals Become Roman Catholic," *Journal of the Evangelical Theological Society* 45, no. 3 (2002): 451–452.

28. Ibid., 470.

29. John Henry Newman, *Certain Difficulties Felt by Anglicans in Catholic Teaching: In Twelve Lectures Addressed in 1850 to the Party of the Religious Movement of 1833*, vol. 1 (Longmans, Green, 1901), 383, http://www.newman-reader.org/works/anglicans/volume1/index.html.

CHAPTER 4

1. Richard Travisano, "Alternation and Conversion as Qualitatively Different Transformations.," in *Social Psychology Through Symbolic Interaction*, ed. G. P. Stone and H. A. Farberman (Waltham, MA: Ginn-Blaisdel, 1970), 594–606.

2. D. A. Snow and R. Machalek, "The Sociology of Conversion," *Annual Review of Sociology* 10, no. 1 (1984): 167–190.

3. John Lofland and Norman Skonovd, "Conversion Motifs," *Journal for the Scientific Study of Religion* 20, no. 4 (1981): 373–385.

4. Henri Gooren, "Reassessing Conventional Approaches to Conversion: Toward a New Synthesis," *Journal for the Scientific Study of Religion* 46, no. 3 (September 2007): 337–353.

5. David K. O'Rourke, *A Process Called Conversion* (Garden City, NY: Knopf Doubleday Publishing Group, 1985), 12, 34.

6. Ibid., 37.

7. Some social science positions, for example psychological behaviorism, would deny the importance or even existence of internal ideas or beliefs in affecting human behavior. Without getting distracted by a refutation of this view, which I hold to be reductionistic, I would point out that my analysis here, with respect to such concerns, is positivistic. The participants we interviewed clearly understood their own behavior, in part, in terms of internal forces of belief and commitment. The suspicion that the interior agency they (and I) perceive operating in their choices could be explained in other philosophical terms makes little or no difference to the classification and analysis of it presented here.

8. Max Weber, "'Objectivity' in Social Science and Social Policy," in *The Methodology of the Social Sciences*, ed. Edward Shils and Henry Finch (New York: Free Press, 1949), 90.

9. Scot McKnight, "From Wheaton to Rome: Why Evangelicals Become Roman Catholic," *Journal of the Evangelical Theological Society* 45, no. 3 (2002): 459.

10. Sheldon Vanauken, "The English Channel: Between Canterbury and Rome," in *The New Catholics: Contemporary Converts Tell Their Stories*, ed. Dan O'Neill (New York: Crossroad, 1987), 125.

11. Specifically, 80 percent of the respondents who mentioned women's ordination, and all of the respondents mentioning any other issue.

12. Walker Percy, "Foreword," in *The New Catholics: Contemporary Converts Tell Their Stories*, by Dan O'Neill (New York: Crossroad, 1987), xv.

13. Lofland and Skonovd, "Conversion Motifs," 376.

14. Ibid., 380.

15. Stephen Joseph Fichter, "Shepherding in Greener Pastures: Causes and Consequences of the Dual Transition of Celibate Catholic Priests into Married Protestant Ministry" (Ph.D. Dissertation, Rutgers University, New Brunswick, NJ, 2009).

16. Ibid., 139.

17. Fichter's sample also included priests who had become ministers in Methodist, Lutheran, and Congregationalist churches, although 87 percent of those he studied were Episcopal priests. Thirty-four percent of all priests in his study gave "reasons of the head"; the proportion of Episcopal priests doing so is not reported, but must be close to this number. It should be noted, however, that on other measures the Episcopal priests were somewhat less affectional, or more intellectual, than former Catholic priests ministering in the other three denominations.

18. Norman W. H. Blaikie, *The Plight of the Australian Clergy: To Convert, Care or Challenge?* (St. Lucia: University of Queensland Press, 1979).

19. Matthew 13:45–46, KJV.

20. From here forward, "double converts" includes all priests with two or more conversions.

21. These differences are not related to formation in an Episcopalian seminary, since about the same proportion (66–70 percent) of all three groups (single, double, and serial converts) graduated from an Episcopal seminary.

22. The material in this and the preceding paragraph reflects the results of exploratory factor analysis on the conversion themes. The analysis extracted three factors for each group by means of a principal components analysis, using the standard Kaiser criterion and rotation for maximum separate variance. For the Episcopalian converts, the ordination of women loaded on a single latent factor with abortion, homosexuality, and the issue of authority. Authority also loaded highly with the issue of truth on a separate factor. For the cradle Episcopalians, the issue of truth loaded with concerns for the unity or universality and legitimacy of Anglicanism. While the issues of homosexuality and abortion loaded with the issue of authority, the ordination of women loaded with the view that the Episcopal Church had moved away from a former position as a Catholic (or more Catholic) church.

23. Denominations are classified according to the scheme found in Wade Clark Roof, *American Mainline Religion: Its Changing Shape and Future* (New Brunswick, NJ: Rutgers University Press, 1987).

CHAPTER 5

1. Wallace Denton, *The Role of the Minister's Wife* (Philadelphia: Westminster Press, 1962), 43.
2. Quoted in Mace David and Vera Mace, *What's Happening to Clergy Marriages?* (Nashville, TN: Abingdon, 1980), 127–128.
3. Ashley Brooks, "An Examination of the Role Satisfaction of the Pastor's Wife in the Southern Baptist Convention" (Ph.D. Dissertation, New Orleans Baptist Theological Seminary, 2008).
4. Denton, *The Role of the Minister's Wife*, 30–32.
5. Cleland Boyd McAfee, *Ministerial Practices, Some Fraternal Suggestions* (New York; London: Harper & Brothers, 1928), 168, 173.
6. Denton, *The Role of the Minister's Wife*, 30.
7. Barbara Brown Zikmund, Adair T. Lummis, and Patricia M. Y. Chang, *Clergy Women: An Uphill Calling*, 1st ed. (Louisville, KY: Westminster John Knox Press, 1998), 43.
8. Erik Eckholm, "Single and Evangelical? Good Luck Finding Work as a Pastor," *New York Times*, March 22, 2011, sec. U.S., http://www.nytimes.com/2011/03/22/us/22pastor.html.
9. Mark R. McMinn et al., "Positive Coping among Wives of Male Christian Clergy," *Pastoral Psychology* 56, no. 4 (February 2008): 445–457.
10. Sandi Brunette-Hill, "A Life of Her Own: Role Change among Clergy Wives," *Research in the Social Scientific Study of Religion* 10 (1999): 97.
11. Lorna Dobson, *I'm More Than the Pastor's Wife* (Grand Rapids, MI: Zondervan, 2003); Harley D. Hunt, *The Stained Glass Fishbowl* (Valley Forge, PA: Ministers Council, 1990).
12. McMinn et al., "Positive Coping among Wives of Male Christian Clergy," 445–447.
13. Ashley Brooks, "An Examination of the Role Satisfaction of the Pastor's Wife in the Southern Baptist Convention," 15. See also Lena Anne Brackin, "Loneliness, Depression, Social Support, Marital Satisfaction and Spirituality as Experienced by the Southern Baptist Clergy Wife" (Ph.D. Dissertation, University of Arizona, 2001).
14. William Hollingsworth Whyte, *The Organization Man* (Philadelphia: University of Pennsylvania Press, 2002).
15. Rosabeth Kanter, *Men and Women of the Corporation* (New York: Basic Books, 1993).
16. Ibid., 16, emphasis Kanter's.
17. Ibid., 112.
18. Ibid., 119.
19. Ibid., 113, 119.
20. Ibid., 120–122.
21. Ibid., 125.

22. Denton, *The Role of the Minister's Wife*, 43.

23. Andrew M Greeley, *Priests in the United States; Reflections on a Survey*, 1st ed. (Garden City, NY: Doubleday, 1972), 84.

24. John Henry Morgan and Linda B. Morgan, *Wives of Priests: A Study of Clergy Wives in the Episcopal Church* (Bristol, IN: St. John of the Cross Parish Church Library for the Notre Dame University Parish Life Institute, 1980), 51.

25. William G. T. Douglas, *Ministers' Wives* (New York: Harper & Row, 1965). Douglas divided the latter two types based on motivations, producing five categories overall.

26. Kanter, *Men and Women of the Corporation*, 107.

27. Morgan and Morgan, *Wives of Priests*, 160.

28. The statistic here is Spearman's rho, since happiness and reception are ordinal measures. The corresponding Pearson correlation coefficients are .51 and .42, respectively. All associations are significant at .05.

29. Ten percent is the approximate rate of natural biological infertility, and does not take into account either medical interventions to improve chances of pregnancy or couples who are childless by choice.

30. Douglas, *Ministers' Wives*, 85.

31. Ibid., 86.

32. Morgan and Morgan, *Wives of Priests*, 172–173.

33. Zikmund, Lummis, and Chang, *Clergy Women*, 43.

34. Ibid., see chart p. 143. The 1996 Presbyterian Panel Survey also reports a divorce rate of 20 percent for pastors.

35. See, e.g., David L. Smith, "Some Thoughts on the Preserving of Clergy Marriages," *Didaskalia* 7, no. 1 (September 1, 1995): 61–65, which begins: "Marriage breakdown among the clergy is rising at a terrifying rate."; Cameron Lee, "Patterns of Stress and Support among Adventist Clergy: Do Pastors and Their Spouses Differ?" *Pastoral Psychology* 55 (2007): 761–771, notes, "Non-empirical works offer numerous case examples of troubled clergy marriages as well as insiders' advice to couples on facing unrealistic expectations and ministry myths"; for an example, see Dean Merrill, *Clergy Couples in Crisis: The Impact of Stress on Pastoral Marriages* (Carol Stream, IL: CTI Publications, 1985).

36. McMinn et al., "Positive Coping among Wives of Male Christian Clergy."

37. Andrew J. Cherlin, *The Marriage-Go-Round: The State of Marriage and the Family in America Today*, 1st Vintage Books ed. (New York: Vintage Books, 2010), 90.

CHAPTER 6

1. The number of Pastoral Provision priests since 2008 has remained about the same, as new ordinations have been more or less balanced by attrition due to death or defection. By the end of 2012, the newly established Ordinariate of the Chair of St. Peter had received 28 new Anglican convert priests, most of them married, putting the estimated number of married priests in the American Catholic Church at the beginning of 2013 at about 100.

2. These men converted from the Antiochian Orthodox Church; Charismatic Episcopal Church; Lutheran Church of America; Lutheran Church, Augustana Synod; and the United Methodist Church. No central records are kept of such exceptional ordinations in the United States, and, while we have searched thoroughly to identify married priests outside the Pastoral Provision, it is quite possible that there are others we did not find.

3. Franjo Seper (Archbishop), Prefect of the Sacred Congregation for the Doctrine of the Faith, "Letter to Archbishop Quinn Outlining the Pastoral Provision, July 22, 1980," in *Into Full Communion: Pastoral Provision for Former Clergy of the Episcopal Church* (Office of the U.S. Ecclesiastical Delegate for the Pastoral Provision, 2009), 13, http://www.pastoralprovision.org/.

4. Ibid., 14.

5. The correlation (Gamma) is negative .72.

6. Dean R. Hoge and Jacqueline Wenger, *Survey of American Catholic Priests [machine-readable data file]*, 2001, Association of Religion Data Archives, www.thearda.com.

7. G. Johnston, "The Case for Priestly Celibacy," *Crisis Magazine*, January 1, 2006, http://www.crisismagazine.com/2006/why-not-married-priests-the-case-for-clerical-celibacy.

8. Compensation and benefits data for celibate priests are based on data from the National Federation of Priests Councils and the National Association of Church Personnel Administrators. Technical details of the compensation factors and estimates involved are presented in the Appendix, Part V.

9. Mary Gautier, "Recession's Impact on Catholic Parish Life," *CARA Report*, Spring 2011, 1, reports the average 2011 parish budget, after contraction due to the recession, to be $350,000.

10. "Into Full Communion: Pastoral Provision for Former Clergy of the Episcopal Church" (Office of the US Ecclesiastical Delegate for the Pastoral Provision, 2009), 21, http://www.pastoralprovision.org/.

11. Seper (Archbishop), Prefect of the Sacred Congregation for the Doctrine of the Faith, "Letter Outlining the Pastoral Provision," 20.

12. Douglas T. Hall and Benjamin Schneider, *Organizational Climates and Careers: The Work Lives of Priests* (New York: Seminar Press, 1973), 30.

13. The statistical model discussed was a linear regression analysis predicting a bishop's agreement with the statement "I would welcome the opportunity to ordain a Pastoral Provision priest" from three variables, reported here followed by the corresponding model standardized coefficient: I personally feel a strong sense of support for the Pastoral Provision (.32); the Church should expand the Pastoral Provision, e.g., to other countries (.31); and in light of the irregularity of such ordinations and the importance of the rule of celibacy, it would be prudent to ordain only a very few married Anglican converts (−.33). The predictor variables were selected from all 13 opinion statements shown in Table 6.1 by means of a forward stepwise elimination process. This was a robust model with strong

coefficients and explanatory range. All three coefficients were statistically significant at .001, and model R-square was .53.

14. This paragraph reports the results of a logistic regression model predicting the presence or absence of a Pastoral Provision priest in the diocese. Only diocesan bishops are included. As an indicator of ordinations, this dependent variable obviously includes some noise, since a bishop may have transferred into a diocese with preexisting married priests; such transfers, however, are in the minority and are probably random with respect to married priests. Starting with the fourteen variables shown in Table 6.1, after backward elimination based on conditional significance, only three independent variables remained mutually significant. With the corresponding coefficient, expressed as its exponent, and significant, these were: I have a good general understanding of the Pastoral Provision (1.69, .013); I personally feel a strong sense of support for the Pastoral Provision (0.59, .081); and I generally admire the Pastoral Provision priests I have known (3.26, .001). The elimination criterion was inclusively set at .10. The Hosmer-Lemeshow test had a significance of .50, indicating a good model fit; model R-square was .21 (Nagelkerke).

CHAPTER 7

1. Two examples of such multiple-issue critiques from Catholic sources are David Gibson, *The Coming Catholic Church: How the Faithful Are Shaping a New American Catholicism*, 1st ed. (San Francisco: HarperSanFrancisco, 2003); and Richard A. Schoenherr, *Goodbye Father: The Celibate Male Priesthood and the Future of the Catholic Church* (Oxford; New York: Oxford University Press, 2002). Gibson links an end to required clergy celibacy with a move to more democratic governance in Church; Schoenherr links it with the ordination of women as priests. There are, of course, many general critiques of Catholic doctrines and practices, including clergy celibacy, written by non-Catholic apologists.

2. Mark 1:30 refers to Peter's mother-in-law, whom Jesus healed. In Matthew 19:12, Jesus commends men "who have made themselves eunuchs for the sake of the kingdom of heaven. Let anyone accept this who can." In I Corinthians 9:5, St. Paul asks: "Do we not have the right to be accompanied by a believing wife, as do the other apostles and the brothers of the Lord and Cephas (Peter)?"

3. I Corinthians 7:1–7; I Timothy 3:2–4. The phrase "husband of one wife" may not imply that the bishop need be married, but only that he must not be in a second or subsequent marriage. The NRSV translates the phrase as "married only once."

4. Technically, the restriction on marriage occurred when a man entered into minor orders, as exorcist or sub-deacon, which are preliminary steps to the priesthood.

5. As with many contested issues, historical accounts of clergy celibacy vary greatly, more or less reflecting the present convictions of the historian, particularly with regard to the early centuries of the Church. Advocates of the Protestant or Eastern Catholic practice generally argue that clergy marriage was more widespread and supporters of the Catholic practice arguing that celibacy was more widespread. See William E. Phipps, *Clerical Celibacy: The Heritage* (New York: Continuum, 2004); and André-Marie Charue, *Priesthood and Celibacy* (Milano-Roma: Àncora, 1972), for good recent examples of such dueling histories. Some recent Catholic apologists for celibacy also maintain that married men were required to abstain from sexual relations with their wives after ordination, as in Alphonso M. Stickler, *The Case for Clerical Celibacy: Its Historical Development and Theological Foundations* (San Francisco: Ignatius Press, 1995). The classic and still most extensive history from a Protestant perspective, which uniformly links celibacy with clerical immorality, is Philip Schaff and David Schley Schaff, *History of the Christian Church*, 8 vols. (New York: C. Scribner's Sons, 1907). All such attempts to impose a uniform practice on the history of this era confront the problem of having to explain away the abundant evidence of practices contradictory to their thesis.

6. Luther was particularly explicit on this point; the only alternatives for men were marriage or masturbation. Gerald Strauss, *Luther's House of Learning: Indoctrination of the Young in the German Reformation* (Baltimore, MD: Johns Hopkins University Press, 1978), 103. See also Martin Luther, *The Table Talk or Familiar Discourse of Martin Luther* (London: D. Bogue, 1848), 300. For a discussion of the Reformation polemics on celibacy and marriage, see Joel Francis Harrington, *Reordering Marriage and Society in Reformation Germany* (Cambridge: Cambridge University Press, 1995), chap. 2.

7. Andrew M Greeley, *Priests in the United States; Reflections on a Survey*, 1st ed. (Garden City, NY: Doubleday, 1972), 77.

8. Richard A. Schoenherr and Andrew M. Greeley, "Role Commitment Processes and the American Catholic Priesthood," *American Sociological Review* 39, no. 3 (June 1, 1974): 407.

9. The 2001 results are reported in Dean R. Hoge, *Evolving Visions of the Priesthood: Changes from Vatican II to the Turn of the New Century* (Collegeville, MN: Liturgical Press, 2003), 217. The book erroneously reports agreement of 56 percent, perhaps due to a rounding error or an unreported weight factor. The number of 55 percent and the 1985 proportion reported in the text are derived directly from the original survey data, collected by Dean Hoge, and downloaded from the Association of Religion Data Archives, www.TheARDA.com. Neither data set permits distinguishing diocesan from religious priests.

10. I Corinthians 7:33–34 (New Revised Standard Version). Quoted at Catholic Church, *Catechism of the Catholic Church*, 2nd ed. (New York: Doubleday Religion, 2003), sec. 1599.

11. Canon 277, §1, in Canon Law Society of America, *Code of Canon Law, Latin-English Edition: Translation* (Washington, DC: Canon Law Society of America, 1983), pt. 277. Text also available online at http://www.vatican.va/archive/ENG1104/_INDEX.HTM.

12. I Corinthians 7:25 (NRSV).

13. Reported in Stephen Joseph Fichter, "Shepherding in Greener Pastures: Causes and Consequences of the Dual Transition of Celibate Catholic Priests into Married Protestant Ministry" (Ph.D. Dissertation, Rutgers University, New Brunswick, NJ, 2009), 67.

14. I Corinthians 7:28–29, 31 (NRSV).

15. In Chapter 4, these respondents were included in the "one day off" category.

16. Hessel J. Zondag, "Involved, Loyal, Alienated, and Detached: The Commitment of Pastors," *Pastoral Psychology* 49, no. 4 (March 2001): 312. See this article for a review of the literature on job satisfaction and commitment among clergy.

17. Arthur G. Cryns, "Dogmatism of Catholic Clergy and Ex-Clergy: A Study of Ministerial Role Perseverance and Open-Mindedness," *Journal for the Scientific Study of Religion* 9, no. 3 (October 1, 1970): 239–243, doi: 10.2307/1384826. Schoenherr and Greeley, "Role Commitment Processes and the American Catholic Priesthood," 422.

18. The correlation between job fulfillment and happiness was .41 for the married priests but only .31 for the celibate priests.

19. Fichter, "Shepherding in Greener Pastures," 160–161.

20. Ibid., 160.

21. Ibid., 161.

22. The correlation (Kendall's tau) = .26. P-value is .04. Kendall's tau, a nonparametric measure of association that is interpreted like a Pearson correlation coefficient, is more accurate when, as here, the associated variables are ordinal measures with limited variation.

CHAPTER 8

1. Philip Schaff, *History of the Christian Church: The Middle Ages 1049–1294 [1882]*, vol. 5 (Grand Rapids, MI: Christian Classics Ethereal Library, 2002), 24.

2. Carl Olson, ed., *Celibacy and Religious Traditions* (New York: Oxford University Press, 2008), presents an excellent collection of such treatments of celibacy in various religious settings. For a classic discussion of Catholic clergy from this perspective, see Lewis A. Coser, *Greedy Institutions: Patterns of Undivided Commitment* (New York: Free Press, 1974).

3. Leslie Woodcock Tentler, "'God's Representative in Our Midst': Toward a History of the Catholic Diocesan Clergy in the United States," *Church History* 67, no. 2 (June 1, 1998): 329.

4. Draper cites statistics from the National Center for Missing and Exploited Children and insurance risk analysts to make this point in "Catholic Priests No Guiltier of Sex Abuse Than Other Clergy," *Hark*, accessed April 24, 2014, http://blogs. denverpost.com/hark/2010/05/25/scandal-creates-contempt-for-catholic-clergy /39/. The most comprehensive study of Catholic priest pedophilia concluding that it is a false perception resulting from media bias rather than an objectively higher predisposition of celibate priests for sexual misconduct is Philip Jenkins, *Pedophiles and Priests: Anatomy of a Contemporary Crisis* (New York: Oxford University Press, 1996).

5. John Jay College, *The Nature and Scope of the Problem of Sexual Abuse of Minors by Catholic Priests and Deacons in the US*, Commissioned by the US Catholic Bishops (February 27, 2004), fig. 2.3.3, http://www.usccb.org/ issues-and-action/child-and-youth-protection/upload/The-Nature-and-S cope-of-Sexual-Abuse-of-Minors-by-Catholic-Priests-and-Deacons-in-the-United-States-1950-2002.pdf.

6. For a review, see Gerard J. McGlone, "Prevalence and Incidence of Roman Catholic Clerical Sex Offenders," *Sexual Addiction & Compulsivity* 10, no. 2–3 (January 1, 2003): 114–116.

7. The 2002 *Los Angeles Times* survey found that 15 percent of Catholic priests identified themselves at above 3 on the Kinsey scale, that is, either homosexual or inclined to homosexual desires. Similar surveys of the US population put the proportion of self-identified homosexual men at about 1.5 percent. Such surveys may well understate the true prevalence of homosexual men due to selective non-response, that is, the fact that homosexual men are less likely to respond to the survey at all or to pertinent questions on the survey. More subjective but possibly valid analyses by Sipe and Cozzens estimate the proportion of homosexual Catholic priests at 30 percent and 50 percent, respectively. Likewise, estimates based on clinical or non-random samples suggest that the rate of homosexuality among American men may be larger than 1.5 percent.

8. Dean R. Hoge and Jacqueline E. Wenger, *Evolving Visions of the Priesthood: Changes from Vatican II to the Turn of the New Century* (Collegeville, MN: Liturgical Press, 2003), 97.

9. Donald B. Cozzens, *The Changing Face of the Priesthood: A Reflection on the Priest's Crisis of Soul* (Liturgical Press, 2000), 109.

10. A. W. Richard Sipe, *A Secret World: Sexuality and the Search for Celibacy* (New York: Routledge, 1990); Hoge and Wenger, *Evolving Visions of the Priesthood*, 178, call this "the most influential book on sexuality of priests"; A. W. Richard Sipe, *Sex, Priests, and Power: Anatomy of a Crisis* (New York: Brunner/ Mazel, 1995); A. W. Richard Sipe, *Celibacy in Crisis: A Secret World Revisited* (New York: Routledge, 2003); A. W. Richard Sipe, *A Secret World: Sexuality and the Search for Celibacy*, 2nd ed. (New York: Routledge, 2013).

11. Sipe, *A Secret World* (1990), 110.

12. The question was, "In the seminary you attended, was there a homosexual subculture at the time?" On the 2001 priest survey by the *Los Angeles Times*, 53 percent of recently ordained priests responded "yes." A concurrent survey by Dean Hoge of The Catholic University of America yielded 55 percent "yes" to the identical question; as reported in *Evolving Visions of the Priesthood*, 101–102.

13. Dean R. Hoge, *The First Five Years of the Priesthood: A Study of Newly Ordained Catholic Priests* (Collegeville, MN: Liturgical Press, 2002), 31.

14. Hoge and Wenger, *Evolving Visions of the Priesthood*, 110.

15. Ibid.

16. Congregation for Catholic Education, "Instruction Concerning the Criteria for the Discernment of Vocations with Regard to Persons with Homosexual Tendencies in View of Their Admission to the Seminary and to Holy Orders," November 4, 2005, http://www.vatican.va/roman_curia/congregations/ccatheduc/documents/rc_con_ccatheduc_doc_20051104_istruzione_en.html.

17. Cozzens, *The Changing Face of the Priesthood*, 110.

18. Sipe, *A Secret World* (1990), 265.

19. "Letter to the German Nobility" (1520), documented in Martin Luther, Henry Eyster Jacobs, and Adolph Spaeth, *Works of Martin Luther: With Introductions and Notes* (Philadelphia, PA: A. J. Holman, 1915), 122.

20. Erik Seeman, "Sarah Prentice and the Immortalists: Sexuality, Piety, and the Body in Eighteenth-Century New England," in *Sex and Sexuality in Early America*, ed. Merril D. Smith (New York: New York University Press, 1998), 125.

21. Erving Goffman, *Asylums: Essays on the Social Situation of Mental Patients and Other Inmates (1961)* (New Brunswick, NJ: Transaction Publishers, 2007), 5–6.

22. Douglas T. Hall and Benjamin Schneider, *Organizational Climates and Careers: The Work Lives of Priests* (New York: Seminar Press, 1973), xvii.

23. Ibid.

24. Ibid.

25. The proportion of Protestant ministers who report that their fathers were ministers ranges from 7.3 percent (for Southern Baptists) to 15.1 percent (Seventh-Day Adventists), according to the 2001 US Congregational Life Survey. The data, collected by a team led by Cynthia Woolever and Keith Wulff, sampled ministers from seven representative Protestant denominations, and were downloaded from the Association of Religion Data Archives, www.TheARDA.com.

26. François Guizot, *History of Civilization in Europe* (London: Cassell, 1911), 229.

27. Eldon Curtiss, "Crisis in Vocations? What Crisis?" *Christian Order*, March 1996, http://www.christianorder.com/contents/1990s/contents_1995.html.

28. Andrew Yuengert, "Do Bishops Matter? A Cross-Sectional Study of Ordinations to the U.S. Catholic Diocesan Priesthood," *Review of Religious Research* 42, no. 3 (March 1, 2001): 307.

29. Roger Finke and Rodney Stark, *The Churching of America, 1776–2005: Winners and Losers in Our Religious Economy* (New Brunswick, NJ: Rutgers University Press, 2005), 238.

30. Ibid., 270.

31. Ibid., 271.

32. Ibid., 263.

33. In Catholic dioceses, the culture of the diocese largely reflects the character and priorities of the bishop. It is very likely that the knowledgeable third-party raters they consulted reflected their knowledge of the bishop in rating dioceses as traditional or progressive. As Yuengert's research shows, moreover, the bishop's conservatism is related to increased ordinations in much the same manner as is what Finke and Stark call diocesan culture.

34. Center for Applied Research in the Apostolate, "Top 20 Dioceses by Ordinand-to-Catholic Ratio," *CARA Report*, Winter 2011, 8.

35. The dual-listed diocese is the Diocese of Lincoln, which is a unique outlier producing far more ordinations for its size than any other US diocese. Due to the possible biasing effect, Finke and Stark reported results both with and without this diocese included. Lincoln was not among the sample dioceses for the *Los Angeles Times* 2002 priest survey, so is not included in the results that I report.

36. François Guizot, *General History of Civilization in Europe, from the Fall of the Roman Empire to the French Revolution* (New York: D. Appleton, 1846), 215.

37. Guizot, *History of Civilization in Europe*, 229.

38. Guizot, *General History of Civilization in Europe, from the Fall of the Roman Empire to the French Revolution*, 10.

39. Jaime Luciano Balmes, *European Civilization: Protestantism and Catholicity Compared*, 7th ed. (Baltimore: Murphy, 1861), 331.

40. The most well-known sociologist making this argument is Rodney Stark, in such works as Rodney Stark, *The Rise of Christianity: A Sociologist Reconsiders History* (Princeton, NJ: Princeton University Press, 1996); and Rodney Stark, *The Victory of Reason: How Christianity Led to Freedom, Capitalism, and Western Success*, 1st ed. (New York: Random House, 2005). This thesis is also put forth by the Catholic philosopher Michael Novak in *The Spirit of Democratic Capitalism* (New York: Simon & Schuster, 1982) and by Pope Benedict XVI in *Christianity and the Crisis of Cultures* (San Francisco: Ignatius Press, 2006). The original, still compelling, statement of the socially rationalizing effect of Christian virtues is found in Max Weber, *The Protestant Ethic and the Spirit of Capitalism (1905)*, Routledge Classics (London; New York: Routledge, 2001).

41. Weber, *The Protestant Ethic and the Spirit of Capitalism (1905)*, 105.

42. Olson, *Celibacy and Religious Traditions*, 13.

CONCLUSION

1. Franjo Seper (Archbishop), Prefect of the Sacred Congregation for the Doctrine of the Faith, "Letter to Archbishop Quinn Outlining the Pastoral Provision, July 22, 1980," in *Into Full Communion: Pastoral Provision for Former Clergy of the Episcopal Church* (Office of the US Ecclesiastical Delegate for the Pastoral Provision, 2009), 11–13, http://www.pastoralprovision.org/.

2. Kenneth Woodward, "The First Married Priests," *Newsweek*, September 1, 1980. See also Chapter 2 of this volume, n. 20–22.

3. "Catholics Request Married Priests for Everyone, Not Just Anglican Converts—FutureChurch Press Release," October 21, 2009, http://future-church.org/press/091020.htm.

4. "A Brief History of Celibacy—FutureChurch," accessed March 26, 2013, http://www.futurechurch.org/fpm/history.htm.

5. Mary Gail Frawley-O'Dea, *Perversion of Power: Sexual Abuse in the Catholic Church*, 1st ed. (Nashville, TN: Vanderbilt University Press, 2007), 108.

6. Edward Peters, "Diaconal Categories and Clerical Celibacy," *Chicago Studies* 49 (2010): 113–114.

7. Franjo Seper (Archbishop), Prefect of the Sacred Congregation for the Doctrine of the Faith, "Letter Outlining the Pastoral Provision."

8. "Complementary Norms for the Apostolic Constitution Anglicanorum Coetibus," November 4, 2009, para. 5, sec. 1, http://www.vatican.va/roman_curia/congregations/cfaith/documents/rc_con_cfaith_doc_20091104_norme-anglicanorum-coetibus_en.html.

9. Ibid., para. 9, sec. 1.

10. Charlotte Hays, "No Ordinary Year for the U.S. Anglican Ordinariate," *National Catholic Register*, January 8, 2013, http://www.ncregister.com/daily-news/no-ordinary-year-for-the-u.s.-anglican-ordinariate/. This article reports 36 communities in the Ordinariate; however, as of mid-2013 the Ordinariate lists only 28 communities. I have characterized this number, no doubt in flux, as "about 30."

11. "Personal Ordinariate: F.A.Q.," accessed September 13, 2013, http://www.usordinariate.org/faq.html. See also http://ordinariate.net/q-a. Among the four "large" parishes reported on this page are Christ the King, Towson, and St. Luke's, Bladensburg. In mid-2012, 125 members were received to form Christ the King, Towson; the previous November fewer than 100 were received to form St. Luke's, Bladensburg.

12. Hays, "No Ordinary Year for the U.S. Anglican Ordinariate."

13. GianPaolo Salvini, "Priests Who 'Desert,' Priests Who 'Come Back,'" trans. Matthew Sherry, *La Civilta Cattolica* 3, no. 3764 (April 21, 2007): 148–155.

14. Ibid., 151.

15. Ibid., 154.

16. Ibid., 155.

17. Karol Wojtyla (Pope John Paul II), *Sign of Contradiction* (New York: Seabury Press, 1979).

APPENDIX

1. The results are published in Andrew Greeley and Richard Schoenherr, *The Catholic Priest in the United States: Sociological Investigations* (Washington, DC: Publications Office, US Catholic Conference, 1972). For political reasons, the publisher of the cited work removed Richard Schoenherr's name as co-author of the book (over Greeley's objection). While citing the book as published, I have chosen to honor Greeley's request by acknowledging Schoenherr's contribution in references to the book in the text.

2. All three surveys were funded by the National Federation of Priests' Councils (NFPC), with support from various foundations. Findings from the 1985 and 1993 surveys were reported in National Federation of Priests Councils, *Project Future Directions: Survey Reports*, 1994; the 2001 survey forms the basis for Dean R. Hoge and Jacqueline E. Wenger, *Evolving Visions of the Priesthood: Changes from Vatican II to the Turn of the New Century* (Collegeville, MN: Liturgical Press, 2003). Unless noted otherwise, the current study cites the original raw data files for these surveys, obtained from the Association of Religion Data Archives (www.thearda.com).

3. *Los Angeles Times* Polls, *Dataset Abstract: Catholic Priests in the United States [USLAT2002-471]*, 2002, The Roper Center for Public Opinion Research, http://webapps.ropercenter.uconn.edu., Los Angeles Times Survey Staff, A Survey of Roman Catholic Priests in the United States (Los Angeles: Los Angeles Times, 2002), available online (as of September 1, 2009) at http://www.latimesinteractive.com/pdfarchive/special/la-timespollpriests-471book.pdf, reports on the methods and findings of the 2002 survey. Greeley himself uses the *LA Times* Surveys to replicate and extend his 1970 findings, in Andrew M. Greeley, *Priests: A Calling in Crisis* (Chicago: University of Chicago Press, 2004).

4. This is not to say that all six surveys are equally valid. The response rate is much higher for the Hoge and Greeley surveys (above 75 percent) than for the *Los Angeles Times* surveys (less than 40 percent). Response bias (sampled priests who decline to return the questionnaire due to mistrust or disapproval of the organization sponsoring the survey) may also be a concern for the *Los Angeles Times* surveys, particularly in 2002, when there was much negative publicity about Catholic priests due to the sex abuse scandal. For this reason the researchers statistically adjusted some of the distributions for this survey to correspond to those of a similar 1999 CARA survey. For the Greeley study, sponsored by the NCCB, and the Hoge studies, which were independently administered by the Catholic University of America, response bias is likely minimal.

5. J. Monahan, "The Prediction of Violent Behavior: Toward a Second Generation of Theory and Policy," *The American Journal of Psychiatry* 141, no. 1 (January 1, 1984): 10–15; R. Karl Hanson, "The Psychological Assessment of Risk for Crime and Violence," *Canadian Psychology/Psychologie Canadienne* 50, no. 3 (2009): 172–182.

6. James F. Hemphill, Robert D. Hare, and Stephen Wong, "Psychopathy and Recidivism: A Review," *Legal and Criminological Psychology* 3, no. 1 (1998): 139–170.

7. David J. Cooke and Christine Michie, "Limitations of Diagnostic Precision and Predictive Utility in the Individual Case: A Challenge for Forensic Practice," *Law & Human Behavior* 34, no. 4 (August 2010): 259.

8. Brian R. Abbott, "Throwing the Baby Out with the Bath Water: Is It Time for Clinical Judgment to Supplement Actuarial Risk Assessment?" *Journal of the American Academy of Psychiatry and the Law Online* 39, no. 2 (April 2011): 222–230.

9. William P. Daly, *The Laborer is Worthy of His Hire*, (Chicago: National Federation of Priests Councils, 2008).

10. Although Daly, "Laborer," reports aggregate priest salary and total compensation numbers as a "median," what is intended by this label is not an arithmetic median in the usual sense. The numbers are more properly described as adjusted means. The NFPC researchers attempted to obtain an average salary figure for each diocese. Some dioceses reported a high and low amount, in which case the researchers averaged the two numbers; others reported their diocesan pay scale rather than actual salaries, in which case the researchers reported the average of the high and low ends of the salary scale. Since these averages represent the midpoint of the actual or stipulated salary range in the diocese, they were reported as a median, though they are really an average. The national aggregate number reported is the mean of these diocesan averages. There is no adjustment for diocesan size (number of priests), so smaller dioceses are somewhat overweighted (William Daly, telephone conversation, January 31, 2013). The aggregate salary amounts, in fact, are reported variably as the "average" or "median" salary throughout the document. This confusion applies only to the salary number; all the other aggregate amounts reported, which are summed to produce the total compensation number, are true means. Although imprecise in a number of ways, the salary data in Daly, "Laborer," are the best available. Furthermore, the report notes of the "median" salary amounts: "The medians reported probably understate what priests actually receive, since, because of their long tenure, the priests in a given diocese will, on average, be somewhat beyond the median step of their salary schedule" (p. 90). This probable understatement increases confidence that the comparison of celibate and married priest salaries reported in the text is conservative in that it does not minimize the difference between them. For comparability in

the analysis, the corresponding married priest amounts reported are also averages. The average 2007 salary for parish-based married priests, at $59,290, was very close to the median salary of $60,000.

11. Daly, "Laborer."

12. Draft language provided by several dioceses for stipulating the clergy housing allowance in a parish employment agreement make this point clear: "The parish provides rectory room and board with an estimated fair market value of _____ per day" (available at home.catholicweb.com/covingtonfinance as of February 4, 2013). In Daly, "Laborer," a minority of dioceses acknowledged or included in the clergy housing allowance amounts reflecting housekeeping (35 percent of dioceses did this), laundry (30 percent), and telephone, cable, and Internet services (37 percent); about half (46 percent) included at least some food preparation cost in the food allowance. According to the author of the report, as far as can be determined, this variation represents differences in reporting, not differences in practice (William Daly, telephone conversation, January 31, 2013). This opinion is confirmed by the nature of the data; it is implausible that the provision of these services would vary by diocese, and be restricted to only a third of Catholic dioceses; and the average housing amount reported by dioceses that did not include them is not less than for those that did. For these reasons, the stipulated designations in Daly, "Laborer," do not provide any reliable guidance to estimate the cost or extent of these affiliated in-kind services.

13. Bureau of Labor Statistics, *Consumer Expenditures in 2007 (Report 1016)* (US Department of Labor, April 2009), reporting data from the Consumer Expenditures Survey, a component of the Consumer Price Index.

14. Property liability insurance expense is from Bureau of Labor Statistics, *Consumer Expenditures in 2007*, reporting data from the National Association of Insurance Commissioners.

15. The "housing allowance" received by Catholic priests who reside in a rectory should not be confused with the housing allowance often received by clergy who own their own home, and sometimes by other professionals, which does usually include funds to pay for utilities and other housing expenses. The housing allowance of a priest who lives in a rectory is not an actual cash payment, but the estimated value of residing in the rectory, a number that is provided to him for the purpose of reporting his income for tax purposes.

16. The 2008 Official Catholic Directory, reporting data from 2007, records that in 2007 there were 19,181 active diocesan priests (a total of 27,614 less 8,433 classed as retired, sick, or absent) and 13,037 parishes pastored by a resident diocesan priest, for a ratio of 1.47 priests per parish. I am indebted to Dr. Mary Gautier of Georgetown University and the Center for Applied Research in the Apostolate for this analysis.

17. National Association of Church Personnel Administrators, *Pay and Benefits Survey of Catholic Parishes,* January 2011, 11, 82.

18. One-fifth of parishes reported employing a rectory housekeeper/cook for an average of 20 hours per week (half-time), an average of one-tenth of a position per parish overall at an average cost, including benefits, of $3,192.50 per parish.

19. National Association of Church Personnel Administrators, *Pay and Benefits Survey of Catholic Parishes,* 11, 82.

20. In addition to those referenced in the test, other reported positions that typically included care of the rectory were facilities maintenance supervisor and facilities maintenance coordinator. Altogether, the 566 responding parishes reported by the National Association of Church Personnel Administrators accounted for 612 such positions, an average just over one position (1.08) per parish. Estimates for the amount of staff expense devoted to rectory maintenance and upkeep vary widely; two knowledgeable experts I consulted respectively characterized them as "enormous" and "minuscule." As a minimal estimate, if only one-tenth of the facilities-related staff time was devoted to the rectory building and grounds, a proportion that roughly corresponds to the size of the rectory and grounds relative to other parish structures, these services would comprise an additional $3,073.50, on average.

21. Unless noted otherwise, comparative numbers for US priests are derived from a mailed survey administered to a national random sample of 1,800 US Catholic priests in 2001 by the National Federation of Priests Councils (reported in Dean Hoge and Jacqueline Wenger, *Evolving Visions of the Priesthood* (Collegeville, MN: Liturgical Press, 2003). This survey obtained 1,279 responses, a response rate of 71 percent. Where the NFPC survey does not have comparable data, numbers are most often reported from a 2002 mailed survey by the *Los Angeles Times.* These items are indicated in the tables with the letter "L" in parentheses. The *Los Angeles Times* survey yielded 1,854 responses from a national random sample of 5,000 Catholic priests, a response rate of 38 percent. Despite the large difference in response, the results of these two surveys generally agree. For some items where neither of these surveys has comparable data, other recent surveys of Catholic priests are used for comparison, as indicated in the tables involved. For many questions there are slight variations in question wording and/or response categories among the surveys compared. I have reported the wording used in the Pastoral Provision survey.

Bibliography

Abbott, Brian R. "Throwing the Baby Out with the Bath Water: Is It Time for Clinical Judgment to Supplement Actuarial Risk Assessment?" *Journal of the American Academy of Psychiatry and the Law Online* 39, no. 2 (April 2011): 222–230.

"A Brief History of Celibacy—FutureChurch." Accessed March 26, 2013. http://www.futurechurch.org/fpm/history.htm.

Ad Hoc Committee for Convert Married Ministers. "Report in Response to Bishop Marshall's Memo and Outline." Unpublished manuscript, September 16, 1977. Archived at the American Catholic History Research Center, The Catholic University of America.

Allitt, Patrick. *Catholic Converts: British and American Intellectuals Turn to Rome.* Ithaca, NY: Cornell University Press, 1997.

Anglican–Roman Catholic Joint Preparatory Commission. *The Malta Report*, 1968. http://www.vatican.va/roman_curia/pontifical_councils/chrstuni/angl-comm-docs/rc_pc_chrstuni_doc_19680102_malta-report_en.html.

"Anglicans Admitted into Catholic Church on 'Common Identity.'" *Religion News Service*, August 20, 1980.

Balmes, Jaime Luciano. *European Civilization: Protestantism and Catholicity Compared.* 7th ed. Baltimore, MD: Murphy, 1861.

Baylor Institute for Studies of Religion. *The Baylor Religion Survey [machine-readable data file]*, 2005. Association of Religion Data Archives, www.thearda.com.

Benedict. *Christianity and the Crisis of Cultures.* San Francisco: Ignatius Press, 2006.

Bibby, Reginald W., and Merlin B. Brinkerhoff. "The Circulation of the Saints: A Study of People Who Join Conservative Churches." *Journal for the Scientific Study of Religion* 12, no. 3 (September 1, 1973): 273–283. doi: 10.2307/1384428.

Blaikie, Norman W. H. *The Plight of the Australian Clergy: To Convert, Care Or Challenge?* St. Lucia: University of Queensland Press, 1979.

Brackin, Lena Anne. "Loneliness, Depression, Social Support, Marital Satisfaction and Spirituality as Experienced by the Southern Baptist Clergy Wife." Ph.D. Dissertation, The University of Arizona, 2001.

Brooks, Ashley. "An Examination of the Role Satisfaction of the Pastor's Wife in the Southern Baptist Convention." Ph.D. Dissertation, New Orleans Baptist Theological Seminary, 2008.

Brunette-Hill, Sandi. "A Life of Her Own: Role Change among Clergy Wives." *Research in the Social Scientific Study of Religion* 10 (1999): 77–90.

Bureau of Labor Statistics. *Consumer Expenditures in 2007 (Report 1016)*. US Department of Labor, April 2009.

Canon Law Society of America. *Code of Canon Law, Latin-English Edition: Translation.* Washington, DC: Canon Law Society of America, 1983.

Carroll, Colleen. *The New Faithful: Why Young Adults Are Embracing Christian Orthodoxy.* Chicago: Loyola Press, 2002.

Catholic Church. *Catechism of the Catholic Church.* 2nd ed. New York: Doubleday Religion, 2003.

Catholic Church in England and Wales. "Liturgical Calendar | National Calendar for England II." Accessed August 15, 2013. http://www.liturgyoffice.org.uk/Calendar/National/England2.shtml#May4.

"Catholic Priests No Guiltier of Sex Abuse Than Other Clergy." *Hark.* Accessed April 24, 2014. http://blogs.denverpost.com/hark/2010/05/25/scandal-creates-contempt-for-catholic-clergy/39/.

"Catholics Request Married Priests for Everyone, Not Just Anglican Converts—FutureChurch Press Release," October 21, 2009. http://future-church.org/press/091020.htm.

Center for Applied Research in the Apostolate. "Top 20 Dioceses by Ordinand-to-Catholic Ratio." *CARA Report*, Winter 2011.

Charue, André-Marie. *Priesthood and Celibacy.* Milano-Roma: Àncora, 1972.

Cherlin, Andrew J. *The Marriage-Go-Round: The State of Marriage and the Family in America Today.* 1st Vintage Books ed. New York: Vintage Books, 2010.

Committee on Priestly Life and Formation. *Program of Priestly Formation.* US Conference of Catholic Bishops, 2006.

"Complementary Norms for the Apostolic Constitution Anglicanorum Coetibus," November 4, 2009. http://www.vatican.va/roman_curia/congregations/cfaith/documents/rc_con_cfaith_doc_20091104_norme-anglicanorum-coetibus_en.html.

Congregation for Catholic Education. "Instruction Concerning the Criteria for the Discernment of Vocations with Regard to Persons with Homosexual Tendencies in View of Their Admission to the Seminary and to Holy Orders," November 4, 2005. http://www.vatican.va/roman_curia/congregations/ccatheduc/documents/rc_con_ccatheduc_doc_20051104_istruzione_en.html.

Congregation for the Doctrine of the Faith. *Observations on the Final Report of ARCIC—ANIMADVERSIONES*, 1982. http://www.vatican.va/roman_curia/congregations/cfaith/documents/rc_con_cfaith_doc_19820327_animadversiones_en.html.

Connor, Charles P. *Classic Catholic Converts*. San Francisco: Ignatius Press, 2001.

Cooke, David J., and Christine Michie. "Limitations of Diagnostic Precision and Predictive Utility in the Individual Case: A Challenge for Forensic Practice." *Law & Human Behavior* 34, no. 4 (August 2010): 259–274.

Coser, Lewis A. *Greedy Institutions: Patterns of Undivided Commitment*. New York: Free Press, 1974.

Cozzens, Donald B. *The Changing Face of the Priesthood: A Reflection on the Priest's Crisis of Soul*. Collegeville, MN: Liturgical Press, 2000.

Creamer, Anita. "Former Lutheran to Be Sacramento Diocese's First Married Catholic Priest." *McClatchy—Tribune Business News*. December 12, 2010. 817202798. ABI/INFORM Complete.

Cryns, Arthur G. "Dogmatism of Catholic Clergy and Ex-Clergy: A Study of Ministerial Role Perseverance and Open-Mindedness." *Journal for the Scientific Study of Religion* 9, no. 3 (October 1, 1970): 239–243. doi: 10.2307/1384826.

Currie, David B. *Born Fundamentalist, Born Again Catholic*. San Francisco: Ignatius Press, 1996.

Curtiss, Eldon. "Crisis in Vocations? What Crisis?" *Christian Order*, March 1996. http://www.christianorder.com/contents/1990s/contents_1995.html.

Daly, William P. *Early Career Resignations from the Priesthood*. Chicago: National Federation of Priests Councils, 2001.

Daly, William P. *The Laborer Is Worthy of His Hire*. Chicago: National Federation of Priests Councils, 2008.

David, Mace, and Vera Mace. *What's Happening to Clergy Marriages?* Nashville, TN: Abingdon, 1980.

Davidson, James D. *The Search for Common Ground: What Unites and Divides Catholic Americans*. Huntington, IN: Our Sunday Visitor, 1997.

Davidson, James D. (Principal Investigator). *Catholic Pluralism Projects Survey [machine-readable data file]*, 1995. Association of Religion Data Archives, www.thearda.com.

Denton, Wallace. *The Role of the Minister's Wife*. Philadelphia: Westminster Press, 1962.

Dobson, Lorna. *I'm More Than the Pastor's Wife*. Grand Rapids, MI: Zondervan, 2003.

Douglas, William G. T. *Ministers' Wives*. New York: Harper & Row, 1965.

Eckholm, Erik. "Single and Evangelical? Good Luck Finding Work as a Pastor." *New York Times*, March 22, 2011, sec. U.S. http://www.nytimes.com/2011/03/22/us/22pastor.html.

Ellis, John Tracy. *American Catholics and the Intellectual Life*. 1st ed. Chicago: Heritage Foundation, 1956.

"Episcopal Bishop Criticizes Action by Roman Catholics on Dissidents." *New York Times*, September 29, 1980, 66.

Fichter, Stephen Joseph. "Shepherding in Greener Pastures: Causes and Consequences of the Dual Transition of Celibate Catholic Priests into Married

Protestant Ministry." Ph.D. Dissertation, Rutgers University, New Brunswick, NJ, 2009.

Finke, Roger, and Rodney Stark. *The Churching of America, 1776–2005: Winners and Losers in Our Religious Economy.* New Brunswick, NJ: Rutgers University Press, 2005.

Frawley-O'Dea, Mary Gail. *Perversion of Power: Sexual Abuse in the Catholic Church.* 1st ed. Nashville, TN: Vanderbilt University Press, 2007.

"Gallup Beliefs and Values Polls 2006–2008." Accessed March 30, 2009. www.gallup.com.

"Gallup Polls May 6–9, 2002," May 16, 2002. www.gallup.com.

Gautier, Mary. "Recession's Impact on Catholic Parish Life." *CARA Report,* Spring 2011.

Gautier, Mary, Mary Bendyna, and Melissa Cidade. *The Class of 2009: Survey of Ordinands to the Priesthood.* Committee for Applied Research in the Apostolate, April 2009. http://www.usccb.org/beliefs-and-teachings/vocations/ordination-class/upload/Ordination-Class-of-2009-Report.pdf.

Gibson, David. *The Coming Catholic Church: How the Faithful Are Shaping a New American Catholicism.* 1st ed. San Francisco: HarperSanFrancisco, 2003.

Goffman, Erving. *Asylums: Essays on the Social Situation of Mental Patients and Other Inmates (1961).* New Brunswick, NJ: Transaction Publishers, 2007.

Gooren, Henri. "Reassessing Conventional Approaches to Conversion: Toward a New Synthesis." *Journal for the Scientific Study of Religion* 46, no. 3 (September 2007): 337–353.

Gordon-Gorman, William J. *Converts to Rome.* London: Sands, 1910.

Greeley, Andrew M. *Priests: A Calling in Crisis.* Chicago: University of Chicago Press, 2004.

Greeley, Andrew M. *Priests in the United States; Reflections on a Survey.* 1st ed. Garden City, NY: Doubleday, 1972.

Greeley, Andrew, and Richard Schoenherr. *The Catholic Priest in the United States: Sociological Investigations.* Washington, DC: Publications Office, United States Catholic Conference, 1972.

Guizot, François. *General History of Civilization in Europe, from the Fall of the Roman Empire to the French Revolution.* New York: D. Appleton, 1846.

Guizot, François. *History of Civilization in Europe.* London: Cassell, 1911.

Hall, Douglas T., and Benjamin Schneider. *Organizational Climates and Careers: The Work Lives of Priests.* New York: Seminar Press, 1973.

Hanson, R. Karl. "The Psychological Assessment of Risk for Crime and Violence." *Canadian Psychology/Psychologie Canadienne* 50, no. 3 (2009): 172–182.

Harrington, Joel Francis. *Reordering Marriage and Society in Reformation Germany.* Cambridge: Cambridge University Press, 1995.

Hays, Charlotte. "No Ordinary Year for the U.S. Anglican Ordinariate." *National Catholic Register,* January 8, 2013. http://www.ncregister.com/daily-news/no-ordinary-year-for-the-u.s.-anglican-ordinariate/.

Hemphill, James F., Robert D. Hare, and Stephen Wong. "Psychopathy and Recidivism: A Review." *Legal and Criminological Psychology* 3, no. 1 (1998): 139–170.

Hoge, Dean R. *Experiences of Priests Ordained Five to Nine Years*. Washington, DC: National Catholic Educational Association, 2006.

Hoge, Dean R. *The First Five Years of the Priesthood: A Study of Newly Ordained Catholic Priests*. Collegeville, MN: Liturgical Press, 2002.

Hoge, Dean R., and Jacqueline Wenger. *Survey of American Catholic Priests [machine-readable data file]*, 2001. Association of Religion Data Archives, www.thearda.com.

Hoge, Dean R., and Jacqueline E. Wenger. *Evolving Visions of the Priesthood: Changes from Vatican II to the Turn of the New Century*. Collegeville, MN: Liturgical Press, 2003.

Hunt, Harley D. *The Stained Glass Fishbowl*. Valley Forge, PA: Ministers Council, 1990.

"Into Full Communion: Pastoral Provision for Former Clergy of the Episcopal Church." Office of the US Ecclesiastical Delegate for the Pastoral Provision, 2009. http://www.pastoralprovision.org/.

Jenkins, Philip. *Pedophiles and Priests: Anatomy of a Contemporary Crisis*. New York: Oxford University Press, 1996.

John Jay College. *The Nature and Scope of the Problem of Sexual Abuse of Minors by Catholic Priests and Deacons in the US*. Commissioned by the US Catholic Bishops, February 27, 2004. http://www.usccb.org/issues-and-action/child-and-youth-protection/upload/The-Nature-and-Scope-of-Sexual-Abuse-of-Minors-by-Catholic-Priests-and-Deacons-in-the-United-States-1950-2002.pdf.

John Paul II. *Pastores Dabo Vobis* [Post-Synodal Apostolic Exhortation on the Formation of Priests in the Circumstances of the Present Day]. 1992.

John Paul II (Pope). *Ad Tuendam Fidem* [Apostolic Letter Motu Proprio to Protect the Faith]. 1998.

Johnston, G. "The Case for Priestly Celibacy." *Crisis Magazine*, September 2006. http://www.crisismagazine.com/2006/why-not-married-priests-the-case-for-clerical-celibacy.

Kanter, Rosabeth. *Men and Women of the Corporation*. New York: Basic Books, 1993.

Kenedy and Sons, ed. *The Official Catholic Directory*. New Providence, NJ: P. J. Kenedy & Sons, Annual.

Langer, Gary (Principal Investigator). *ABC News/Washington Post Poll*, October 9, 2003. American Religious Data Archive, www.thearda.com.

Laumann, Edward O., ed. *The Social Organization of Sexuality: Sexual Practices in the United States*. Chicago: University of Chicago Press, 1994.

Law, Bernard (Bishop). "A Progress Report to the Sacred Congregation for the Faith from Its Ecclesiastical Delegate for the Pastoral Provision," December 1982. Archived at the American Catholic History Research Center, The Catholic University of America.

Lee, Cameron. "Patterns of Stress and Support Among Adventist Clergy: Do Pastors and Their Spouses Differ?" *Pastoral Psychology* 55 (2007): 761–771.

Leo XIII (Pope). *Apostolicae Curae* [Encyclical Letter on the Invalidity of Anglican Orders]. 1896.

Lofland, John, and Norman Skonovd. "Conversion Motifs." *Journal for the Scientific Study of Religion* 20, no. 4 (1981): 373–385.

Los Angeles Times Polls. *Dataset Abstract: Catholic Priests in the United States* [*USLAT2002-471*], 2002. The Roper Center for Public Opinion Research. http://webapps.ropercenter.uconn.edu.

Luther, Martin. *The Table Talk or Familiar Discourse of Martin Luther.* London: D. Bogue, 1848.

Luther, Martin, Henry Eyster Jacobs, and Adolph Spaeth. *Works of Martin Luther: With Introductions and Notes.* Philadelphia: A. J. Holman, 1915.

McAfee, Cleland Boyd. *Ministerial Practices, Some Fraternal Suggestions.* New York; London: Harper & Brothers, 1928.

McGlone, Gerard J. "Prevalence and Incidence of Roman Catholic Clerical Sex Offenders." *Sexual Addiction & Compulsivity* 10, no. 2–3 (January 1, 2003): 111–121.

McKnight, Scot. "From Wheaton to Rome: Why Evangelicals Become Roman Catholic." *Journal of the Evangelical Theological Society* 45, no. 3 (2002): 451–472.

McMinn, Mark R., Sarah P. Kerrick, Susan J. Duma, Emma R. Campbell, and Jane B. Jung. "Positive Coping among Wives of Male Christian Clergy." *Pastoral Psychology* 56, no. 4 (February 2008): 445–457.

Menendez, Albert J. *The Road to Rome: An Annotated Bibliography.* New York: Garland, 1986.

Merrill, Dean. *Clergy Couples in Crisis: The Impact of Stress on Pastoral Marriages.* Carol Stream, IL: CTI Publications, 1985.

Monahan, J. "The Prediction of Violent Behavior: Toward a Second Generation of Theory and Policy." *The American Journal of Psychiatry* 141, no. 1 (January 1, 1984): 10–15.

Moore, David. "American Catholics Revere Pope, Disagree with Some Major Teachings." Gallup Research Reports, April 1, 2005. www.gallup.com.

Morgan, John Henry, and Linda B. Morgan. *Wives of Priests: A Study of Clergy Wives in the Episcopal Church.* Bristol, IN: St. John of the Cross Parish Church Library for the Notre Dame University Parish Life Institute, 1980.

National Association of Church Personnel Administrators. *Pay and Benefits Survey of Catholic Parishes,* January 2011, http://www.nacpa.org/live/index.htm.

National Federation of Priests Councils. *Project Future Directions: Survey Reports,* 1994, http://nfpc.org/.

Newman, John Henry. *Certain Difficulties Felt by Anglicans in Catholic Teaching: In Twelve Lectures Addressed in 1850 to the Party of the Religious Movement of 1833.* Vol. 1. Longmans, Green, 1901. http://www.newmanreader.org/works/anglicans/volume1/index.html.

Newport, Frank. "Catholics Similar to Mainstream on Abortion, Stem Cells." Gallup Research Reports, March 30, 2009. www.gallup.com.

Newsome, David. *The Parting of Friends: The Wilberforces and Henry Manning.* Grand Rapids, MI; Leominster, UK: Eerdmans; Gracewing, 1993.

Novak, Michael. *The Spirit of Democratic Capitalism.* New York: Simon & Schuster, 1982.

Olson, Carl, ed. *Celibacy and Religious Traditions.* New York: Oxford University Press, 2008.

O'Rourke, David K. *A Process Called Conversion.* Garden City, NY: Knopf Doubleday Publishing Group, 1985.

Parker, James. "The Reverend James Parker: A Married Catholic Priest?" In *The New Catholics: Contemporary Converts Tell Their Stories,* edited by Dan O'Neill, Ch. 16. New York: Crossroad, 1987.

Paul VI (Pope). *Gaudium et Spes* [Pastoral Constitution of the Second Vatican Council on the Church in the Modern World]. Vatican City, 1965.

Paul VI (Pope). *Lumen Gentium* [Dogmatic Constitution of the Second Vatican Council on the Church]. Vatican City, 1964.

Paul VI (Pope). *Sacerdotalis Caelibatus* [Encyclical Letter on the Celibacy of the Priest]. Vatican City, 1967.

Pearce, Joseph. *Literary Converts: Spiritual Inspiration in an Age of Unbelief.* San Francisco: Ignatius Press, 2000.

Percy, Walker. "Foreword." In *The New Catholics: Contemporary Converts Tell Their Stories,* edited by Dan O'Neill. New York: Crossroad, 1987.

"Personal Ordinariate: F.A.Q." Accessed September 13, 2013. http://www.usordinariate.org/q-a.

Peters, Edward. "Diaconal Categories and Clerical Celibacy." *Chicago Studies* 49 (2010): 100–116.

Phipps, William E. *Clerical Celibacy: The Heritage.* New York: Continuum, 2004.

Ray, Stephen K. *Crossing the Tiber: Evangelical Protestants Discover the Historical Church.* San Francisco: Ignatius Press, 1997.

Roof, Wade Clark. *American Mainline Religion: Its Changing Shape and Future.* New Brunswick, NJ: Rutgers University Press, 1987.

Sacred Congregation for the Doctrine of the Faith. *The Ordination of Women: Official Commentary from the Sacred Congregation for the Doctrine of the Faith on Its Declaration Inter Insigniores ('Women and the Priesthood') of 15th October 1976 Together with the Exchange of Correspondence in 1975 and 1976 Between His Grace the Most Reverend Dr. Frederick Donald Coggan, Archbishop of Canterbury and His Holiness Pope Paul VI.* London: Catholic Truth Society, 1977.

Salvini, GianPaolo. "Priests Who 'Desert,' Priests Who 'Come Back.'" Translated by Matthew Sherry. *La Civilta Cattolica* 3, no. 3764 (April 21, 2007): 148–155.

Schaff, Philip. *History of the Christian Church: The Middle Ages 1049–1294 [1882].* Vol. 5. Christian Classics Ethereal Library, 2002, http://www.ccel.org/.

Schaff, Philip, and David Schley Schaff. *History of the Christian Church*. 8 vols. New York: C. Scribner's Sons, 1907.

Schoenherr, Richard A. *Goodbye Father: The Celibate Male Priesthood and the Future of the Catholic Church*. Oxford; New York: Oxford University Press, 2002.

Schoenherr, Richard A., and Andrew M. Greeley. "Role Commitment Processes and the American Catholic Priesthood." *American Sociological Review* 39, no. 3 (June 1, 1974): 407–426.

Schoenherr, Richard A., and Lawrence A. Young. "Quitting the Clergy: Resignations in the Roman Catholic Priesthood." *Journal for the Scientific Study of Religion* 29, no. 4 (December 1, 1990): 463–481.

Seeman, Erik. "Sarah Prentice and the Immortalists: Sexuality, Piety, and the Body in Eighteenth-Century New England." In *Sex and Sexuality in Early America*, edited by Merril D. Smith. New York: New York University Press, 1998.

Seper, Franjo (Archbishop), Prefect of the Sacred Congregation for the Doctrine of the Faith. "Letter to Archbishop Quinn Outlining the Pastoral Provision, July 22, 1980." In *Into Full Communion: Pastoral Provision for Former Clergy of the Episcopal Church*, 11–13. Office of the US Ecclesiastical Delegate for the Pastoral Provision, 2009. http://www.pastoralprovision.org/.

Shea, Mark P. *By What Authority?: An Evangelical Discovers Catholic Tradition*. Huntington, IN: Our Sunday Visitor, 1996.

Sipe, A. W. Richard. *A Secret World: Sexuality and the Search for Celibacy*. New York: Routledge, 1990.

Sipe, A. W. Richard. *A Secret World: Sexuality and the Search for Celibacy*. 2nd ed. New York: Routledge, 2013.

Sipe, A. W. Richard. *Celibacy in Crisis: A Secret World Revisited*. New York: Routledge, 2003.

Sipe, A. W. Richard. *Sex, Priests, and Power: Anatomy of a Crisis*. New York: Brunner/Mazel, 1995.

Smith, David L. "Some Thoughts on the Preserving of Clergy Marriages." *Didaskalia* 7, no. 1 (September 1, 1995): 61–65.

Smith, Peter Marsden, Michael Hout, and Jibum Kim. *General Social Surveys 1972–2010 [machine-readable data file]*. Chicago: National Opinion Research Center, 2010. Storrs, CT: The Roper Center for Public Opinion Research.

Snow, D. A., and R. Machalek. "The Sociology of Conversion." *Annual Review of Sociology* 10, no. 1 (1984): 167–190.

Society of the Holy Cross. "Rule of Life," n.d. http://www.sscamericas.org/resources/rule.html.

Stanford, Peter. *Cardinal Hume and the Changing Face of English Catholicism*. London: Continuum, 1999.

Stark, Rodney. *The Rise of Christianity: A Sociologist Reconsiders History*. Princeton, NJ: Princeton University Press, 1996.

Stark, Rodney. *The Victory of Reason: How Christianity Led to Freedom, Capitalism, and Western Success.* 1st ed. New York: Random House, 2005.

Stickler, Alphonso M. *The Case for Clerical Celibacy: Its Historical Development and Theological Foundations.* San Francisco: Ignatius Press, 1995.

Strauss, Gerald. *Luther's House of Learning: Indoctrination of the Young in the German Reformation.* Baltimore, MD: Johns Hopkins University Press, 1978.

Sullins, D. Paul. "Institutional Selection for Conformity: The Case of U.S. Catholic Priests." *Sociology of Religion* 74, no. 1 (March 1, 2013): 56–81.

Sullins, D. Paul. "Switching Close to Home: Volatility or Coherence in Protestant Affiliation Patterns?" *Social Forces* 72, no. 2 (December 1, 1993): 399–419. doi: 10.1093/sf/72.2.399.

Sullins, D. Paul. "The History and Development of the Anglican Pastoral Provision." *Catholic Historical Review* (forthcoming), 2017.

Surprised by Truth: Eleven Converts Give the Biblical and Historical Reasons for Becoming Catholic. San Diego: Basilica Press, 1994.

Tanner, Mary, and Andrew Faley. "Anglican-Roman Catholic Relations: A Kick Start?" Society for Ecumenical Studies, May 30, 2007. sfes.faithweb.com/0705sfesagmanglicancatholic.pdf.

Tentler, Leslie Woodcock. "'God's Representative in Our Midst': Toward a History of the Catholic Diocesan Clergy in the United States." *Church History* 67, no. 2 (June 1, 1998): 326–349.

Travisano, Richard. "Alternation and Conversion as Qualitatively Different Transformations." In *Social Psychology Through Symbolic Interaction,* edited by G. P. Stone and H. A. Farberman, 594–606. Waltham, MA: Ginn-Blaisdel, 1970.

United States Conference of Catholic Bishops. "Ordination Class Reports." Accessed March 27, 2014. http://www.usccb.org/beliefs-and-teachings/vocations/ ordination-class/.

Vanauken, Sheldon. "The English Channel: Between Canterbury and Rome." In *The New Catholics: Contemporary Converts Tell Their Stories,* edited by Dan O'Neill, Ch. 12. New York: Crossroad, 1987.

"Vatican to Allow Ordination of Dissident Episcopal Priests." *Washington Post,* August 21, 1980.

"Washington Dateline-PM Cycle." *Associated Press,* August 20, 1980.

Weber, Max. "'Objectivity' in Social Science and Social Policy." In *The Methodology of the Social Sciences,* edited by Edward Shils and Henry Finch, 89–99. New York: Free Press, 1949.

Weber, Max. *The Protestant Ethic and the Spirit of Capitalism (1905).* Routledge Classics. London; New York: Routledge, 2001.

Weber, Max. *The Theory of Social and Economic Organization.* 1st American ed. New York: Oxford University Press, 1947.

Whyte, William Hollingsworth. *The Organization Man.* Philadelphia: University of Pennsylvania Press, 2002.

Wilcox, W. Bradford. "A River Runs to It: A New Exodus of Protestants Streams to Rome." *Crisis Magazine*, May 1999, https://www.crisismagazine. com/1999/a-river-runs-to-it-a-new-exodus-of-protestants-streams-to-rome.

Wojtyla, Karol (Pope John Paul II). *Sign of Contradiction*. New York: Seabury Press, 1979.

Woodward, Kenneth. "The First Married Priests." *Newsweek*, September 1, 1980.

Woolever, Cynthia, and Keith Wulff. *U.S. Congregational Life Surveys*, 2001. The Association of Religion Data Archives, www.TheARDA.com.

Yearbook of American and Canadian Churches. New York: National Council of Churches USA, 2006.

Yuengert, Andrew. "Do Bishops Matter? A Cross-Sectional Study of Ordinations to the U.S. Catholic Diocesan Priesthood." *Review of Religious Research* 42, no. 3 (March 1, 2001): 294–312.

Zikmund, Barbara Brown, Adair T. Lummis, and Patricia M. Y. Chang. *Clergy Women: An Uphill Calling*. 1st ed. Louisville, KY: Westminster John Knox Press, 1998.

Zondag, Hessel J. "Involved, Loyal, Alienated, and Detached: The Commitment of Pastors." *Pastoral Psychology* 49, no. 4 (March 2001): 311–323.

Index